1992

Ethics at Work

ETHICS AT WORK

A Harvard Business Review Paperback

Harvard Business Review paperback No. 90077

ISBN 0-87584-286-0

The *Harvard Business Review* articles in this collection are
available individually, except "Case of the Disputed Dismissal" by David W. Ewing. Discounts apply to quantity pur-
chases. For information and ordering contact Operations
Department, Harvard Business School Publishing Division,
Boston, MA 02163. Telephone: (617) 495-6192, 9 a.m. to 5
p.m. Eastern Time, Monday through Friday. Fax: (617)
495-6985, 24 hours a day.

Editor's Note: Some articles in this book may have been written before authors and editors began to take into consideration the role of women in management. We hope the archaic
usage representing all managers as male does not detract from
the usefulness of the collection.

Printed in the United States of America by Harvard
University, Office of the University Publisher.
93 92 91 5 4 3 2 1

Contents

Ethics and Executive Action

Ethical Managers Make Their Own Rules
Sir Adrian Cadbury
3

The chairman of Cadbury Schweppes describes an attitude and approach for dealing with the ethical dimensions of business decisions.

Why "Good" Managers Make Bad Ethical Choices
Saul W. Gellerman
9

The situation is depressingly familiar: a manager with years of honorable service makes a decision that is patently immoral. Or worse: the manager engages in a pattern of action that is morally indefensible. How does this happen? Individuals often resort to certain rationalizations that appear to justify questionable behavior.

Nobody Trusts the Boss Completely—Now What?
Fernando Bartolomé
15

Proclaiming the importance of honesty and trust in an organization is admirable, but the realities of organizations and human nature place practical limits on both. Managers must therefore work hard to make their parts of the organization safe for candor and trust.

How Selfish Are People—Really?
David Warsh
23

Economics has performed an elegant reduction on the motives of ethical behavior: strict self-interest. Two recent studies call into question the appealing simplicity of this definition. The pure pursuit of self-interest may turn out to be incompatible with achieving it.

A Traveler's Guide to Gifts and Bribes
Jeffrey A. Fadiman
29

The Western businessperson overseas can be faced with requests that serve local tradition, courtesy, or personal friendship but to Western eyes look like bribery attempts. Here is a primer on the variation of business ethics from one culture to another, with a focus on payoffs.

The Ethics of Business Organizations

Ethics in Practice
Kenneth R. Andrews
39

The problem of corporate ethics has three dimensions: the individual manager, the organization, and the company strategy and mission. The most influential individuals in this ethical setting are a company's leaders, who uphold values both explicitly and implicitly.

142,512

Why Be Honest If Honesty Doesn't Pay
Amar Bhide and Howard Stevenson
45

Ethical behavior gives a company few if any material rewards. And contrary to conventional wisdom, the consequences of dishonesty and trust-breaking are often nil. Moral behavior, then, is primarily—and almost strictly—a moral choice.

Values Make the Company: An Interview with Robert Haas
Robert Howard
54

Under Robert Haas, Levi Strauss has a six-point "Aspirations Statement." Unlike other pro forma charters, this statement of values is being used by managers to reshape the company.

Moral Mazes: Bureaucracy and Managerial Work
Robert Jackall
67

How does bureaucracy shape managerial ethics? In ways that aren't especially healthy, according to this study. Getting ahead in a bureaucracy can invite game playing by rules that stray far from ethical behavior.

The Poletown Dilemma
Joseph Auerbach
81

As part of a modernization program, General Motors asked the City of Detroit to acquire part of a neighborhood for a new plant. The deal wound up in court, which ruled for GM. The case nevertheless raises important questions about a company's responsibility to the communities in which it operates.

Reading Fiction to the Bottom Line
Benjamin DeMott
89

Many businesspeople believe the worlds of art and business are emphatically separate. Distinct they may be, but interconnected, says the author of this article. Literary thinking can give priceless early indications of shifts in values and ideas that will impinge on business.

Case Studies

Case of the Disputed Dismissal
David W. Ewing
99

An outspoken public health employee is a thorn in the side of the city manager and the board of health. Does his behavior justify termination? Just as important, what sort of hearing does the employee deserve before termination?

The Case of the Willful Whistle-Blower
Sally Seymour
107

A long-buried report surfaces that implicates Fairway Electric in wrongdoing: it knowingly sold a flawed power plant design. The report triggers a crisis of integrity, loyalty, and business ethics.

The Case of the Mismanaged Ms.
Sally Seymour
115

When an ambitious female executive runs afoul of the old-boy network, a company must decide where normal human behavior ends and sexual discrimination begins.

The Case of the Omniscient Organization
Gary T. Marx
127

Dominion-Swann Industries improved productivity with a comprehensive set of personnel policies, some of which involved intrusive high-tech monitoring of employees. How much control of employees is appropriate?

Ethics and Executive Action

Ethical managers make their own rules

Ethics prize winner

Sir Adrian Cadbury

In 1900 Queen Victoria sent a decorative tin with a bar of chocolate inside to all of her soldiers who were serving in South Africa. These tins still turn up today, often complete with their contents, a tribute to the collecting instinct. At the time, the order faced my grandfather with an ethical dilemma. He owned and ran the second-largest chocolate company in Britain, so he was trying harder and the order meant additional work for the factory. Yet he was deeply and publicly opposed to the Anglo-Boer War. He resolved the dilemma by accepting the order, but carrying it out at cost. He therefore made no profit out of what he saw as an unjust war, his employees benefited from the additional work, the soldiers received their royal present, and I am still sent the tins.

My grandfather was able to resolve the conflict between the decision best for his business and his personal code of ethics because he and his family owned the firm which bore their name. Certainly his dilemma would have been more acute if he had had to take into account the interests of outside shareholders, many of whom would no doubt have been in favor both of the war and of profiting from it. But even so, not all my grandfather's ethical dilemmas could be as straightforwardly resolved.

So strongly did my grandfather feel about the South African War that he acquired and financed the only British newspaper which opposed it. He was also against gambling, however, and so he tried to run the paper without any references to horse racing. The effect on the newspaper's circulation was such that he had to choose between his ethical beliefs. He decided, in the end, that it was more important that the paper's voice be heard as widely as possible than that gambling should thereby receive some mild encouragement. The decision was doubtless a relief to those working on the paper and to its readers.

The way my grandfather settled these two clashes of principle brings out some practical points about ethics and business decisions. In the first place, the possibility that ethical and commercial considerations will conflict has always faced those who run companies. It is not a new problem. The difference now is that a more widespread and critical interest is being taken in our decisions and in the ethical judgments which lie behind them.

Secondly, as the newspaper example demonstrates, ethical signposts do not always point in the same direction. My grandfather had to choose between opposing a war and condoning gambling. The rule that it is best to tell the truth often runs up against the rule that we should not hurt people's feelings unnecessarily. There is no simple, universal formula for solving ethical problems. We have to choose from our own codes of conduct whichever rules are appropriate to the case in hand; the outcome of those choices makes us who we are.

Lastly, while it is hard enough to resolve dilemmas when our personal rules of conduct conflict, the real difficulties arise when we have to make decisions which affect the interests of others. We can work out what weighting to give to our own rules through trial and error. But business decisions require us to do the same for others by allocating weights to all the con-

George Adrian Hayhurst Cadbury is chairman of Cadbury Schweppes PLC. Readers who would like to know more about Sir Adrian's views on management practice and ethics can read "Cadbury Schweppes: More Than Chocolate and Tonic," an interview with HBR that appeared in January-February 1983.

The editors of Harvard Business Review *are glad to announce that "Ethical Managers Make Their Own Rules" has won* HBR's *1986 Ethics in Business Prize for the best original article written and submitted by a corporate manager on the ethical problems business executives face.*

flicting interests which may be involved. Frequently, for example, we must balance the interests of employees against those of shareholders. But even that sounds more straightforward than it really is, because there may well be differing views among the shareholders, and the interests of past, present, and future employees are unlikely to be identical.

Eliminating ethical considerations from business decisions would simplify the management task, and Milton Friedman has urged something of the kind in arguing that the interaction between business and society should be left to the political process. "Few trends could so thoroughly undermine the very foundation of our free society," he writes in *Capitalism and Freedom*, "as the acceptance by corporate officials of a social responsibility other than to make as much money for their shareholders as possible."

But the simplicity of this approach is deceptive. Business is part of the social system and we cannot isolate the economic elements of major decisions from their social consequences. So there are no simple rules. Those who make business decisions have to assess the economic and social consequences of their actions as best as they can and come to their conclusions on limited information and in a limited time.

We judge companies—and managers— by their actions, not their pious statements of intent.

As will already be apparent, I use the word ethics to mean the guidelines or rules of conduct by which we aim to live. It is, of course, foolhardy to write about ethics at all, because you lay yourself open to the charge of taking up a position of moral superiority, of failing to practice what you preach, or both. I am not in a position to preach nor am I promoting a specific code of conduct. I believe, however, that it is useful to all of us who are responsible for business decisions to acknowledge the part which ethics plays in those decisions and to encourage discussion of how best to combine commercial and ethical judgments. Most business decisions involve some degree of ethical judgment; few can be taken solely on the basis of arithmetic.

While we refer to a company as having a set of standards, that is a convenient shorthand. The people who make up the company are responsible for its conduct and it is their collective actions which determine the company's standards. The ethical standards of a company are judged by its actions, not by pious statements of intent put out in its name. This does not mean that those who head companies should not

set down what they believe their companies stand for—hard though that is to do. The character of a company is a matter of importance to those in it, to those who do business with it, and to those who are considering joining it.

What matters most, however, is where we stand as individual managers and how we behave when faced with decisions which require us to combine ethical and commercial judgments. In approaching such decisions, I believe it is helpful to go through two steps. The first is to determine, as precisely as we can, what our personal rules of conduct are. This does not mean drawing up a list of virtuous notions, which will probably end up as a watered-down version of the Scriptures without their literary merit. It does mean looking back at decisions we have made and working out from there what our rules actually are. The aim is to avoid confusing ourselves and everyone else by declaring one set of principles and acting on another. Our ethics are expressed in our actions, which is why they are usually clearer to others than to ourselves.

Once we know where we stand personally we can move on to the second step, which is to think through who else will be affected by the decision and how we should weight their interest in it. Some interests will be represented by well-organized groups; others will have no one to put their case. If a factory manager is negotiating a wage claim with employee representatives, their remit is to look after the interests of those who are already employed. Yet the effect of the wage settlement on the factory's costs may well determine whether new employees are likely to be taken on. So the manager cannot ignore the interest of potential employees in the outcome of the negotiation, even though that interest is not represented at the bargaining table.

Black and white alternatives are a regrettable sign of the times.

The rise of organized interest groups makes it doubly important that managers consider the arguments of everyone with a legitimate interest in a decision's outcome. Interest groups seek publicity to promote their causes and they have the advantage of being single-minded: they are against building an airport on a certain site, for example, but take no responsibility for finding a better alternative. This narrow focus gives pressure groups a debating advantage against managements, which cannot evade the responsibility for taking decisions in the same way.

In *The Hard Problems of Management*, Mark Pastin has perceptively referred to this phenomenon as the ethical superiority of the uninvolved, and there is a good deal of it about. Pressure groups are skilled at seizing the high moral ground and arguing that our judgment as managers is at best biased and at worst influenced solely by private gain because we have a direct commercial interest in the outcome of our decisions. But as managers we are also responsible for arriving at business decisions which take account of all the interests concerned; the uninvolved are not.

At times the campaign to persuade companies to divest themselves of their South African subsidiaries has exemplified this kind of ethical high-handedness. Apartheid is abhorrent politically, socially, and morally. Those who argue that they can exert some influence on the direction of change by staying put believe this as sincerely as those who favor divestment. Yet many anti-apartheid campaigners reject the proposition that both sides have the same end in view. From their perspective it is self-evident that the only ethical course of action is for companies to wash their hands of the problems of South Africa by selling out.

Managers cannot be so self-assured. In deciding what weight to give to the arguments for and against divestment, we must consider who has what at stake in the outcome of the decision. The employees of a South African subsidiary have the most direct stake, as the decision affects their future; they are also the group whose voice is least likely to be heard outside South Africa. The shareholders have at stake any loss on divestment, against which must be balanced any gain in the value of their shares through severing the South African connection. The divestment lobby is the one group for whom the decision is costless either way.

What is clear even from this limited analysis is that there is no general answer to the question of whether companies should sell their South African subsidiaries or not. Pressure to reduce complicated issues to straightforward alternatives, one of which is right and the other wrong, is a regrettable sign of the times. But boards are rarely presented with two clearly opposed alternatives. Companies faced with the same issues will therefore properly come to different conclusions and their decisions may alter over time.

A less contentious divestment decision faced my own company when we decided to sell our foods division. Because the division was mainly a U.K. business with regional brands, it did not fit the company's strategy, which called for concentrating resources behind our confectionery and soft drinks brands internationally. But it was an attractive business in its own right and the decision to sell prompted both a management bid and external offers.

Employees working in the division strongly supported the management bid and made their views felt. In this instance, they were the best orga-nized interest group and they had more information available to them to back their case than any of the other parties involved. What they had at stake was also very clear.

From the shareholders' point of view, the premium over asset value offered by the various bidders was a key aspect of the decision. They also had an interest in seeing the deal completed without regulatory delays and without diverting too much management attention from the ongoing business. In addition, the way in which the successful bidder would guard the brand name had to be considered, since the division would take with it products carrying the parent company's name.

In weighing the advantages and disadvantages of the various offers, the board considered all the groups, consumers among them, who would be affected by the sale. But our main task was to reconcile the interests of the employees and of the shareholders. (The more, of course, we can encourage employees to become shareholders, the closer together the interests of these two stakeholders will be brought.) The division's management upped its bid in the face of outside competition, and after due deliberation we decided to sell to the management team, believing that this choice best balanced the diverse interests at stake.

Actions are unethical if they won't stand scrutiny.

Companies whose activities are international face an additional complication in taking their decisions. They aim to work to the same standards of business conduct wherever they are and to behave as good corporate citizens of the countries in which they trade. But the two aims are not always compatible: promotion on merit may be the rule of the company and promotion by seniority the custom of the country. In addition, while the financial arithmetic on which companies base their decisions is generally accepted, what is considered ethical varies among cultures.

If what would be considered corruption in the company's home territory is an accepted business practice elsewhere, how are local managers expected to act? Companies could do business only in countries in which they feel ethically at home, provided always that their shareholders take the same view. But this approach could prove unduly restrictive, and there is also a certain arrogance in dismissing foreign codes of conduct without considering why they may be different. If companies find, for example, that they have to pay customs officers in another country just to do their job, it may be that the state is simply transferring its responsibilities to the private sector as an alternative to using taxation less efficiently to the same end.

Nevertheless, this example brings us to one of the most common ethical issues companies face – how far to go in buying business? What payments are legitimate for companies to make to win orders and, the reverse side of that coin, when do gifts to employees become bribes? I use two rules of thumb to test whether a payment is acceptable from the company's point of view: Is the payment on the face of the invoice? Would it embarrass the recipient to have the gift mentioned in the company newspaper?

The first test ensures that all payments, however unusual they may seem, are recorded and go through the books. The second is aimed at distinguishing bribes from gifts, a definition which depends on the size of the gift and the influence it is likely to have on the recipient. The value of a case of whiskey to me would be limited, because I only take it as medicine. We know ourselves whether a gift is acceptable or not and we know that others will know if they are aware of the nature of the gift.

As for payment on the face of the invoice, I have found it a useful general rule precisely because codes of conduct do vary round the world. It has legitimized some otherwise unlikely company payments, to the police in one country, for example, and to the official planning authorities in another, but all went through the books and were audited. Listing a payment on the face of the invoice may not be a sufficient ethical test, but it is a necessary one; payments outside the company's system are corrupt and corrupting.

The logic behind these rules of thumb is that openness and ethics go together and that actions are unethical if they will not stand scrutiny. Openness in arriving at decisions reflects the same logic. It gives those with an interest in a particular decision the chance to make their views known and opens to argument the basis on which the decision is finally taken. This in turn enables the decision makers to learn from experience and to improve their powers of judgment.

Openness is also, I believe, the best way to disarm outside suspicion of companies' motives and actions. Disclosure is not a panacea for improving the relations between business and society, but the willingness to operate an open system is the foundation of those relations. Business needs to be open to the views of society and open in return about its own activities; this is essential for the establishment of trust.

For the same reasons, as managers we need to be candid when making decisions about other people. Dr. Johnson reminds us that when it comes to lapidary inscriptions, "no man is upon oath." But what should be disclosed in references, in fairness to those looking for work and to those who are considering employing them?

The simplest rule would seem to be that we should write the kind of reference we would wish to read. Yet "do as you would be done by" says nothing about ethics. The actions which result from applying it could be ethical or unethical, depending on the standards of the initiator. The rule could be adapted to help managers determine their ethical standards, however, by reframing it as a question: If you did business with yourself, how ethical would you think you were?

Anonymous letters accusing an employee of doing something discreditable create another context in which candor is the wisest course. Such letters cannot by definition be answered, but they convey a message to those who receive them, however warped or unfair the message may be. I normally destroy these letters, but tell the person concerned what has been said. This conveys the disregard I attach to nameless allegation, but preserves the rule of openness. From a practical point of view, it serves as a warning if there is anything in the allegations; from an ethical point of view, the degree to which my judgment of the person may now be prejudiced is known between us.

Shelving hard decisions is the least ethical course.

The last aspect of ethics in business decisions I want to discuss concerns our responsibility for the level of employment; what can or should companies do about the provision of jobs? This issue is of immediate concern to European managers because unemployment is higher in Europe than it is in the United States and the net number of new jobs created has been much lower. It comes to the fore whenever companies face decisions which require a trade-off between increasing efficiency and reducing numbers employed.

If you believe, as I do, that the primary purpose of a company is to satisfy the needs of its customers and to do so profitably, the creation of jobs cannot be the company's goal as well. Satisfying customers requires companies to compete in the marketplace, and so we cannot opt out of introducing new technology, for example, to preserve jobs. To do so would be to deny consumers the benefits of progress, to shortchange the shareholders, and in the longer run to put the jobs of everyone in the company at risk. What destroys jobs certainly and permanently is the failure to be competitive.

Experience says that the introduction of new technology creates more jobs than it eliminates, in ways which cannot be forecast. It may do so, however, only after a time lag, and those displaced may not, through lack of skills, be able to take advantage of the new opportunities when they arise. Nevertheless, the company's prime responsibility to everyone who has a stake in it is to retain its competitive edge, even if this means a loss of jobs in the short run.

Where companies do have a social responsibility, however, is in how we manage that situation, how we smooth the path of technological change. Companies are responsible for the timing of such changes and we are in a position to involve those who will be affected by the way in which those changes are introduced. We also have a vital resource in our capacity to provide training, so that continuing employees can take advantage of change and those who may lose their jobs can more readily find new ones.

In the United Kingdom, an organization called Business in the Community has been established to encourage the formation of new enterprises. Companies have backed it with cash and with secondments. The secondment of able managers to worthwhile institutions is a particularly effective expression of concern, because the ability to manage is such a scarce resource. Through Business in the Community we can create jobs collectively, even if we cannot do so individually, and it is clearly in our interest to improve the economic and social climate in this way.

Throughout, I have been writing about the responsibilities of those who head companies and my emphasis has been on taking decisions, because that is what directors and managers are appointed to do. What concerns me is that too often the public pressures which are put on companies in the name of ethics encourage their boards to put off decisions or to wash their hands of problems. There may well be commercial reasons for those choices, but there are rarely ethical ones. The ethical bases on which decisions are arrived at will vary among companies, but shelving those decisions is likely to be the least ethical course.

The company which takes drastic action in order to survive is more likely to be criticized publicly than the one which fails to grasp the nettle and gradually but inexorably declines. There is always a temptation to postpone difficult decisions, but it is not in society's interests that hard choices should be evaded because of public clamor or the possibility of legal action. Companies need to be encouraged to take the decisions which face them; the responsibility for providing that encouragement rests with society as a whole.

Society sets the ethical framework within which those who run companies have to work out their own codes of conduct. Responsibility for decisions, therefore, runs both ways. Business has to take account of its responsibilities to society in coming to its decisions, but society has to accept its responsibilities for setting the standards against which those decisions are made. ▽

Reprint 87502

Saul W. Gellerman

Why 'good' managers make bad ethical choices

How could top-level executives at the Manville Corporation have suppressed evidence for decades that proved that asbestos inhalation was killing their own employees?

What could have driven the managers of Continental Illinois Bank to pursue a course of action that threatened to bankrupt the institution, ruined its reputation, and cost thousands of innocent employees and investors their jobs and their savings?

Why did managers at E.F. Hutton find themselves pleading guilty to 2,000 counts of mail and wire fraud, accepting a fine of $2 million, and putting up an $8 million fund for restitution to the 400 banks that the company had systematically bilked?

How can we explain the misbehavior that took place in these organizations — or in any of the others, public and private, that litter our newspapers' front pages: workers at a defense contractor who accused their superiors of falsifying time cards; alleged bribes and kickbacks that honeycombed New York City government; a company that knowingly marketed an unsafe birth control device; the decision-making process that led to the space shuttle Challenger tragedy.

"When in doubt, don't."

The stories are always slightly different; but they have a lot in common since they're full of the oldest questions in the world, questions of human behavior and human judgment applied in ordinary day-to-day situations. Reading them we have to ask how usually honest, intelligent, compassionate human beings could act in ways that are callous, dishonest, and wrongheaded.

In my view, the explanations go back to four rationalizations that people have relied on through

Mr. Gellerman is dean of the University of Dallas Graduate School of Management. He is the author of eight books on management and of the HBR article "Supervision: Substance and Style" (March-April 1976).

the ages to justify questionable conduct: believing that the activity is not "really" illegal or immoral; that it is in the individual's or the corporation's best interest; that it will never be found out; or that because it helps the company the company will condone it. By looking at these rationalizations in light of these cases, we can develop some practical rules to more effectively control managers' actions that lead to trouble — control, but not eliminate. For the hard truth is that corporate misconduct, like the lowly cockroach, is a plague that we can suppress but never exterminate.

Three cases

Amitai Etzioni, professor of sociology at George Washington University, recently concluded that in the last ten years, roughly two-thirds of America's 500 largest corporations have been involved, in varying degrees, in some form of illegal behavior. By taking a look at three corporate cases, we may be able to identify the roots of the kind of misconduct that not only ruins some people's lives, destroys institutions, and gives business as a whole a bad name but that also inflicts real and lasting harm on a large number of innocent people. The three cases that follow should be familiar. I present them here as examples of the types of problems that confront managers in all kinds of businesses daily.

Manville Corporation

A few years ago, Manville (then Johns Manville) was solid enough to be included among the giants of American business. Today Manville is in the process of turning over 80% of its equity to a trust representing people who have sued or plan to sue it for liability in connection with one of its principal former products, asbestos. For all practical purposes, the entire company was brought down by questions of corporate ethics.

More than 40 years ago, information began to reach Johns Manville's medical department—and through it, the company's top executives—implicating asbestos inhalation as a cause of asbestosis, a debilitating lung disease, as well as lung cancer and mesothelioma, an invariably fatal lung disease. Manville's managers suppressed the research. Moreover, as a matter of policy, they apparently decided to conceal the information from affected employees. The company's medical staff collaborated in the cover-up, for reasons we can only guess at.

Money may have been one motive. In one particularly chilling piece of testimony, a lawyer recalled how 40 years earlier he had confronted Manville's corporate counsel about the company's policy of concealing chest X-ray results from employees. The lawyer had asked, "Do you mean to tell me you would let them work until they dropped dead?" The reply was, "Yes, we save a lot of money that way."

Based on such testimony, a California court found that Manville had hidden the asbestos danger from its employees rather than looking for safer ways to handle it. It was less expensive to pay workers' compensation claims than to develop safer working conditions. A New Jersey court was even blunter: it found that Manville had made a conscious, cold-blooded business decision to take no protective or remedial action, in flagrant disregard of the rights of others.

How can we explain this behavior? Were more than 40 years' worth of Manville executives all immoral?

Such an answer defies common sense. The truth, I think, is less glamorous—and also less satisfying to those who like to explain evil as the actions of a few misbegotten souls. The people involved were probably ordinary men and women for the most part, not very different from you and me. They found themselves in a dilemma, and they solved it in a way that seemed to be the least troublesome, deciding not to disclose information that could hurt their product. The consequences of what they chose to do—both to thousands of innocent people and, ultimately, to the corporation—probably never occurred to them.

The Manville case illustrates the fine line between acceptable and unacceptable managerial behavior. Executives are expected to strike a difficult balance—to pursue their companies' best interests but not overstep the bounds of what outsiders will tolerate.

Even the best managers can find themselves in a bind, not knowing how far is too far. In retrospect, they can usually easily tell where they should have drawn the line, but no one manages in retrospect. We can only live and act today and hope that whoever looks back on what we did will judge that we struck the proper balance. In a few years, many of us may be found delinquent for decisions we are making now about tobacco, clean air, the use of chemicals, or some other seemingly benign substance. The managers at Manville may have believed that they were acting in the company's best interests, or that what they were doing would never be found out, or even that it wasn't really wrong. In the end, these were only rationalizations for conduct that brought the company down.

Continental Illinois Bank

Until recently the ninth largest bank in the United States, Continental Illinois had to be saved from insolvency because of bad judgment by management. The government bailed it out, but at a price. In effect it has been socialized: about 80% of its equity now belongs to the Federal Deposit Insurance Corporation. Continental seems to have been brought down by managers who misunderstood its real interests. To their own peril, executives focused on a single-minded pursuit of corporate ends and forgot about the means to the ends.

In 1976, Continental's chairman declared that within five years the magnitude of its lending would match that of any other bank. The goal was attainable; in fact, for a time, Continental reached it. But it dictated a shift in strategy away from conservative corporate financing and toward aggressive pursuit of borrowers. So Continental, with lots of lendable funds, sent its loan officers into the field to buy loans that had originally been made by smaller banks that had less money.

The practice in itself was not necessarily unsound. But some of the smaller banks had done more than just lend money—they had swallowed hook, line, and sinker the extravagant, implausible dreams of poorly capitalized oil producers in Oklahoma, and they had begun to bet enormous sums on those dreams. Eventually, a cool billion dollars' worth of those dreams found their way into Continental's portfolio, and a cool billion dollars of depositors' money flowed out to pay for them. When the price of oil fell, a lot of dry holes and idle drilling equipment were all that was left to show for most of the money.

Continental's officers had become so entranced by their lending efforts' spectacular results that they hadn't looked deeply into how they had been achieved. Huge sums of money were lent at fat rates of interest. If the borrowers had been able to repay the loans, Continental might have become the eighth or even the seventh largest bank in the country. But that was a very big "if." Somehow there was a failure of control and judgment at Continental—probably because the officers who were buying those shaky loans

"...So that's how the destabilization is going down here. How's the deregulation going up there!"

were getting support and praise from their superiors. Or at least they were not hearing enough tough questions about them.

At one point, for example, Continental's internal auditors stumbled across the fact that an officer who had purchased $800 million in oil and gas loans from the Penn Square Bank in Oklahoma City had also borrowed $565,000 for himself from Penn Square. Continental's top management investigated and eventually issued a reprimand. The mild rebuke reflected the officer's hard work and the fact that the portfolio he had obtained would have yielded an average return of nearly 20% had it ever performed as planned. In fact, virtually all of the $800 million had to be written off. Management chose to interpret the incident charitably; federal prosecutors later alleged a kickback.

On at least two other occasions, Continental's own control mechanisms flashed signals that something was seriously wrong with the oil and gas

portfolio. A vice president warned in a memo that the documentation needed to verify the soundness of many of the purchased loans had simply never arrived. Later, a junior loan officer, putting his job on the line, went over the heads of three superiors to tell a top executive about the missing documentation. Management chose not to investigate. After all, Continental was doing exactly what its chairman had said it would do: it was on its way to becoming the leading commercial lender in the United States. Oil and gas loans were an important factor in that achievement. Stopping to wait for paperwork to catch up would only slow down reaching the goal.

Eventually, however, the word got out about the instability of the bank's portfolio, which led to a massive run on its deposits. No other bank was willing to come to the rescue, for fear of being swamped by Continental's huge liabilities. To avoid going under, Continental in effect became a ward of the federal government. The losers were the bank's shareholders, some officers who lost their jobs, at least one who was indicted, and some 2,000 employees (about 15% of the total) who were let go, as the bank scaled down to fit its diminished assets.

Once again, it is easy for us to sit in judgment after the fact and say that Continental's loan officers and their superiors were doing exactly what bankers shouldn't do: they were gambling with their depositors' money. But on another level, this story is more difficult to analyze—and more generally a part of everyday business. Certainly part of Continental's problem was neglect of standard controls. But another dimension involved ambitious corporate goals. Pushed by lofty goals, managers could not see clearly their real interests. They focused on ends, overlooked the ethical questions associated with their choice of means—and ultimately hurt themselves.

E.F. Hutton

The nation's second largest independent broker, E.F. Hutton & Company, recently pleaded guilty to 2,000 counts of mail and wire fraud. It had systematically bilked 400 of its banks by drawing against uncollected funds or in some cases against nonexistent sums, which it then covered after having enjoyed interest-free use of the money. So far, Hutton has agreed to pay a fine of $2 million as well as the government's investigation costs of $750,000. It has set up an $8 million reserve for restitution to the banks—which may not be enough. Several officers have lost their jobs, and some indictments may yet follow.

But worst of all, Hutton has tarnished its reputation, never a wise thing to do—certainly not when your business is offering to handle other people's money. Months after Hutton agreed to appoint new directors – as a way to give outsiders a solid majority on the board – the company couldn't find people to accept the seats, in part because of the bad publicity.

Apparently Hutton's branch managers had been encouraged to pay close attention to cash management. At some point, it dawned on someone that using other people's money was even more profitable than using your own. In each case, Hutton's overdrafts involved no large sums. But cumulatively, the savings on interest that would otherwise have been owed to the banks was very large. Because Hutton always made covering deposits, and because most banks did not object, Hutton assured its managers that what they were doing was sharp – and not shady. They presumably thought they were pushing legality to its limit without going over the line. The branch managers were simply taking full advantage of what the law and the bankers' tolerance permitted. On several occasions, the managers who played this game most astutely were even congratulated for their skill.

Hutton probably will not suffer a fate as drastic as Manville's or Continental Illinois's. Indeed, with astute damage control, it can probably emerge from this particular embarrassment with only a few bad memories. But this case has real value because it is typical of much corporate misconduct. Most improprieties don't cut a corporation off at the knees the way Manville's and Continental Illinois's did. In fact, most such actions are never revealed at all – or at least that's how people figure things will work out. And in many cases, a willingness to gamble thus is probably enhanced by the rationalization – true or not – that everyone else is doing something just as bad or would if they could; that those who wouldn't go for their share are idealistic fools.

Four rationalizations

Why do managers do things that ultimately inflict great harm on their companies, themselves, and people on whose patronage or tolerance their organizations depend? These three cases, as well as the current crop of examples in each day's paper, supply ample evidence of the motivations and instincts that underlie corporate misconduct. Although the particulars may vary – from the gruesome dishonesty surrounding asbestos handling to the mundanity of illegal money management – the motivating beliefs are pretty much the same. We may examine them in the context of the corporation, but we know that these feelings are basic throughout society; we find them wherever we go because we take them with us.

When we look more closely at these cases, we can delineate four commonly held rationalizations that can lead to misconduct:

> A belief that the activity is within reasonable ethical and legal limits – that is, that it is not "really" illegal or immoral.

> A belief that the activity is in the individual's or the corporation's best interests – that the individual would somehow be expected to undertake the activity.

> A belief that the activity is "safe" because it will never be found out or publicized; the classic crime-and-punishment issue of discovery.

> A belief that because the activity helps the company the company will condone it and even protect the person who engages in it.

☐   The idea that an action is not really wrong is an old issue. How far is too far? Exactly where is the line between smart and too smart? Between sharp and shady? Between profit maximization and illegal conduct? The issue is complex: it involves an interplay between top management's goals and middle managers' efforts to interpret those aims.

Put enough people in an ambiguous, ill-defined situation, and some will conclude that whatever hasn't been labeled specifically wrong must be OK – especially if they are rewarded for certain acts. Deliberate overdrafts, for example, were not proscribed at Hutton. Since the company had not spelled out their illegality, it could later plead guilty for itself while shielding its employees from prosecution.

Top executives seldom ask their subordinates to do things that both of them know are against the law or imprudent. But company leaders sometimes leave things unsaid or give the impression that there are things they don't want to know about. In other words, they can seem, whether deliberately or otherwise, to be distancing themselves from their subordinates' tactical decisions in order to keep their own hands clean if things go awry. Often they lure ambitious lower level managers by implying that rich rewards await those who can produce certain results – and that the methods for achieving them will not be examined too closely. Continental's simple wrist-slapping of the officer who was caught in a flagrant conflict of interest sent a clear message to other managers about what top management really thought was important.

How can managers avoid crossing a line that is seldom precise? Unfortunately, most know that they have overstepped it only when they have gone too far. They have no reliable guidelines about what will be overlooked or tolerated or what will be condemned or attacked. When managers must operate in murky borderlands, their most reliable guideline is an old principle: when in doubt, don't.

That may seem like a timid way to run a business. One could argue that if it actually took hold among the middle managers who run most companies, it might take the enterprise out of free enterprise. But there is a difference between taking a worthwhile economic risk and risking an illegal act to make more money.

The difference between becoming a success and becoming a statistic lies in knowledge—including self-knowledge—not daring. Contrary to popular mythology, managers are not paid to take risks; they are paid to know which risks are worth taking. Also, maximizing profits is a company's second priority, not its first. The first is ensuring its survival.

All managers risk giving too much because of what their companies demand from them. But the same superiors who keep pressing you to do more, or to do it better, or faster, or less expensively, will turn on you should you cross that fuzzy line between right and wrong. They will blame you for exceeding instructions or for ignoring their warnings. The smartest managers already know that the best answer to the question, "How far is too far?" is don't try to find out.

☐   Turning to the second reason why people take risks that get their companies into trouble, believing that unethical conduct is in a person's or corporation's best interests nearly always results from a parochial view of what those interests are. For example, Alpha Industries, a Massachusetts manufacturer of microwave equipment, paid $57,000 to a Raytheon manager, ostensibly for a marketing report. Air force investigators charged that the report was a ruse to cover a bribe: Alpha wanted subcontracts that the Raytheon manager supervised. But those contracts ultimately cost Alpha a lot more than they paid for the report. After the company was indicted for bribery, its contracts were suspended and its profits promptly vanished. Alpha wasn't unique in this transgression: in 1984, the Pentagon suspended 453 other companies for violating procurement regulations.

Ambitious managers look for ways to attract favorable attention, something to distinguish them from other people. So they try to outperform their peers. Some may see that it is not difficult to look remarkably good in the short run by avoiding things that pay off only in the long run. For example, you can skimp on maintenance or training or customer service, and you can get away with it—for a while.

The sad truth is that many managers have been promoted on the basis of "great" results obtained in just those ways, leaving unfortunate successors to inherit the inevitable whirlwind. Since this is not necessarily a just world, the problems that such people create are not always traced back to them. Companies cannot afford to be hoodwinked in this way. They must be concerned with more than just results. They have to look very hard at how results are obtained.

Evidently, in Hutton's case there were such reviews, but management chose to interpret favorably what government investigators later interpreted unfavorably. This brings up another dilemma: management quite naturally hopes that any of its borderline actions will be overlooked or at least interpreted charitably if noticed. Companies must accept human nature for what it is and protect themselves with watchdogs to sniff out possible misdeeds.

An independent auditing agency that reports to outside directors can play such a role. It can provide a less comfortable, but more convincing, review of how management's successes are achieved. The discomfort can be considered inexpensive insurance and serve to remind all employees that the real interests of the company are served by honest conduct in the first place.

☐   The third reason why a risk is taken, believing that one can probably get away with it, is perhaps the most difficult to deal with because it's often true. A great deal of proscribed behavior escapes detection.

We know that conscience alone does not deter everyone. For example, First National Bank of Boston pleaded guilty to laundering satchels of $20 bills worth $1.3 billion. Thousands of satchels must have passed through the bank's doors without incident before the scheme was detected. That kind of heavy, unnoticed traffic breeds complacency.

How can we deter wrongdoing that is unlikely to be detected? Make it more likely to be detected. Had today's "discovery" process—in which plaintiff's attorneys can comb through a company's records to look for incriminating evidence—been in use when Manville concealed the evidence on asbestosis, there probably would have been no cover-up. Mindful of the likelihood of detection, Manville would have chosen a different course and could very well be thriving today without the protection of the bankruptcy courts.

The most effective deterrent is not to increase the severity of punishment for those caught but to heighten the perceived probability of being caught in the first place. For example, police have found that parking an empty patrol car at locations where motorists often exceed the speed limit reduces the frequency of speeding. Neighborhood "crime watch" signs that people display decrease burglaries.

Simply increasing the frequency of audits and spot checks is a deterrent, especially when combined with three other simple techniques: scheduling audits irregularly, making at least half of them unannounced, and setting up some checkups soon after others. But frequent spot checks cost more than big sticks, a fact that raises the question of which approach is more cost-effective.

A common managerial error is to assume that because frequent audits uncover little behavior that is out of line, less frequent, and therefore less costly, auditing is sufficient. But this condition overlooks the important deterrent effect of frequent checking. The point is to prevent misconduct, not just to catch it.

A trespass detected should not be dealt with discreetly. Managers should announce the misconduct and how the individuals involved were punished. Since the main deterrent to illegal or unethical behavior is the perceived probability of detection, managers should make an example of people who are detected.

☐ Let's look at the fourth reason why corporate misconduct tends to occur, a belief that the company will condone actions that are taken in its interest and will even protect the managers responsible. The question we have to deal with here is, How do we keep company loyalty from going berserk?

That seems to be what happened at Manville. A small group of executives and a succession of corporate medical directors kept the facts about the lethal qualities of asbestos from becoming public knowledge for decades, and they managed to live with that knowledge. And at Manville, the company—or really, the company's senior management—did condone their decision and protect those employees.

Something similar seems to have happened at General Electric. When one of its missile projects ran up costs greater than the air force had agreed to pay, middle managers surreptitiously shifted those costs to projects that were still operating under budget. In this case, the loyalty that ran amok was primarily to the division: managers want their units' results to look good. But GE, with one of the finest reputations in U.S. industry, was splattered with scandal and paid a fine of $1.04 million.

One of the most troubling aspects of the GE case is the company's admission that those involved were thoroughly familiar with the company's ethical standards before the incident took place. This suggests that the practice of declaring codes of ethics and teaching them to managers is not enough to deter unethical conduct. Something stronger is needed.

Top management has a responsibility to exert a moral force within the company. Senior executives are responsible for drawing the line between loy-alty to the company and action against the laws and values of the society in which the company must operate. Further, because that line can be obscured in the heat of the moment, the line has to be drawn well short of where reasonable men and women could begin to suspect that their rights had been violated. The company has to react long before a prosecutor, for instance, would have a strong enough case to seek an indictment.

Executives have a right to expect loyalty from employees against competitors and detractors, but not loyalty against the law, or against common morality, or against society itself. Managers must warn employees that a disservice to customers, and especially to innocent bystanders, cannot be a service to the company. Finally, and most important of all, managers must stress that excuses of company loyalty will not be accepted for acts that place its good name in jeopardy. To put it bluntly, superiors must make it clear that employees who harm other people allegedly for the company's benefit will be fired.

The most extreme examples of corporate misconduct were due, in hindsight, to managerial failures. A good way to avoid management oversights is to subject the control mechanisms themselves to periodic surprise audits, perhaps as a function of the board of directors. The point is to make sure that internal audits and controls are functioning as planned. It's a case of inspecting the inspectors and taking the necessary steps to keep the controls working efficiently. Harold Geneen, former head of ITT, has suggested that the board should have an independent staff, something analogous to the Government Accounting Office, which reports to the legislative rather than the executive branch. In the end, it is up to top management to send a clear and pragmatic message to all employees that good ethics is still the foundation of good business. ▽

Reprint 86402

*How to overcome
the limits of trust and the
fear of candor*

Nobody Trusts the Boss Completely— Now What?

by Fernando Bartolomé

Managers who can head off serious problems before they blow up in the company's face are two steps ahead of the game. Their employers avoid needless expense or outright disaster, and they themselves get the promotions they deserve for running their departments smoothly and nipping trouble neatly in the bud.

 ## Subordinates are never eager to give the boss bad news.

In practice, of course, it's never this easy. Everyone knows that one trick to dealing with problems is to learn about them early. But what's the trick to learning about them early? How do effective managers find out that trouble is brewing? What are their warning systems?

All good managers have their own private information networks, and many develop a kind of sixth sense for the early signs of trouble. But by far the simplest and most common way to find out about problems is to be told, usually by a subordinate.

It is easy to get information when things are going well. People love to give the boss good news. But subordinates are never eager to tell their supervisors that the latest scheme isn't working, to assume ownership of a problem by giving it a name, to look like an informer, or to sound like Chicken Little. A subordinate's reluctance to be frank about problems is also related to risk. While it's fairly easy to tell the boss that the machines sent over by the purchasing department aren't working properly, it's much harder to admit responsibility for the malfunction, and harder still—and perhaps dangerous—to blame it on the boss. Yet it is terribly important to get subordinates to convey unpleasant messages. The sooner a problem is disclosed, diagnosed, and corrected, the better for the company.

Almost any organization would operate more effectively with completely open and forthright employees, but absolute frankness is too much to hope for (and probably too much to bear). Candor depends upon trust, and in hierarchical organizations, trust has strict natural limits.

The Limits of Trust and Candor

In a hierarchy, it is natural for people with less power to be extremely cautious about disclosing weaknesses, mistakes, and failings—especially when the more powerful party is also in a position to evaluate and punish. Trust flees authority, and, above all, trust flees a judge. Managers are inescapably positioned to judge subordinates. Good managers may be able to confine evaluation to formal occasions, to avoid all trace of judgmental style in other settings, even to communicate criticism in a positive, constructive way. But there is no way to escape completely a subordinate's inclination to see superiors as judges.

So one of the limits on candor is self-protection. For example, people often hide the failures of their own departments and hope they will correct themselves. In one typical case, the development group for a piece of special software fell terribly behind on its

Fernando Bartolomé is professor of management at Bentley College in Waltham, Massachusetts. He is also guest lecturer at the European Institute of Business Administration (INSEAD) in France and at the Oxford Centre for Management Studies in England. He consults frequently in Europe, the United States, and Latin America. This is his fifth article for HBR.

*"Don't you have any feeling for this car, Mr. Geller?
Don't you ever communicate with it?"*

Sometimes a subordinate may try to protect a client. In one case, a salesman withheld the information that one of his largest customers was in financial trouble. The customer went bankrupt, and the company lost $500,000.

We can only guess at the salesman's motives—eagerness to get his commission before the troubled company failed, fear of losing an old customer, reluctance to give official warning of a danger that might be exaggerated. The fact remains that he failed to communicate the problem, his boss saw no sign of danger, and the company lost half a million dollars.

Often the motive for silence is at least superficially praiseworthy: people keep quiet about a developing problem while trying to solve it. Most believe solving problems on their own is what they're paid to do, and in many cases, they're right. Subordinates are not paid to run to their bosses with every glitch and hiccup. As problems grow more serious, however, managers need to know about them.

schedule, but no one told the manager until the delivery date could no longer be met. Delivery was three months late, and the company had to absorb a financial penalty.

The lack of candor was not self-protective in the long run, of course, because the development group was ultimately held responsible for the delay. But human beings are often shortsighted. At one time or another, most of us have chosen an uncertain future calamity over today's immediate unpleasantness.

A variation on this theme is when subordinates protect their own subordinates in order to protect themselves, as in the following example:

☐ I was vice president of finance for a large manufacturing company and supervised a staff of 27. One new hire was failing on an important assignment. Her supervisor—who had hired her—withheld this information from me until her failure could no longer be corrected without serious disruption. He didn't tell me because he knew I would make him face up to the problem and deal with it, which he knew he would find very difficult to do.

The difficulty here lies in the bewildering territory between minor snags and major disasters. Handled promptly and decisively, the problems in this gray area sometimes turn out to be insignificant, but self-confident supervisors, particularly inexperienced ones, are perhaps too eager to prove they can cope on their own. This case is typical:

☐ I am head of medical research in a pharmaceutical company. My job is part of R&D and is on the critical path to marketing any new product. One of my managers saw that we weren't receiving data critical to the timely generation of a licensing package for worldwide registration of a new drug. He spent four months trying to get the data on his own, or proceed without it, and didn't inform me of the problem. We suffered an eight-month delay in applying for a license to sell. That represents 10% of the patent life of the product, which has estimated peak worldwide sales of $120 million a year.

Politics is another common obstacle to candor. Organizations are political systems, and employees are often involved in political struggles. There is no guarantee your subordinates will be on your side.

A U.S. engineering-products company manufactured a successful product on license from a Swedish company, but the American CEO heartily disliked his Swedish counterpart and came to the private conclusion that the licensing fees were out of line. Knowing that his senior staff would object, he began confidential acquisition talks with one of the Swedish corporation's competitors, a much smaller and technically less sophisticated company. Because the negotiations were too complex for him to handle alone, he circumvented the vice presidents who would have opposed the move and secretly enlisted the help of their subordinates. By the time the negotiations became public, it was too late for the senior staff to stop the deal. The Swedish company canceled its license, and the U.S. company has not sold a single piece of new technology since the acquisition.

This CEO made a grave error in letting his personal feelings interfere with his business judgment, but his incompetence, however great, is not the point. The point is that certain employees concealed information from their immediate superiors. Their motives are easy to guess at and perhaps understandable—after all, they were acting on orders from the CEO. But the fact remains that not one of them spoke up, their superiors suspected nothing, and the consequences for the company were extremely negative.

In these days of mergers and acquisitions, political infighting is often acute after absorption of—or by—another company. Restructuring and consolidation can produce epidemic fear and rupture lines of communication, as this case illustrates:

☐ My electronics corporation acquired a division of another company and merged it with two existing subsidiaries. Many employees were let go in the process of the merger and consolidation. I was named president and CEO of the new company one year after its formation. The new company had its headquarters on the East Coast and its research facilities

> ## Mergers, acquisitions, and office politics can all choke off the flow of essential information.

in the West. The VP for research—whose office was in California—did not tell me that the merger, the layoffs, and the new company policies and procedures had had a terrible impact on employee morale. I was completely unaware of the problem for four months.

Then I visited the research facility to announce a new benefits package. After announcing the plan, I asked for questions. All hell broke loose. For the next year and a half I spent about a third of my time and a great deal of other people's time trying to build bridges and establish trust, hoping to lower turnover, improve productivity, and get those Californians to feel like part of the total company.

Why wasn't I told? My guess is that the subordinate who kept me in the dark was afraid for his own job. Or else he felt he had something to gain by undermining my position. I don't know, but it was an expensive failure of communication.

Building and Destroying Trust

Given the natural obstacles to trust and candor—fear, pride, politics, dislike—managers need to make the most of whatever opportunities they have to increase subordinates' trust. Trust is not easy to build in the best of cases, and the kind of trust that concerns us here has to grow on rocky ground—between people at different levels of authority.

The factors affecting the development of trust and candor fall into six categories: communication, support, respect, fairness, predictability, and competence.

Communication is a matter of keeping subordinates informed, providing accurate feedback, explaining decisions and policies, being candid about one's own problems, and resisting the temptation to hoard information for use as a tool or a reward.

For several years, the founder and CEO of a small, South American conglomerate had addressed the needs of each of his six divisions separately. He treated his vice presidents like the CEOs of the divisions, cutting deals with each of them independently and keeping each in the dark about his arrangements with the others. He had always solved problems on this ad hoc basis, and it worked reasonably well. The company had grown swiftly and steadily. But now times were tougher, the company was bigger, and he began getting complaints from his VPs about resource allocation. None of them was satisfied with his own division's share, but none was in a position to consider the needs of the company as a whole.

At this point, the CEO recognized that his way of managing was part of the problem, did an abrupt about-face, and created an executive committee comprising himself and his six VPs. They all took part in setting priorities, allocating resources, and planning company strategy. Conflicts remained, of course, as each vice president fought for resources for his division. But trust increased substantially, and for the first time there was communication between divisions and a willingness and opportunity for the company's leadership to work together as a team.

Another CEO moved the offices of his small company without notice. His staff simply arrived at work one Monday morning to learn that the movers were coming on Tuesday. When asked to explain, the man gave his reasons but clearly didn't feel his employees needed to know. He insulted and belittled the people he depended on for information and support.

It is important to communicate with subordinates not only as a group but also as individuals. This woman's boss may have believed money spoke for itself:

☐ I have been working for my current boss for two years and never had a performance appraisal. I guess I'm doing okay because I get good raises every year. But I have no idea what the future may hold for me in this company.

Middle- to upper-level managers often find it difficult to talk with superiors about their own perfor-

Resist the temptation to use information as a tool or a reward.

mance and career prospects. When they feel they aren't getting the feedback they need, they are uncomfortable asking for it. Communication must flow in both directions if it is to flow at all. Information won't surge up where it barely trickles down.

Support means showing concern for subordinates as people. It means being available and approachable. It means helping people, coaching them, encouraging their ideas, and defending their positions. It may mean socializing with them. It certainly means taking an interest in their lives and careers. Here are three examples of good and poor support:

☐ During one period of my life, I had some serious personal problems that affected my work. My boss protected me at work and gave me a lot of moral support. Eventually, I was able to solve my problems, thanks in part to her help. That strengthened our professional relationship enormously.
☐ I presented a proposal to the executive committee. Some members were in favor, others against. I was so young and nervous, I didn't see how I could possibly convince them I was right. Then my boss took on the

defense of my proposal, argued energetically in favor of it, and we won. When I think back on it now, I realize that few events in my career have pleased me more or given me a more genuine sense of gratitude.
☐ I approved a credit and had been authorized by my boss to waive certain credit warranties. Then some other people started questioning what I had done and throwing doubt on my competence. Instead of supporting me, my boss took the side of my critics.

It is often tempting to abandon an employee who is in trouble, out of favor, or simply unpopular, but the extra effort expended in behalf of such a person can pay big dividends later. When you have to terminate employees, the worst possible method is to let them twist in the wind. Get rid of those you have to get rid of. Support the others for all you're worth. Subordinates trust most deeply the superiors they feel will stand by them when the chips are down.

Respect feeds on itself. The most important form of respect is delegation, and the second most important is listening to subordinates and acting on their opinions. In the first two examples below, the boss shows genuine respect for the subordinate's judgment and intelligence. In the third, the relationship actually deteriorates in the course of the meeting.

☐ My boss put me in charge of a project. It involved a big risk for me, but an even bigger risk for her if I failed. I asked her how she wanted me to do it and who else I should contact for clearance. She said, "You have free rein on this. Whatever you do is okay with me."
☐ Six years ago, just after I joined the bank, my boss told me he had decided to buy a company and asked me to look into it and give him my opinion. I did my homework and told him I thought it was a bad idea. So he eliminated me from the team he had put together to manage the acquisition. Somehow I succeeded in persuading him to listen to a fuller presentation of my analysis. He not only took the time, he really listened to my arguments and finally canceled the purchase.
☐ My boss and I agreed that we had to reduce the personnel in my department. I wanted to cut five positions; he wanted to cut eight. I argued my case for an hour. In the end he forced me to cut eight jobs, without even answering my arguments, and I realized he hadn't paid attention to anything I'd said.

In interpersonal relations, the law of reciprocity tends to rule. When supervisors use a lot of fine words about trust and respect but behave disdainfully, subordinates are likely to respond in kind.

Fairness means giving credit where it's due, being objective and impartial in performance appraisals, giving praise liberally. The opposite kind of behavior —favoritism, hypocrisy, misappropriating ideas and accomplishments, unethical behavior—is difficult to forgive and hugely destructive of trust. These two examples make the point well:

☐ One of my subordinates had what I thought was a terrific idea, and I told my boss. He agreed and immediately dictated a memo to the division manager outlining the idea and giving full credit where it was due. I learned sometime later that he never sent that memo but substituted another in which he took a good share of the credit for himself—and gave an equal share to me. I not only felt cheated, I felt I had somehow taken part in a plot to cheat the person who had the idea in the first place. It not only destroyed my relationship with that boss, it almost ruined my relationship with my subordinate.

☐ We were involved in a very difficult lawsuit with a former client. The battle lasted four years, and in the end we lost the case before the Supreme Court. When I gave the news to my boss, I was afraid he would take it badly, as a kind of personal failure. But he understood that we lost because of factors completely out of our control, and, instead of criticizing us, he praised our hard work and dedication.

Chronic lack of fairness will dry up trust and candor quickly, but every act of support and fair play will prime the pump.

Predictability is a matter of behaving consistently and dependably and of keeping both explicit and implicit promises. A broken promise can do considerable damage, as this example illustrates:

☐ When my boss hired me, she promised me a percentage of the profits on the project I was to manage. My arrival was delayed, so I took over the project as it

Not giving credit where it's due is hugely destructive of trust.

was winding down—without any profits to speak of. As soon as I cleaned up the loose ends, I took over a new project that was my responsibility from the outset. I managed it well, and profits were substantial. I felt badly cheated when I was told that my percentage deal applied to the first project only, that I had no such agreement on the second. I complained bitterly, and the company made it right. But it left a bad taste in my mouth, and I left shortly afterward.

Another form of predictability is consistency of character, which is, after all, the best proof of authenticity.

Competence, finally, means demonstrating technical and professional ability and good business sense. Employees don't want to be subordinate to people they see as incompetent. Trust grows from seeds of decent behavior, but it thrives on the admiration and respect that only a capable leader can command.

Learning to Recognize Signs of Trouble

Building trust and candor is a gradual process, a long chain of positive experiences: trusting employees with important assignments, publicly defending their positions and supporting their ideas, showing candor and fairness in evaluating their work, and so forth. And because trust takes time to build and has natural limits once achieved, it is easy to destroy. Betraying a confidence, breaking a promise, humiliating an employee in public, lying, withholding information, or excluding subordinates from groups in which they feel they rightly belong—any of these can do instant and irreparable damage to a trust relationship that has taken months or years to develop.

Given these limitations, can managers rely on subordinates to come forward with problems before they become critical?

The obvious answer is no, not entirely. Honest, forthright communication is the best source of information about problems that managers have, and good ones make the most of it. At the same time, they learn to recognize subtle signs of danger, and they develop and refine alternative sources of information to fill in the gaps. My interviews indicate that there are several important warning signs that managers can look for.

Decline in information flow is often a first sign of trouble. Streams of information suddenly go dry. Subordinates communicate less, express opinions reluctantly, avoid discussions—even meetings. Reports are late, subordinates are more difficult to reach, and follow-up has to be more thorough and deliberate. In this example, the first warning was a series of glib reassurances that didn't quite jibe with reality:

☐ I was exploration manager for an oil company in Venezuela. I began to notice that when I asked about one particular project, I got very short and superficial answers assuring me that everything was okay. But there were some contradictory signals. For example, labor turnover in the project was quite high. I had a gut feeling that something was seriously wrong. I contacted the area manager, but he couldn't put his finger on any specific problem. I called the field supervisor and still got no clear answers. I went to the field location and spent two days. Nothing. Then I sent a trustworthy young assistant to work with the field crews for a week, and he uncovered the problem. Local labor subcontractors were bribing the workers, increasing turnover, and taking in a lot of money for supplying replacements. We were not only spending more on labor bounties, we were often working with green hands instead of well-trained workers.

Deterioration of morale can reveal itself in lack of enthusiasm, reduced cooperation, increased complaints about workload, a tendency to dump more minor problems on the boss's desk. At a more advanced stage, absenteeism starts to rise and aggressive behavior—increased criticism, irritability, finger pointing, and the like—appears.

Ambiguous verbal messages come from subordinates who aren't quite comfortable with the information they are passing on. They may be reluctant to blow a potential problem out of proportion, or they may be testing to see if the door is open for a more serious discussion.

In one example, the head of an R&D lab asked the woman in charge of a large research project how a newly hired scientist was working out. The woman said, "He's very bright, but a bit strange. But he's working very hard and is extremely enthusiastic. He's okay." The boss missed the message. "I'm glad everything's okay" was all he said.

In this case, the woman's answer was a typical sign of trouble in sandwich form—positive, negative, positive. The subordinate who answers this way may simply be testing her boss's attention. When he failed to pick up on the "he's a bit strange" remark, she dropped the matter. Her boss never found out that she felt threatened by the scientist's brilliance and that his prima donna behavior made her angry. The friction between them grew, and she eventually took a job with another division.

Nonverbal signals can take a wide variety of forms, from body language to social behavior to changes in routines and habits.

The director of the international division of a major U.S. bank noticed that his chief of Asian operations had begun to work with his office door closed during his frequent visits to New York. This was unusual behavior: he was a gregarious soul, always available for lunch or a chat, and a closed door was out of character.

After two or three such visits, the director invited him to lunch to talk business. After a bottle of good wine, the younger man brought up what was really on his mind. He had heard rumors that his name had come up to head the European division—the most prestigious foreign assignment—and that the director had opposed him. The rumors were wrong. In fact, the bank was looking for someone to take the director's job, as he was about to be promoted, and the Asian operations chief was a prime candidate.

Consciously or unconsciously, the man sent a signal by closing his door. The lunch invitation was a nonthreatening way of finding out what the signal meant. At the time this took place, business had not yet begun to suffer, but more serious trouble might have

"It's a hostile attempt to take the company public!"

erupted if this man had continued to brood over false rumors. This prompt response to a nonverbal signal kept a small problem from growing into a big one.

Body language, incidentally, is easily misinterpreted. Popular books have encouraged many people to believe they are experts, but interpreting body language is risky business. Distress signals may be triggered by events in a person's private life, for example, and have nothing to do with the office. A more prudent approach is to see body language merely as an indication of a potential problem, without jumping to conclusions about what the problem may be.

Outside signals, such as customer complaints and problems spotted by other company divisions, are also clear warnings, but they often come too late. By this time, the trouble has usually reached the stage of impaired results—decreasing productivity, deteriorating quality, dwindling orders, declining numbers. By now the manager has long since failed.

Turning Hints into Information

When experienced managers see changes in the behavior of the people they supervise, they do their best to amplify hints and gather supplemental information.

As I pointed out at the beginning of this article, by far the easiest way of obtaining information is to get it from a subordinate, in plain English. Managers who have built good relationships with their subordinates often rely on this method. When they see the early warning signs of trouble, they ask questions.

As I have stressed, the answers to their questions will be only as honest as subordinates want to and dare to give. In other words, successful questioning depends partly on the level of trust. However, it also depends partly on a manager's ability to peel away superficial and sometimes misleading symptoms, much like the outside layers of an onion. Effective managers have good clinical sense. This man, for example, had a gut feeling that he had not yet reached the core of the problem:

□ My department was responsible for trade with the Far East, and I needed a good manager for China. I found what I thought was the perfect man. He not only knew all the traders but also spoke fluent English, French, Chinese, and Japanese. The new position was a promotion for him in terms of title and meant a big salary increase.

For the first year, he worked hard, things went well, and we made a lot of money. At the same time, he started to complain about his salary, arguing that other managers reporting to me and doing the same kind of work were getting 20% more—which was true. I told him he'd already had a 25% increase and that if he continued doing well, he could expect further raises over the next couple of years.

Then I began hearing his complaint from third parties all over the Far East. I discussed the matter with him many times, and eventually his salary rose to within 5% of the other managers. But something was still wrong. Then he suddenly got sick and disappeared from the office for two weeks. When he returned, his opening words were about salary.

Over the next couple of months, however, his health continued to deteriorate, and I began to wonder if salary was the real problem after all. I had several long talks with him and finally learned the truth. His deteriorating health was related to the job and the level of responsibility, which was too great for him to handle. He was so anxious that he couldn't sleep and was having problems with his family. As soon as we both understood the cause of his problem, I promised him a different job with less stress and frustration. He immediately became more relaxed and happier with his salary and his life.

The salary issue was only a symptom—a particularly misleading one, since the man was in fact underpaid by comparison with his colleagues. Notice also the escalation of symptoms from complaints to illness and the fact that it took the narrator several discussions to get at the actual truth. His persistence grew from a gut feeling that salary was not the real problem but rather a masking symptom.

> The best, the most common, and the hardest way of getting information is face to face, in plain English.

When conflicts arise between superiors and subordinates, the most common method of punishing the boss is to withhold information. So the greater the conflict is, the less effective direct questioning will be. Furthermore, if an honest answer means pointing out some of the boss's own shortcomings, almost anyone will think twice.

One way of circumventing this difficulty is to design anonymous forms of communication—suggestion boxes, questionnaires, and performance appraisals of managers by the people who work for them.

One manager took advantage of an odd condition in his office space to coax anonymous information from his staff. The offices were on the ninth and tenth floors of an office building and had two elevators of their own, which every employee rode several times a day. The boss put a bulletin board in each of them and posted frequent notices, including a weekly newsletter about office activities, personnel changes, and industry developments. He then let it be known informally that the bulletin boards were open to everyone—no approvals required—and when the first employee notices appeared, he made a point of leaving them in place for a full week. There were only two rules. First, no clippings from newspapers and magazines—contributions had to be original. Second, nothing tasteless or abusive—but complaints and bellyaching were okay.

The bulletin boards flourished, partly because most people had at least an occasional chance to ride alone and post their own views in private. For a while, there was even an anonymous weekly newspaper that handed out praise and criticism pretty

Using information properly is largely a matter of not *misusing* it.

freely and irreverently. It made some people uncomfortable, but it had no more avid reader than the boss, who learned volumes about the problems and views of his staff and organization.

Criticizing the boss's managerial style and professional competence is probably the hardest thing for employees to do. Remember two critical points: First, top performers are the most likely to feel secure enough to criticize, so ask them first. Second, many of your subordinates have learned the hard way that

honest negative feedback can be dangerous. Never ask for it unless you are certain you can handle it.

Building Information Networks

There are big differences between consuming, disseminating, and creating information. Effective managers seem to have a talent for all three.

Using information well is primarily a matter of not *misusing* it—of being discreet about its sources, of using it not as a weapon but only as a means of solving problems and improving the quality of work life.

Spreading information well means not spreading gossip but also not hoarding the truth. People in organizations want—and have a right to—information that will help them do their jobs better or otherwise affect their lives. In general, they also work better and suffer less stress and fewer complications when they are well informed. At the same time—and more important for this discussion—information attracts information. Managers who are generous with what they know seem to get as much as they give.

Creating information, finally, is a question of assembling scattered facts and interpreting them for others. Shaping data in this way is a skill that needs exercise. It is an act of education and, of course, an act of control.

The final positive outcome for information-rich individuals is that information flows to them as well as away from them. This ability to attract, create, and disseminate information can become an immense managerial asset, a self-perpetuating information network, and a means of creating the trust that the upward flow of candid information depends on. ⊟

Reprint 89203

FOR THE MANAGER'S BOOKSHELF

How Selfish Are People—Really?

Adam Smith and Charles Darwin gave us the economic explanation of ethics: self-interest.

by David Warsh

The Evolution of Cooperation
by Robert Axelrod
New York: Basic Books, 1984
241 pages. $8.95.

Passions Within Reason:
The Strategic Role of the Emotions
by Robert H. Frank
New York: W.W. Norton &
Company, 1988
304 pages. $19.95.

Events of the last ten years have sparked considerable controversy about the teaching and learning of ethics. But relatively little has been said concerning the deep-down underpinnings of our feelings about insider trading, malfeasance, and other betrayals of trust. This is too bad, because some important new thinking about our conception of ourselves as human beings is going on—thinking that so far has attracted only a small audience outside the technical precincts where it is taking place.

Two broad historical streams contribute to our ideas of right and wrong. One is the ancient tradition of religious, philosophical, and moral discourse, the province of the Golden Rule, the Ten Commandments, the Sermon on the Mount. Call this the humanist tradition. The other is the comparatively young tradition of the biological and social sciences. Chief among these is economics, with its central tenet that people, when they are able, tend to look out for themselves, choosing to maximize their advantage. Perhaps because it is cloaked in the mantle of science, the rhetoric and content of the latter tradition has become increasingly influential in our public life, often eclipsing religion and other traditional sources of instruction.

This eclipse began with two disarmingly simple sentences published by Adam Smith in *The Wealth of Nations* in 1776. "It is not from the benevolence of the butcher, the brewer, or the baker that we expect our dinner, but from their regard to their own interest. We address ourselves not to their humanity but to their self-love and never talk to them of our own necessities but of their advantages," Smith wrote. He then cobbled up his shrewd view of persons

as calculating and self-interested into the familiar "invisible hand," a sweeping vision of the interdependence of all markets everywhere. In Smith's world, competition among persons who pursue their own interest promotes the general welfare of society more effectively than the efforts of any individual who might deliberately set out to promote it. Better to open a shop, then, or manufacture a product than to curse the darkness; the market will harmonize self-interests more surely than usury laws and regulatory bodies.

Some 80 years later, Charles Darwin offered a second and perhaps even more powerful justification for selfish behavior—his theory of natural selection. Aptly described as "survival of the fittest," Darwin's evolutionary account of biological diversity was a powerful story of adaptation through the continuous variation of traits and the selection of those that improved "fitness." Differential reproduction and survival rates determined who survived and prospered and who didn't. Those who were capable of "looking out for number one" in a biological sense would survive, while natural selection would quickly sweep away the less fit.

Darwin's insights were immediately translated into a coarse social gospel that was itself quickly swept away. In a far more sophisticated and compelling form, his theory returned 100 years later as sociobiology. But in economics, the self-interest model of Adam Smith immediately acquired a deep hold on the popular imagination. Critics like Thorstein Veblen railed at the assumption of rational self-interest that was at the heart of the new conception—the view of man as "a lightning calculator of pleasures and pains, who oscillates like a homogenous globule of desire," as Veblen snorted. But the successes of the new approach were very great. The universal "laws" of supply and

David Warsh writes on economics for the Boston Globe, *where his column, "Economic Principals," appears regularly. He is the author of* The Idea of Economic Complexity *(Viking Press, 1984).*

demand could explain relative prices, differing wage rates, the composition of production: people really did build smaller houses if the price of fuel went up! And as economists refined their analyses, they extended their searchlight into new and unfamiliar areas.

For example, the American astronomer-turned-economist Simon Newcomb appalled outsiders in 1885 when he discussed the willingness of citizens to give dimes to the homeless in terms of the "demand for beggars," no different in principle from children giving pennies to organ-grinders in exchange for their services. "Mendicity will exist according to the same laws that govern the existence of other trades and occupations," Newcomb wrote. And, after all, who could doubt that plentiful alms might have an effect on the size of the street population? The emotion of pity was thus recast as a taste for a warm glow that the consumer included in his or her utility function.

Indeed, a word must be said here about the "utility function" that economists build into their models of consumer behavior. The idea of a single mathematical function capable of expressing complex systems of psychological motivation is an old one in economics; at the hands of statisticians and theorists it has been refined to a remarkable extent as something called "subjective expected utility" theory. As Nobel laureate Herbert Simon has explained, the model assumes that decision makers contemplate, in one comprehensive view, everything that lies before them; that they understand the range of alternative choices open to them, not only at the moment but also in the future; that they understand the consequences of every possible choice; and that they have reconciled all their conflicting desires into a single undeviating principle designed to maximize their gain in any conceivable situation.

Emotions such as love, loyalty, and outrage, like a sense of fairness, have little or no place in most of today's utility functions; a narrow selfishness is pervasive. Undoubtedly, as Si-

mon says, this construction is one of the impressive intellectual achievements of the first half of the twentieth century; after all, he is one of its architects. It is an elegant machine for applying reason to problems of choice. Equally certainly, however (and again following Simon), this Olympian stereotype is also a wildly improbable account of how human beings actually operate, and a preoccupation with it is doing economists more harm than good.

Nevertheless, so powerful is the optimizing cost-benefit approach that economists have applied it to an ever-increasing range of human experience in the years since World War II, always with illuminating results.

Economics transforms all human experience into a calculation of personal gain.

Education has become human capital. Job hunting is now a matter of search costs, tacit contracts, and a desire for leisure. Segregation laws are explained as a preference for discrimination and a willingness to pay the higher prices it entails. Love is an exchange relationship; decisions to bear children are analyzed as the purchase of "durable goods" of varying quality. Addiction, terrorism, arms control, the pace of scientific discovery—all have come under the economic magnifying glass.

Gary Becker, the foremost of the theorists who extended economic analysis into new areas, some years ago staked the claim that economics was the universal social science that could explain everything. George Stigler, himself an economics Nobel prizewinner, joked that he looked forward to the day when there would be only two Nobel prizes, "one for economics, and one for fiction."

At a certain point, all this rhetoric began to have real repercussions on everyday life. It's one thing just to talk about the demand for beggars;

it's another actually to calculate the lifetime "consumption of pleasure" for an accident victim. One group has extended the calculus of costs and benefits into law, seeking to substitute them for "fuzzy" notions of fairness and justice. Another group has analyzed the motives of interest groups and laid the foundations for deregulation. Still another has discovered what it calls "the market for corporate control" and touched off the restructuring of American industry. "Public choice" economics has brought to bear a withering analysis of self-interest in political and bureaucratic behavior. Indeed, there is hardly an area into which the steady gaze of economics has failed to penetrate—all of it a vision built on a conception of man as inherently, relentlessly self-aggrandizing. Long before there was a "Me-decade," academics had taught us to see ourselves as Economic Man.

But how realistic is this conception? How selfish are people, really? For the most part, humanists have simply ignored the spread of the new economic ideas. Instead, they have continued to talk about right and wrong in their accustomed frameworks—everything from sermons to novels to TV scripts. With the exception of the brilliant 30-year campaign against perfect rationality by Herbert Simon (and the guerrilla war of John Kenneth Galbraith), the major universities have produced no sustained criticism by economists of the central tenets of utility theory.

Psychologists and sociologists, confronted with ubiquitous theorizing about the economics of decisions they previously considered their domain, have been quick to complain of "economic imperialism" but rather slow to launch counterattacks. In the last few years, however, a small but growing number of persons has begun to come to grips with assumptions underlying economic interpretations of human nature. Robert B. Reich and Jane Mansbridge have grappled with the significance of the self-interest paradigm for political philosophy, for example. Howard Margolis and Amitai Etzioni have propounded theories of a dual human nature, competitive and altruistic by turns. Sometimes these disagreements come to the attention of outsiders in the press, like me, on the reasonable grounds that arguments over what constitutes human nature are too important to be left entirely to the experts.

There is, however, also a reexamination of rationality going on inside the economics business. This effort seeks not so much to overturn the idea of universal competition as to

> ## Economics replaces emotions with math. Love is an exchange relationship.

take it to a new and subtler level of understanding. If history is any guide, this is the development to watch, for as Paul Samuelson likes to say, economics will be changed by its friends, not its critics. Change there certainly is. Efforts to produce a theory of cooperation or of altruism suggest that much of the certitude about the nature of man that economists have advanced these last 100 years may have been misleading. There may be a good and logical foundation for doctrines of loyalty and sympathetic understanding after all.

Perhaps the best-known book to have opened up new avenues in the study of human behavior (at least along the economic axis) is Robert Axelrod's *The Evolution of Cooperation*. From its beginnings nine years ago as a report published in the *Journal of Conflict Resolution* on a computer tournament among diverse strategies, the argument grew to become a highly successful article in *Science* magazine (it won the Newcomb Cleveland prize in 1981), then a book published to wide acclaim in 1984, then a paperback issued a year later. Since then, it has been extensively discussed, taught in business schools, employed in arms limitation talks, consulted by labor negotiators.

Axelrod begins his analysis with the familiar prisoners' dilemma, an illustrative exercise that has been one of the dominating features of the landscape since game theory first brought considerations of strategic behavior to economic theory 40 years ago. In this situation, two prisoners are accused of a crime, which they did in fact commit. The jailers structure the payoffs to encourage each prisoner to confess: if neither prisoner confesses, both are given light jail sentences of, say, one year. If one prisoner confesses while the other remains silent, the first goes free while the other receives a heavy sentence of, say, ten years. If both prisoners confess, both get the heavy sentence, but with time off for good behavior – say, five years. Neither one knows what the other is going to do.

Clearly, each player does better by confessing than by remaining silent: if he confesses and his partner doesn't, he goes home immediately, while if he and his partner both confess, they each get five years instead of ten. So the question is, why would either ever stand pat and say nothing? How is it that cooperation ever gets started?

The answer, it turns out, lies in repeated play. Researchers before Axelrod had noted that the tendency to cooperate in prisoners' dilemma games increased dramatically whenever a player was paired repeatedly with the same partner. In these circumstances, a strategy called Tit for Tat quickly emerged: cooperate on the first move, then follow suit on each successive move; cooperate if your partner cooperates, defect if he defects, at least until the end of the game is in sight (then defect no matter what). This strategy has, of course, been known at least since Biblical times as "an eye for an eye, a tooth for a tooth."

What Axelrod forcefully contributed was the much-prized quality of robustness. He showed that Tit for Tat players in reiterated games would find each other and accumulate higher scores than meanies who always defected. He demonstrated how clusters of Tit for Tat players might invade an evolutionary game and win. He generalized the strategy

and found that Tit for Tat worked well against a wide range of counterstrategies simulated on computers as well as in biological systems from bacteria to the most complex species. He published his computer tournament results and proofs of his theoretical propositions.

For nonexperts, the real persuasive power of Axelrod's argument lay in the variety of real world situations he found to which Tit for Tat applied. Businesses really did cooperate, extending each other reciprocal credit, until liquidation loomed. Then trust fell apart, and even old associates vied with each other to see who could file the quickest writs. Elected representatives really did learn to cooperate, for if they didn't learn to produce legislative results through logrolling, they weren't reelected.

But the dramatic centerpiece of Axelrod's book is a long analysis of the live-and-let-live system that evolved in between the large battles of World War I. Generals could force soldiers into battle whenever they could directly monitor their behavior; but when headquarters wasn't watching, the soldiers restored tacit truces. The key to the system was that soldiers in the trenches rarely moved; they got to know each other, and became, in essence, partners in an oft-repeated prisoners' dilemma game. When one player "defected," the common penalty response was an exchange of two-for-one or three-for-one. A French soldier explained, "We fire two shots for every one fired at us, but we never fire first." This brief historical excursion is a convincing proof that cooperation could evolve among even the most desperate of egoists, those who had been issued rifles and ordered to kill.

In a recent survey of the work since the publication of his book, Axelrod wrote that cooperation based on reciprocity had been noted in everything from vampire bats to vervet monkeys to stickleback fish, and that advice based on the theory had been offered for problems in breaches of contract, child custody arrangements, superpower negotiations, and international trade. We were constantly gaining a better understand-

THINGS PUT INTO PERSPECTIVE

WHILE·U·WAIT

ing of the conditions in which cooperation would arise, he said; light had been cast on the significance of variations in the number of players, the payoff structure, population structure and dynamics, and the "shadow of the future," meaning the prospect of retaliation. The study of cooperation was well established and growing, Axelrod said; cooperative behavior could be taught.

For humanists, however, and those scientists who are troubled by the conviction that there is more to human nature than the purely selfish, even this description of cooperation through reciprocity is disappointing. Axelrod's work is built firmly on the foundation of self-interest. In a sense, his prisoners' dilemma is no dilemma at all to those who see human choice as strictly rational. There is no divided loyalty here, no painful choice, just a simple calculation. Choose the course with the bigger payoff now: cooperate if you think you are going to play again, stiff your partner if you think you won't see him again. There is no reason to feel embarrassment; cheating is the rational thing to do as long as you don't expect to be caught.

The trouble is that there is a wide range of familiar, everyday behavior

that we all know doesn't square with this logic. Travelers still leave the requisite tip in restaurants in cities to which they will never return. Citizens vote in elections even though they know that their vote is extremely unlikely to make a difference. People help strangers in trouble. They willingly bear costs in the name of fair play. They remain married in situations in which it would clearly pay to cut and run. A highly imaginative approach for dealing with such instances, and for extending economics to the realm of the emotions in general, is proposed in a new book by Robert H. Frank.

Frank, a Cornell University professor, spent ten years performing the comparatively humdrum duties of a teacher before going to Washington, D.C. as Alfred Kahn's chief economist at the Civil Aeronautics Board. Kahn moved on to serve as President Jimmy Carter's "anti-inflation czar" and Frank remained behind to help close up the CAB. When he returned to Cornell, a couple of remarkable books tumbled out, sufficient to place Frank on leading lists of the half-dozen most interesting mid-life economists working in the United States today. *Choosing the Right Pond: Human Behavior and the*

Quest for Status is an exploration of status fairly bursting with novel ideas about why people tend to organize themselves into leagues. It is the kind of book that any reader, perhaps especially readers of this magazine, can pick up and browse with pleasure.

Now, with *Passions Within Reason*, Frank has written a somewhat tighter and more demanding book. But it is the one that is destined to help change the way we think about the basis of ethical behavior.

Frank's starting point is to take emotions as a given. They exist, he says. They're probably not the "fuzzy thinking" that most economists believe them to be. We see a homeless person, we are moved to pity; we see a child in danger, we are moved to help; we see a sterling baseball play, we are stirred and excited; we imagine our mate with another person, we burn with jealously and rage; we contemplate stealing from an unattended change box, we blush with shame. Thinking as an evolutionist, Frank asks, what useful purpose might these feelings serve?

The answer he gives is that the highly useful function of the emotions is precisely to short-circuit narrowly self-interested behavior, because honest and helpful people are those whom everyone wants for partners, and because nobody messes with people who get angry when they are crossed. It is well known that the ball hog doesn't make the team, that, in the end, the utter egoist doesn't win at romance; the existence of mitigating emotions is evolution's way of making us more "fit" partners.

For Frank, emotions are a way of solving the "commitment problem" —the fact that, for society to work, people have to make binding commitments that can later require otherwise rational actors to behave in ways that seem contrary to their self-interest. There are any number of everyday situations where common sense dictates that it helps to have one's hands tied by emotional predispositions.

If you want people to trust you, it helps, not hurts, to blush when you tell a lie. If you want people not to take advantage of you, it helps, not hurts, to be known as someone who will fly into an irrational rage if you are cheated.

The self-interest model counsels that opportunists have every reason to break the rules when they think no one is looking. Frank says his commitment model challenges this view "to the core," because it suggests a compelling answer to the question, "What's in it for me if I'm honest?" Frank writes, "I am still annoyed if a plumber asks me to pay cash; but now my resentment is tempered by thinking of (my own) tax compliance as an investment in maintaining an honest predisposition. Virtue is not only its own reward here; it may also lead to material rewards in other contexts."

The trick here is that, in order to work, your emotional predisposition must be observable; in order for evolutionary processes to produce the kind of emotionally based, altruistic behavior that interests Frank, cooperators have to be able to recognize each other. Moreover, an emotional commitment must be costly to fake; the Quakers grew rich on the strength of their reputation for honest dealing, partly because it takes just too much time and energy to become a Quaker in order to take advantage of the opportunity to cheat. Any Quaker you meet is almost bound to be honest.

The same principle applies to the rich set of linkages between the brain and the rest of the body, according to Frank. Posture, the rate of breathing, pitch and timbre of the voice, facial muscle tone and expression, eye movement—all these offer clues to a speaker's emotional state. An actor can fake them for a few minutes, but not more. Even a baby can discriminate between a real smile and a forced one. Humans have evolved this complicated signaling apparatus because it is useful in communicating information about character. And forming character and recognizing it is what emotions are all about. For Frank, moral sentiments are like a spinning gyroscope: they are predisposed to maintain their initial orientation. Nature's role is to provide the gyroscope, in the form of "hard wiring" between the body and brain; culture's role is to provide the spin.

In the end, Frank sees his commitment model as a kind of secular substitute for the religious glue that for centuries bound people together in a compact of mutuality and civility. To the question, "Why shouldn't I cheat when no one is looking?" Frank notes that religion always had a compelling answer: "Because God will know!" But the threat of damnation has lost much of its force in the last century or so, and "Smith's carrot and Darwin's stick have by now rendered character development an all but forgotten theme in many industrial countries." The commitment model offers a way back to good behavior based on the logic of self-interest: gains will accrue almost immediately to those who become trustworthy characters. In this view, no man is an island, entire of himself, for each is a part of the other fellow's utility function, thanks to the biological adaptation of the emotions.

Does this make sense? Of course it does. What Axelrod and Frank have in common is that each has offered an account of how "nice" people survive and thrive in the economic world—why they aren't automatically competed out of existence by persons who are more relentlessly self-seeking. What makes Frank's approach more appealing is that it treats emotions as observed facts of life and attempts to account for them rather than immediately rationalizing them away as a regrettable imperfection of the spirit. He gets at what we really mean by "honest"—as opposed to merely prudent behavior.

There are still other explanatory approaches to this situation, in some cases even more promising. Herbert Simon, for example, has proposed a trait he calls "docility"—meaning susceptibility to social influence and instruction—that would contribute to individual fitness and so explain altruism within the framework of natural selection. Such evolutionary approaches may yield more understanding of the rise of the complex organizations that populate the modern world economy than reasoning about the equilibrium of the firm.

Whatever way you cut it, the "news" from economics is beginning to confirm what most working people know in their bones: that integrity and fellow-feeling are highly effective forms of individual fitness. When you consider the amount of time and effort that goes into the moral education of the child, the claim of the economists that there is self-interest and only self-interest is preposterous.

In general, children learn the Golden Rule in kindergarten. Religious traditions introduce them to the absolute prohibitions of the Ten Commandments. In families they learn the role of the conscience and are introduced to many forms of cooperation, including frequent self-sacrifice in the interest of the group.

In schools they learn to be members of cliques, dividing their loyalties between friends inside and outside their gangs. In sports they learn teamwork, including the lesson that nice guys finish all over the standings; as spectators, they learn that fan loyalty may pay off, as may the lack of it.

In love and war they learn sympathetic understanding, and they return constantly to the narrative arts (TV, movies, talk shows, novels, and biographies) to exercise and replenish their understanding. They may even go to military academies or business schools to learn more intricate forms of cooperation before going out into the world of large organizations to practice it.

Character development, in other words, is far from "forgotten" in industrialized countries. Instead, it is simply ignored by most economists while practiced by nearly everyone else—including most economists.

If practitioners may now turn to economics to learn that the conscious pursuit of self-interest is often incompatible with its attainment, so much the better—for economics. Most of us will continue to disregard the utterly premature claims of economics to "scientific" certainty about the intricacies of human nature. We will continue looking to the humanistic tradition for our instruction in ethics, as we have all along. ▽

Reprint 89314

Special Report

A traveler's guide to gifts and bribes

Jeffrey A. Fadiman

"What do I say if he asks for a bribe?" I asked myself while enduring the all-night flight to Asia. Uncertain, I shared my concern with the man sitting beside me, a CEO en route to Singapore. Intrigued, he passed it on to his partners next to him. No one seemed sure.

Among American executives doing business overseas, this uncertainty is widespread. Consider, for example, each of the following situations:

☐ You are invited to the home of your foreign colleague. You learn he lives in a palatial villa. What gift might both please your host and ease business relations? What if he considers it to be a bribe? What if he *expects* it to be a bribe? Why do you feel uneasy?

☐ Your company's product lies on the dock of a foreign port. To avoid spoilage, you must swiftly transport it inland. What "gift," if any, would both please authorities and facilitate your business? What if they ask for "gifts" of $50? $50,000? $500,000? When does a gift become a bribe? When do you stop feeling comfortable?

☐ Negotiations are complete. The agreement is signed. One week later, a minister asks your company for $1 million—"for a hospital"—simultaneously suggesting that "other valuable considerations" might come your way as the result of future favors on both sides. What response, if any, would please him, satisfy you, and help execute the signed agreement?

☐ You have been asked to testify before the Securities and Exchange Commission regarding alleged violations of the Foreign Corrupt Practices Act. How would you explain the way you handled the examples above? Would your explanations both satisfy those in authority and ensure the continued overseas operation of your company?

Much of the discomfort Americans feel when faced with problems of this nature is due to U.S. law. Since 1977, congressional passage of the Foreign Corrupt Practices Act has transformed hypothetical problems into practical dilemmas and has created considerable anxiety among Americans who deal with foreign governments and companies. The problem is particularly difficult for those conducting business in the developing nations, where the rules that govern payoffs may differ sharply from our own. In such instances, U.S. executives may face not only legal but also ethical and cultural dilemmas: How do businesspeople comply with customs that conflict with both their sense of ethics and this nation's law?

One way to approach the problem is to devise appropriate corporate responses to payoff requests. The suggestions that follow apply to those developing Asian, African, and Middle Eastern nations, still in transition toward industrial societies, that have retained aspects of their communal traditions. These approaches do not assume that those who adhere to these ideals exist in selfless bliss, requesting private payments only for communal ends, with little thought of self-enrichment. Nor do these suggestions apply to situations of overt extortion, where U.S. companies are forced to provide funds. Instead they explore a middle way in which non-Western colleagues may have several motives when requesting a payoff, thereby providing U.S. managers with several options.

Decisions & dilemmas

My own first experience with Third World bribery may illustrate the inner conflict Americans can feel when asked to break the rules. It occurred in East Africa and began with this request: "Oh, and Bwana, I would like 1,000 shillings as Zawadi, my gift. And, as we are now friends, for Chai, my tea, an eight-band radio, to bring to my home when you visit."

Both *Chai* and *Zawadi* can be Swahili terms for "bribe." He delivered these requests in respectful tones. They came almost as an afterthought, at the conclusion of negotiations in which we had settled the details of a projected business venture. I had looked forward to buying my counterpart a final drink to complete the deal symbolically in the American fashion. Instead, after we had settled every contractual aspect, he expected money.

The amount he suggested, although insignificant by modern standards, seemed large at the time. Nonetheless, it was the radio that got to me. Somehow it added insult to injury. Outwardly, I kept smiling. Inside, my stomach boiled. My own world view equates bribery with sin. I expect monetary issues to be settled before contracts are signed. Instead, although the negotiations were complete, he expected me to pay out once more. Once? How often? Where would it stop? My reaction took only moments to formulate. "I'm

Jeffrey Fadiman is a professor of international marketing at San Jose State University. He has 22 years of experience in Afro-Asia, including 7 years in Africa's tourist industry.

American," I declared. "I don't pay bribes." Then I walked away. That walk was not the longest in my life. It was, however, one of the least commercially productive.

As it turned out, I had misunderstood him – in more ways than one. By misinterpreting both his language and his culture, I lost an opportunity for a business deal and a personal relationship that would have paid enormous dividends without violating either the law or my own sense of ethics.

Go back through the episode – but view it this time with an East African perspective. First, my colleague's language should have given me an important clue as to how he saw our transaction. Although his limited command of English caused him to frame his request as a command – a phrasing I instinctively found offensive – his tone was courteous. Moreover, if I had listened more carefully, I would have noted that he had addressed me as a superior: he used the honorific *Bwana*, meaning "sir," rather than *Rafiki* (or friend), used between equals. From his perspective, the language was appropriate; it reflected the differences in our personal wealth and in the power of the institutions we each represented.

Having assigned me the role of the superior figure in the economic transaction, he then suggested how I should use my position in accord with his culture's traditions – logically assuming that I would benefit by his prompting. In this case, he suggested that money and a radio would be appropriate gifts. What he did not tell me was that his culture's traditions required him to use the money to provide a feast – in my honor – to which he would invite everyone in his social and commercial circle whom he felt I should meet. The radio would simply create a festive atmosphere at the party. This was to mark the beginning of an ongoing relationship with reciprocal benefits.

He told me none of this. Since I was willing to do business in local fashion, I was supposed to know. In fact, I had not merely been invited to a dwelling but through a gateway into the maze of gifts and formal visiting that linked him to his kin. He hoped that I would respond in local fashion. Instead, I responded according to my cultural norms and walked out both on the chance to do business and on the opportunity to make friends.

The legal side. Perhaps from a strictly legal perspective my American reaction was warranted. In the late 1970s, as part of the national reaction to Watergate, the SEC sued several large U.S. companies for alleged instances of bribery overseas. One company reportedly authorized $59 million in contributions to political parties in Italy, including the Communist party. A second allegedly paid $4 million to a political party in South Korea. A third reportedly provided $450,000 in "gifts" to Saudi generals. A fourth may have diverted $377,000 to fly planeloads of voters to the Cook Islands to rig elections there.

"What may initially appear as begging, bribery, or blackmail may be revealed as local tradition, cross-cultural courtesy, or attempts to make friends."

The sheer size of the payments and the ways they had been used staggered the public. A U.S. senate committee reported "corrupt" foreign payments involving hundreds of millions of dollars by more than 400 U.S. corporations, including 117 of the *Fortune* "500." The SEC described the problem as a national crisis.

In response, Congress passed the Foreign Corrupt Practices Act in 1977. The law prohibits U.S. corporations from providing or even offering payments to foreign political parties, candidates, or officials with discretionary authority under circumstances that might induce recipients to misuse their positions to assist the company to obtain, maintain, or retain business.

The FCPA does not forbid payments to lesser figures, however. On the contrary, it explicitly allows facilitating payments ("grease") to persuade foreign officials to perform their normal duties, at both the clerical and ministerial levels. The law establishes no monetary guidelines but requires

companies to keep reasonably detailed records that accurately and fairly reflect the transactions.

The act also prohibits indirect forms of payment. Companies cannot make payments of this nature while "knowing or having reason to know" that any portion of the funds will be transferred to a forbidden recipient to be used for corrupt purposes as previously defined. Corporations face fines of up to $1 million. Individuals can be fined $10,000 – which the corporation is forbidden to indemnify – and sentenced to a maximum of five years in prison. In short, private payments by Americans abroad can mean violation of U.S. law, a consideration that deeply influences U.S. corporate thinking.

The ethical side. For most U.S. executives, however, the problem goes beyond the law. Most Americans share an aversion to payoffs. In parts of Asia, Africa, and the Middle East, however, certain types of bribery form an accepted element of their commercial traditions. Of course, nepotism, shakedown, and similar practices do occur in U.S. business; these practices, however, are both forbidden by law and universally disapproved.

Americans abroad reflect these sentiments. Most see themselves as personally honest and professionally ethical. More important, they see themselves as preferring to conduct business according to the law, both American and foreign. They also know that virtually all foreign governments – including those notorious for corruption – have rigorously enforced statutes against most forms of private payoff. In general, there is popular support for these anticorruption measures. In Malaysia, bribery is publicly frowned on and punishable by long imprisonment. In the Soviet Union, Soviet officials who solicit bribes can be executed.

Reflecting this awareness, most U.S. businesspeople prefer to play by local rules, competing in the open market according to the quality, price, and services provided by their product. Few, if any, want to make illegal payments of any kind to anybody. Most prefer to obey both local laws and their own ethical convictions while remaining able to do business.

The cultural side. Yet, as my African experience suggests, indigenous traditions often override the law. In some developing nations, payoffs have become a norm. The problem is compounded when local payoff practices are rooted in a "communal heritage," ideals inherited from a preindustrial past where a community leader's wealth—however acquired—was shared throughout the community. Those who hoarded were scorned as antisocial. Those who shared won status and authority. Contact with Western commerce has blurred the ideal, but even the most individualistic businesspeople remember their communal obligations.

Contemporary business practices in those regions often reflect these earlier ideals. Certain forms of private payoff have endured for centuries. The Nigerian practice of *dash* (private payments for private services), for example, goes back to fifteenth century contacts with the Portuguese, in which Africans solicited "gifts" (trade goods) in exchange for labor. Such solicitation can pose a cultural dilemma to Americans who may be unfamiliar with the communal nuances of non-Western commercial conduct. To cope, they may denigrate these traditions, perceiving colleagues who solicit payments as unethical and their culture as corrupt.

Or they may respond to communal business methods by ignoring them, choosing instead to deal with foreign counterparts purely in Western fashion. This approach will usually work—up to a point. Non-Western businesspeople who deal with U.S. executives, for example, are often graduates of Western universities. Their language skills, commercial training, and professional demeanor, so similar to ours, make it comfortable to conduct business. But when these same colleagues shift to non-Western behavior, discussing gifts or bribes, Americans are often shocked.

Obviously, such reactions ignore the fact that foreign businesspeople have more than one cultural dimension. Managers from developing countries may hold conflicting values: one instilled by exposure to the West, the other imposed by local tradition. Non-Western businesspeople may see no conflict in negotiating contracts along Western lines, then reverting to indigenous traditions when discussing private payments. For Americans, however, this transition may be hard to make.

My experience suggests that most non-Westerners are neither excessively corrupt nor completely communal. Rather, they are simultaneously drawn to both indigenous and Western ideals. Many have internalized the Western norms of personal enrichment along with those of modern commerce, while simultaneously adhering to indigenous traditions by fulfilling communal obligations. Requests for payoffs may spring from both these ideals. Corporate responses must therefore be designed to satisfy them both.

Background for payoffs

Throughout non-Western cultures, three traditions form the background for discussing payoffs: the inner circle, future favors, and the gift exchange. Though centuries old, each has evolved into a modern business concept. Americans who work in the Third World need to learn about them so they can work within them.

The inner circle. Most individuals in developing nations classify others into some form of "ins" and "outs." Members of more communal societies, influenced by the need to strive for group prosperity, divide humanity into those with whom they have relationships and those with whom they have none. Many Africans, for instance, view people as either "brothers" or "strangers." Relationships with brothers may be real—kin, however distant—or fictional, extending to comrades or "mates." Comrades, however, may both speak and act like kin, address one another as family, and assume obligations of protection and assistance that Americans reserve for nuclear families.

Together, kin and comrades form an inner circle, a fictional "family," devoted to mutual protection and prosperity. Like the "old boy networks" that operate in the United States, no single rule defines membership in the inner circle. East Africans may include "age mates," individuals of similar age; West Africans, "homeboys," all men of similar region; Chinese, members of a dialect group; Indians, members of a caste. In most instances, the "ins"

include extended families and their friends.

Beyond this magic circle live the "outs": strangers, aliens, individuals with no relationship to those within. Communal societies in Southern Africa, for example, describe these people in all their millions as "predators," implying savage creatures with whom the "ins" lack any common ground. The motives of outsiders inspire fear, not because there is danger but simply because they are unknown. Although conditioned to display courtesy, insiders prefer to restrict both social and commercial dealings to those with whom they have dependable relationships. The ancient principle can still be found in modern commerce; non-Western businesspeople often prefer to restrict commercial relationships to those they know and trust.

Not every U.S. manager is aware of this division. Those who investigate often assume that their nationality, ethnic background, and alien culture automatically classify them as "outs." Non-Western colleagues, however, may regard specific Westerners as useful contacts, particularly if they seem willing to do business in local fashion. They may, therefore, consider bringing certain individuals into their inner circles in such a manner as to benefit both sides.

Overseas executives, if asked to work within such circles, should find their business prospects much enhanced. These understandings often lead to implicit quid pro quos. For example, one side might agree to hire workers from only one clan; in return the other side would guarantee devoted labor. As social and commercial trust grows, the Westerners may be regarded less and less as aliens or predators and more and more as comrades or kin. Obviously, this is a desirable transition, and executives assigned to work within this type of culture may wish to consider whether these inner circles exist, and if so, whether working within them will enhance business prospects.

The future favor. A second non-Western concept that relates to payoffs is a system of future favors. Relationships within the inner circles of non-Western nations function through such favors. In Japan, the corresponding system is known as "inner duty" or *giri*. On Mt. Kenya, it is "inner relation-

"Look, pal, econometrics *aside, will you lend me ten bucks or won't you?"*

These sentiments can also operate within non-Western commercial circles, where business favors can replace hens, but *uthoni* are what sweetens corporate life. Western interest lies in doing business; non-Western, in forming bonds so that business can begin. Westerners seek to discharge obligations; non-Westerners, to create them. Our focus is on producing short-term profit; theirs, on generating future favors. The success of an overseas venture may depend on an executive's awareness of these differences.

The gift exchange. One final non-Western concept that can relate to payoffs is a continuous exchange of gifts. In some developing nations, gifts form the catalysts that trigger future favors. U.S. executives often wish to present gifts appropriate to cultures where they are assigned, to the point where at least one corporation has commissioned a special study of the subject. They may be less aware, however, of the long-range implications of gift giving within these cultures. Two of these may be particularly relevant to CEOs concerned with payoffs.

In many non-Western commercial circles, the tradition of gift giving has evolved into a modern business tool intended to create obligation as well as affection. Recipients may be gratified by what they receive, but they also incur an obligation that they must some day repay. Gift giving in these cultures may therefore operate in two dimensions: one meant to provide short-term pleasure; the other, long-range bonds.

This strategy is common in Moslem areas of Africa and Asia. Within these cultures, I have watched export merchants change Western clientele from browsers to buyers by inviting them to tea. Seated, the customers sip at leisure, while merchandise is brought before them piece by piece. The seller thus achieves three goals. His clients have been honored, immobilized, and placed under obligation.

In consequence, the customers often feel the need to repay in kind. Lacking suitable material gifts, they frequently respond as the merchant intends: with decisions to buy—not because they need the merchandise but to return the seller's gift of hospitality. The buyers, considering their obliga-

ship," *uthoni*. Filipinos describe it as "inner debt," *utani na loob*. All systems of this type assume that any individual under obligation to another has entered a relationship in which the first favor must be repaid in the future, when convenient to all sides.

Neither side defines the manner of repayment. Rather, both understand that some form of gift or service will repay the earlier debt with interest. This repayment places the originator under obligation. The process then begins again, creating a lifelong cycle. The relationship that springs from meeting lifelong obligations builds the trust that forms a basis for conducting business.

My own introduction to the future favors system may illustrate the process. While conducting business on Mt. Kenya in the 1970s, I visited a notable local dignitary. On completing our agenda, he stopped my rush to leave by presenting me a live and angry hen. Surprised, I stammered shaky "thank-yous," then walked down the mountain with my kicking, struggling bird. Having discharged my obligation—at

least in Western terms—by thanking him, I cooked the hen, completed my business, eventually left Kenya, and forgot the incident.

Years later, I returned on different business. It was a revelation. People up and down the mountain called out to one another that I had come back to "return the dignitary's hen." To them, the relationship that had sprung up between us had remained unchanged throughout the years. Having received a favor, I had now come back to renew the relationship by returning it.

I had, of course, no such intention. Having forgotten the hen incident, I was also unaware of its importance to others. Embarrassed, I slipped into a market and bought a larger hen, then climbed to his homestead to present it. Again I erred, deciding to apologize in Western fashion for delaying my return. "How can a hen be late?" he replied. "Due to the bird, we have *uthoni* [obligations, thus a relationship]. That is what sweetens life. What else was the hen for but to bring you here again?"

tion discharged, leave the premises believing relations have ended. The sellers, however, hope they have just begun. Their intent is to create relationships that will cause clients to return. A second visit would mean presentation of another gift, perhaps of greater value. That, in turn, might mean a second purchase, leading to further visits, continued gifts, and a gradual deepening of personal and commercial relations intended to enrich both sides.

The point of the process, obviously, is not the exchanges themselves but the relationships they engender. The gifts are simply catalysts. Under ideal circumstances the process should be unending, with visits, gifts, gestures, and services flowing back and forth among participants throughout their lives. The universally understood purpose is to create reciprocal good feelings and commercial prosperity among all concerned.

Gift giving has also evolved as a commercial "signal." In America, gifts exchanged by business colleagues may signal gratitude, camaraderie, or perhaps the discharge of minor obligations. Among non-Westerners, gifts may signal the desire to begin both social and commercial relationships with members of an inner circle. That signal may also apply to gifts exchanged with Westerners. If frequently repeated, such exchanges may be signals of intent. For Americans, the signal may suggest a willingness to work within a circle of local business colleagues, to assume appropriate obligations, and to conduct business in local ways. For non-Western colleagues, gifts may imply a wish to invite selected individuals into their commercial interactions.

Approaches to payoffs

While U.S. corporations may benefit from adapting to local business concepts, many indigenous business traditions, especially in developing regions, are alien to the American experience and therefore difficult to implement by U.S. field personnel—as every executive who has tried to sit cross-legged for several hours with Third World counterparts will attest.

Conversely, many non-Western administrators are particularly well informed about U.S. business practices, thus permitting U.S. field representatives to function on familiar ground. Nonetheless, those willing to adapt indigenous commercial concepts to U.S. corporate needs may find that their companies can benefit in several ways. Through working with a circle of non-Western business colleagues, and participating fully in the traditional exchange of gifts and favors, U.S. executives may find that their companies increase the chance of preferential treatment; use local methods and local contacts to gain market share; develop trust to reinforce contractual obligations; and minimize current risk, while maximizing future opportunities by developing local expertise.

Corporations that adapt to local business concepts may also develop methods to cope with local forms of payoff. Current approaches vary from culture to culture, yet patterns do appear. Three frequently recur in dealings between Americans and non-Westerners: gifts, bribes, and other considerations.

Gifts: the direct request. This form of payoff may occur when key foreign businesspeople approach their U.S. colleagues to solicit "gifts." Solicitations of this type have no place in U.S. business circles where they could be construed as exploitation. Obviously, the same may hold true overseas, particularly in areas where shakedown, bribery, and extortion may be prevalent. There is, however, an alternative to consider. To non-Western colleagues, such requests may simply be a normal business strategy, designed to build long-term relationships.

To U.S. businesspeople, every venture is based on the bottom line. To non-Western colleagues, a venture is based on the human relationships that form around it. Yet, when dealing with us they often grow uncertain as to how to form these relationships. How can social ties be created with Americans who speak only of business, even when at leisure? How can traditions of gift giving be initiated with people unaware of the traditions? Without the exchange of gifts, how can obligations be created? Without obligations, how can there be trust?

Faced with such questions, non-Western business colleagues may understandably decide to initiate gift-giving relationships on their own. If powerful, prominent, or wealthy, they may simply begin by taking on the role of giver. If less powerful or affluent, some may begin by suggesting they become recipients. There need be no dishonor in such action, since petitioners know they will repay with future favors whatever inner debt they incur.

The hosts may also realize that, as strangers, Americans may be unaware of local forms of gift giving as well as their relationship to business norms. Or they may be cognizant of such relationships but may have no idea of how to enter into them. In such instances, simple courtesy may cause the hosts to indicate—perhaps obliquely—how proper entry into the local system should be made. Such was the unfortunate case with my East African colleague's request for the eight-band radio.

Cultural barriers can be difficult to cross. Most Americans give generously, but rarely on request. When solicited, we feel exploited. Solicitations may seem more relevant, however, if examined from the perspective of the non-Western peoples with whom we are concerned.

Often, in societies marked by enormous gaps between the rich and the poor, acts of generosity display high status. To withhold gifts is to deny the affluence one has achieved. Non-Western counterparts often use lavish hospitality both to reflect and to display their wealth and status within local society. When Americans within these regions both represent great wealth through association with their corporations and seek high status as a tool to conduct business, it may prove more profitable for the corporation to give than to receive.

In short, when asked for "gifts" by foreign personnel, managers may consider two options. The first option is to regard each query as extortion and every petitioner as a potential thief. The second is to consider the request within its local context. In nations where gifts generate a sense of obligation, it may prove best to give them, thereby creating inner debts among key foreign colleagues in the belief that they will repay them over time. If such requests indeed reflect a local way of doing business, they may be gateways into the workings of its commercial world. One U.S. option, therefore, is to consider the effect of providing "gifts"—even on direct request—in terms of the relationships required to implement the corporation's long-range plans.

Bribes: the indirect request. A second approach to payoffs, recurrent in non-Western business circles, is the indirect request. Most Third World people prefer the carrot to the stick. To avoid unpleasant confrontation, they designate third parties to suggest that "gifts" of specified amounts be made to those in local power circles. In explanation they cite the probability of future favors in return. No line exists, of course, dividing gifts from bribes. It seems that direct solicitation involves smaller amounts, while larger ones require go-betweens. On occasion, however, the sums requested can be staggering: in 1976, for example, U.S. executives in Qatar were asked for a $1.5 million "gift" for that nation's minister of oil.

U.S. responses to such queries must preserve both corporate funds and executive relationships with those in power. While smaller gifts may signal a desire to work with the local business circles, a company that supplies larger sums could violate both local antipayoff statutes and the FCPA. Conversely, outright rejection of such requests may cause both the go-betweens and those they represent to lose prestige and thus possibly prompt retaliation.

In such instances, the FCPA may actually provide beleaguered corporate executives with a highly convenient excuse. Since direct compliance with requests for private funds exposes every U.S. company to threats of negative publicity, blackmail, legal action, financial loss, and damage to corporate image, it may prove easy for Americans to say no—while at the same time offering nonmonetary benefits to satisfy both sides.

U.S. competitors may, in fact, be in a better situation than those companies from Europe and Japan that play by different rules. Since the principle of payoffs is either accepted or encouraged by many of their governments, the companies must find it difficult to refuse payment of whatever sums are asked.

Nor should the "right to bribe" be automatically considered an advantage. Ignoring every other factor, this argument assumes contracts are awarded solely on the basis of the largest private payoff. At the most obvious level, it ignores the possibility that products also compete on the basis of quality, price, promotion, and service—factors often crucial to American success abroad. U.S. field representatives are often first to recognize that payoffs may be only one of many factors in awarding contracts. In analyzing U.S. competition in the Middle East, for instance, one executive of an American aircraft company noted: "The French have savoir faire in giving bribes discreetly and well, but they're still not ...backing up their sales with technical expertise." The overseas executive should consider to what degree the right to bribe may be offset by turning the attention of the payoff seekers to other valuable considerations.

Other considerations: the suggested service. A third approach, often used by members of a non-Western elite, is to request that U.S. companies contribute cash to public service projects, often administered by the petitioners themselves. Most proposals of this type require money. Yet if American executives focus too sharply on the financial aspects, they may neglect the chance to work other nonmonetary considerations into their response. In many developing nations, nonmonetary considerations may weigh heavily on foreign colleagues.

Many elite non-Westerners, for example, are intensely nationalistic. They love their country keenly, deplore its relative poverty, and yearn to help it rise. They may, therefore, phrase their requests for payoffs in terms of a suggested service to the nation. In Kenya, for example, ministerial requests to U.S. companies during the 1970s suggested a contribution toward the construction of a hospital. In Indonesia, in the mid-1970s, a top executive of Pertamina, that nation's government-sponsored oil company, requested contributions to an Indonesian restaurant in New York City as a service to the homeland. In his solicitation letter, the executive wrote that the restaurant was in fact intended to "enhance the Indonesian image in the U.S.A.,...promote tourism,...and attract the interest of the U.S. businessmen to investments in Indonesia."

Westerners may regard such claims with cynicism. Non-Westerners may not. They recognize that, even if the notables involved become wealthy, some portion of the wealth, which only they can attract from abroad, will still be shared by other members of their homeland.

That belief is worth consideration, for many elite non-Westerners share a second concern: the desire to meet communal obligations by sharing wealth with members of their inner circle. Modern business leaders in communal cultures rarely simply hoard their wealth. To do so would invite social condemnation. Rather, they provide gifts, funds, and favors to those in their communal settings, receiving deference, authority, and prestige in return.

This does not mean that funds transferred by Western corporations to a single foreign colleague will be parceled out among a circle of cronies. Rather, money passes through one pair of hands over time, flowing slowly in the form of gifts and favors to friends and kin. The funds may even flow beyond this inner circle to their children, most often to ensure their continued education. Such generosity, of course, places both adult recipients and children under a long-term obligation, thereby providing donors both with current status and with assurance of obtaining future favors.

In short, non-Western colleagues who seek payoffs may have concerns beyond their personal enrichment. If motivated by both national and communal idealism, they may feel that these requests are not only for themselves but also a means to aid much larger groups and ultimately their nation.

A donation strategy

Requests for payoffs give executives little choice. Rejection generates resentment, while agreement may lead to prosecution. Perhaps appeals to both communal and national idealism can open up a third alternative. Consider, for example, the possibility of deflecting such requests by transforming private payoffs into public services. One approach would be to respond to requests for private payment with well-publicized, carefully tailored "donations" – an approach that offers both idealistic and practical appeal.

This type of donation could take several forms. The most obvious, a monetary contribution, could be roughly identical to the amount requested in private funds. Donating it publicly, however, would pay off important foreign colleagues in nonmonetary ways.

At the national level, for instance, the most appropriate and satisfying corporate response to ministerial requests for "contributions" toward the construction of a hospital, such as occurred in Kenya, might be actually to provide one, down to the final door and stethoscope, while simultaneously insisting that monetary payments of any kind are proscribed by U.S. law.

The same principle can apply at local levels. Top executives of smaller companies, faced with requests for funds by influential foreign counterparts, might respond by donating to medical, educational, or agricultural projects at the provincial, district, or even village level, focusing consistently on the geographic areas from which those associates come. The donation strategy can even operate at interpersonal levels. How, for example, would my African colleague have reacted had I responded to his request by offering to "donate" whatever would be needed for a special feast – including a radio?

U.S. executives could also weave "other considerations" into the donation, encouraging foreign colleagues to continue business interaction. Many U.S. companies now simply donate funds. Those in Bali, Indonesia, contribute large sums to local temples. Those in Senegal donate to irrigation projects. Companies in South Africa support 150 Bantu schools for black Africans.

Yet donations alone seem insufficient. To serve as an alternative to payoffs, the concept should have practical appeal. Consider, for example, the story of a Western company in Zaire. During the 1970s, Zaire's economy decayed so badly that even ranking civil servants went unpaid. As a result, key Zairian district officials approached officers of the Western company, requesting private funds for future favors. Instead, the company responded with expressions of deference and "donations" of surplus supplies, including goods that could be sold on the black market. The resulting cash flow enabled the officials to continue in their posts. This in turn allowed them to render reciprocal services, both to their district and to the company. By tailoring their contribution to local conditions, the company avoided draining its funds, while providing benefits to both sides.

There are many ways to tailor donations. At the most obvious level, funds can support social projects in the home areas of important local colleagues. Funds or even whole facilities can be given in their names. Production centers can be staffed by members of their ethnic group. Educational, medical, and other social services can be made available to key segments of a target population based on the advice of influential foreign counterparts. Given the opportunity, many non-Westerners would direct the contributions toward members of their inner circles profiting from local forms of recognition and prestige. These practices, often used in one form or another in the United States, can provide non-Western counterparts with local recognition and authority and supply a legal, ethical, and culturally acceptable alternative to a payoff.

Donating services. U.S. companies may also deflect payoff proposals by donating services, gratifying important foreign colleagues in nonmonetary fashion, and thus facilitating the flow of future business. In 1983, for example, a British military unit, part of the Royal Electrical and Mechanical Engineers, planned an African overland vehicle expedition across the Sahara to Tanzania. On arrival, they were "expected" to make a sizable cash donation to that nation to be used in support of its wildlife.

Usually this meant meeting a minister, handing over a check, and taking a picture of the transfer. Instead, the British assembled thousands of dollars worth of tools and vehicle parts, all needed in Tanzanian wildlife areas for trucks on antipoaching patrols. Tanzania's weakened economy no longer permitted the import of enough good tools or parts, which left the wildlife authorities with few working vehicles. As a result, wild-game management had nearly halted. By transporting the vital parts across half of Africa, then working alongside local mechanics until every vehicle was on the road, the British reaped far more goodwill than private payments or even cash donations would have gained. More important, they paved the way for future transactions by providing services meant to benefit both sides.

Donating jobs. A third alternative to private payoffs may be to donate jobs, particularly on projects meant to build goodwill among a host nation's elite. In the 1970s, for example, Coca-Cola was the object of a Middle Eastern boycott by members of the Arab League. Conceivably, Coca-Cola could have sought to win favor with important individuals through gifts or bribes. Instead, the company hired hundreds of Egyptians to plant thousands of acres of orange trees. Eventually the company carpeted a considerable stretch of desert and thereby created both employment and goodwill.

More recently, Mexico refused to let IBM become the first wholly owned foreign company to make personal computers within its borders. Like Coca-Cola in Egypt, IBM employed a strategy of national development: it offered a revised proposal, creating both direct and indirect employment for Mexican nationals, in numbers high enough to satisfy that nation's elite. Such projects do more than generate goodwill. Those able to involve key foreign colleagues in ways that lend prestige on local terms may find they serve as viable alternatives to bribery.

Good ethics, good business

Three strategies do not exhaust the list. U.S. executives in foreign countries should be able to devise their own variants based on local conditions. Each approach should further social progress while offering local status instead of U.S. funds. Americans may find their non-Western colleagues more inclined to do business with corporations that lend prestige than with those whose representatives evade, refuse, or simply walk away. It should not harm a company to gain a reputation for providing social services instead of bribes. A corporation that relies too much on payoffs will be no more respected within non-Western business circles than developing nations that rely too much on payoffs are now respected in U.S. business circles.

Similarly, since the legal dilemma would be resolved, home offices might respond more favorably to overseas requests for funds. Whereas funding for private payments remains illegal, proposals to "donate" the same amounts toward host-nation development could be perceived as public relations and cause-related marketing. Home offices should not fear legal action. While the FCPA prohibits payments to foreign political parties, candidates, or officials with discretionary authority, nowhere does it prohibit the use of funds to aid developing societies, and it requires only that companies keep detailed records that accurately and fairly reflect the transactions.

Businesspeople can also resolve the ethical dilemma. Turning private payoffs into public services should meet both U.S. and corporate moral standards. While one measure of corporate responsibility is to generate the highest possible returns for investors, this can usually be best achieved within a climate of goodwill. In contemporary Third World cultures, this climate can more often be created by public services than by private payoffs. To sell cola, Coke did not bribe ministers, it planted trees. Certainly, host governments will look most favorably on companies that seek to serve as well as to profit, especially through "gifts" that show concern for local ways.

Finally, the cultural dilemmas can also be resolved. Non-Western business practices may be difficult to comprehend, especially when they involve violations of U.S. legal, commercial, or social norms. Nonetheless, U.S. business options are limited only by our business attitudes. If these can be expanded through selective research into those local concepts that relate to payoffs, responses may emerge to satisfy both congressional and indigenous demands. What may initially appear as begging, bribery, or blackmail may be revealed as local tradition, cross-cultural courtesy, or attempts to make friends. More important, when examined from a non-American perspective, mention of "gifts," "bribes," and "other valuable considerations" may signal a wish to do business. ☖

Reprint 86401

The Ethics of Business Organizations

*The values of a company's leaders are evident
in every strategic decision they make.*

Ethics in Practice

by Kenneth R. Andrews

As the 1990s overtake us, public interest in ethics is at a historic high. While the press calls attention to blatant derelictions on Wall Street, in the defense industry, and in the Pentagon, and to questionable activities in the White House, in the attorney general's office, and in Congress, observers wonder whether our society is sicker than usual. Probably not. The standards applied to corporate behavior have risen over time, and that has raised the average rectitude of businesspersons and politicians both. It has been a long time since we could say with Mark Twain that we have the best Senate money can buy or agree with muckrakers like Upton Sinclair that our large companies are the fiefdoms of robber barons. But illegal and unethical behavior persists, even as efforts to expose it often succeed in making its rewards short-lived.

Why is business ethics a problem that snares not just a few mature criminals or crooks in the making but a host of apparently good people who lead exemplary private lives while concealing information about dangerous products or systematically falsifying costs? My observation suggests that the problem of corporate ethics has three aspects: the development of the executive as a moral person; the influence of the corporation as a moral environment; and the actions needed to map a high road to economic and ethical performance – and to mount guardrails to keep corporate wayfarers on track.

Sometimes it is said that wrongdoing in business is an individual failure: a person of the proper moral fiber, properly brought up, simply would not cheat. Because of poor selection, a few bad apples are bound to appear in any big barrel. But these corporate misfits can subsequently be scooped out. Chief executive officers, we used to think, have a right to rely on the character of individual employees without being distracted from business objectives. Moral character is shaped by family, church, and education long before an individual joins a company to make a living.

Kenneth R. Andrews is the Donald K. David Professor of Business Administration, Emeritus, at the Harvard Business School. He was editor of HBR from 1979 to 1985. This article is adapted from his introduction to Ethics in Practice: Managing the Moral Corporation *(Harvard Business School Press, 1989).*

In an ideal world, we might end here. In the real world, moral development is an unsolved problem at home, at school, at church – and at work. Two-career families, television, and the virtual disappearance of the dinner table as a forum for discussing moral issues have clearly outmoded instruction in basic principles at Mother's knee – if that fabled tutorial was ever as effective as folklore would have it. We cannot expect our battered school systems to take over the moral role of the family. Even religion is less help than it once might have been when membership in a distinct community promoted – or coerced – conventional moral behavior. Society's increasing secularization, the profusion of sects, the conservative church's divergence from new lifestyles, pervasive distrust of the religious right – all these mean that we cannot depend on uniform religious instruction to armor business recruits against temptation.

Nor does higher education take up the slack, even in disciplines in which moral indoctrination once flourished. Great literature can be a self-evident source of ethical instruction, for it informs the mind and heart together about the complexities of moral choice. Emotionally engaged with fictional or historic characters who must choose between death and dishonor, integrity and personal advancement, power and responsibility, self and others, we expand our own moral imaginations as well. Yet professors of literature rarely offer guidance in ethical interpretation, preferring instead to stress technical, aesthetic, or historical analysis.

Why do so many good people get caught falsifying costs?

Moral philosophy, which is the proper academic home for ethical instruction, is even more remote, with few professors choosing to teach applied ethics. When you add to that the discipline's studied disengagement from the world of practical affairs, it is not surprising that most students (or managers) find little in the subject to attract them.

What does attract students – in large numbers – is economics, with its theory of human behavior that relates all motivation to personal pleasure, satisfaction, and self-interest. And since self-interest is more easily served than not by muscling aside the self-interest of others, the Darwinian implications of conventional economic theory are essentially immoral. Competition produces and requires the will to win. Careerism focuses attention on advantage. Immature individuals of all ages are prey to the moral flabbiness that William James said attends exclusive service to the bitch goddess Success.

Spurred in part by recent notorious examples of such flabbiness, many business schools are making determined efforts to reintroduce ethics in elective and required courses. But even if these efforts were further along than they are, boards of directors and senior managers would be unwise to assume that recruits could enter the corporate environment without need for additional education. The role of any school is to prepare its graduates for a lifetime of learning from experience that will go better and faster than it would have done without formal education. No matter how much colleges and business schools expand their investment in moral instruction, most education in business ethics (as in all other aspects of business acumen) will occur in the organizations in which people spend their lives.

Making ethical decisions is easy when the facts are clear and the choices black and white. But it is a different story when the situation is clouded by ambiguity, incomplete information, multiple points of view, and conflicting responsibilities. In such situations – which managers experience all the time – ethical decisions depend on both the decision-making process itself and on the experience, intelligence, and integrity of the decision maker.

Responsible moral judgment cannot be transferred to decision makers ready-made. Developing it in business turns out to be partly an administrative process involving: recognition of a decision's ethical implications; discussion to expose different points of view; and testing the tentative decision's adequacy in balancing self-interest and consideration of others, its import for future policy, and its consonance with the company's traditional values. But after all this, if a clear consensus has not emerged, then the executive in charge must decide, drawing on his or her intuition and conviction. This being so, the caliber of the decision maker is decisive – especially when an immediate decision must arise from instinct rather than from discussion.

This existential resolution requires the would-be moral individual to be the final authority in a situation where conflicting ethical principles are joined. It does not rule out prior consultation with others or recognition that, in a hierarchical organization, you might be overruled.

Ethical decisions therefore require of individuals three qualities that can be identified and developed. The first is competence to recognize ethical issues and to think through the consequences of alternative resolutions. The second is self-confidence to seek out different points of view and then to decide what is right at a given time and place, in a particular set of relationships and circumstances. The third is what William James called tough-mindedness, which in management is the willingness to make decisions when all that needs to be known cannot be known and when the questions that press for answers have no established and incontrovertible solutions.

Unfortunately, moral individuals in the modern corporation are too often on their own. But these individuals cannot be expected to remain autonomous, no matter how well endowed they are, without positive organized support. The stubborn persistence of ethical problems obscures the simplicity of the solution—once the leaders of a company decide to do something about their ethical standards. Ethical dereliction, sleaziness, or inertia is not merely an individual failure but a management problem as well.

When they first come to work, individuals whose moral judgment may ultimately determine their company's ethical character enter a community whose values will influence their own. The economic function of the corporation is necessarily one of those values. But if it is the only value, ethical inquiry cannot flourish. If management believes that the invisible hand of the market adequately moderates the injury done by the pursuit of self-interest, ethical policy can be dismissed as irrelevant. And if what people see (while they are hearing about maximizing shareholder wealth) are managers dedicated to their own survival and compensation, they will naturally be more concerned about rewards than about fairness.

For the individual, the impact of the need to succeed is doubtless more direct than the influence of neoclassical economic theory. But just as the corporation itself is saddled with the need to establish competitive advantage over time (after reinvestment of what could otherwise be the immediate profit by which the financial community and many shareholders judge its performance), aspiring managers will also be influenced by the way they are judged. A highly moral and humane chief executive can preside over an amoral organization because the incentive system focuses attention on short-term quantifiable results.

Under pressures to get ahead, the individual (of whose native integrity we are hopeful) is tempted to pursue advancement at the expense of others, to cut corners, to seek to win at all cost, to make things seem better than they are—to take advantage, in sum, of a myopic evaluation of performance. People will do what they are rewarded for doing. The quanti-

fiable results of managerial activity are always much more visible than the quality and future consequences of the means by which they are attained.

By contrast, when the corporation is defined as a socioeconomic institution with responsibilities to other constituencies (employees, customers, and communities, for example), policy can be established to regulate the single-minded pursuit of maximum immediate profit. The leaders of such a company speak of social responsibility, promulgate ethical policy, and make their personal values available for emulation by their juniors. They are respectful of neoclassical economic theory, but find it only partially useful as a management guide.

As the corporation grows beyond its leader's daily direct influence, the ethical consequences of size and geographical deployment come into play. Control and enforcement of all policy becomes more difficult, but this is especially true with regard to policy established for corporate ethics. Layers of responsibility bring communication problems. The possibility of penalty engenders a lack of candor. Distance from headquarters complicates the evaluation of performance, driving it to numbers. When operations are dispersed among different cultures and countries in which corruption assumes exotic guises, a consensus about moral values is hard to achieve and maintain.

Moreover, decentralization in and of itself has ethical consequences, not least because it absolutely requires trust and latitude for error. The inability to monitor the performance of executives assigned to tasks their superiors cannot know in detail results inexorably in delegation. Corporate leaders are accustomed to relying on the business acumen of profit-center managers, whose results the leaders watch with a practiced eye. Those concerned with maintaining their companies' ethical standards are just as dependent on the judgment and moral character of the managers to whom authority is delegated. Beyond keeping your fingers crossed, what can you do?

Fortunately for the future of the corporation, this microcosm of society can be, within limits, what its leadership and membership make it. The corporation is an organization in which people influence one another to establish accepted values and ways of doing things. It is not a democracy, but to be fully effective, the authority of its leaders must be supported by their followers. Its leadership has more power than elected officials do to choose who will join or remain in the association. Its members expect direction to be proposed even as they threaten resistance to change. Careless or lazy managements let their organizations drift, continuing their economic performance along lines previously established and leaving their ethics to chance. Resolute managements find they can surmount the problems I have dwelt on—once they have separated these problems from their camouflage.

It is possible to carve out of our pluralistic, multicultured society a coherent community with a strategy that defines both its economic purposes and the standards of competence, quality, and humanity that govern its activities. The character of a corporation may well be more malleable than an individual's. Certainly its culture can be shaped. Intractable persons can be replaced or retired. Those committed to the company's goals can generate formal and informal sanctions to constrain and alienate those who are not.

Shaping such a community begins with the personal influence of the chief executive and that of the managers who are heads of business units, staff departments, or any other suborganizations to which authority is delegated. The determination of explicit ethical policy comes next, followed by the same management procedures that are used to execute any body of policy in effective organizations.

How can you tell whether managers merit your trust?

The way the chief executive exercises moral judgment is universally acknowledged to be more influential than written policy. The CEO who orders the immediate recall of a product, at the cost of millions of dollars in sales because of a quality defect affecting a limited number of untraceable shipments, sends one kind of message. The executive who suppresses information about a producer's actual or potential ill effects or, knowingly or not, condones overcharging, sends another.

Policy is implicit in behavior. The ethical aspects of product quality, personnel, advertising, and marketing decisions are immediately plain. CEOs say much more than they know in the most casual contacts with those who watch their every move. Pretense is futile. "Do not *say* things," Emerson once wrote. "What you *are* stands over you the while, and thunders so that I can not hear what you say to the contrary." It follows that "if you would not be known to do anything, never do it."

The modest person might respond to this attribution of transparency with a "who, me?" Self-confident sophisticates will refuse to consider themselves so easily read. Almost all executives underestimate their power and do not recognize deference in others. The import of this, of course, is that a CEO should be conscious of how the position amplifies his or her most casual judgments, jokes, and silences. But an even more important implication—given that people cannot hide their characters—is that the selection of a chief executive (indeed of any aspirant to management responsibility) should include an explicit estimate of his or her character. If you ask how to do that, Emerson would reply, "Just look."

Once a company's leaders have decided that its ethical intentions and performance will be managed, rather than left untended in the corrosive environment of unprincipled competition, they must determine their corporate policy and make it explicit much as they do in other areas. The need for written policy is especially urgent in companies without a strong tradition to draw on or where a new era must be launched—after a public scandal, say, or an internal investigation of questionable behavior. Codes of ethics are now commonplace. But in and of themselves they are not effective, and this is especially true when they are so broadly stated that they can be dismissed as merely cosmetic.

Internal policies specifically addressed to points of industry, company, and functional vulnerability make compliance easier to audit and training easier to conduct. Where particular practices are of major concern—price fixing, for example, or bribery of government officials or procurement—compliance can be made a condition of employment and certified annually by employees' signatures. Still, the most pervasive problems cannot be foreseen, nor can the proper procedures be so spelled out in advance as to tell the person on the line what to do. Unreasonably repressive rules undermine trust, which remains indispensable.

What executives can do is advance awareness of the kinds of problems that are foreseeable. Since policy cannot be effective unless it is understood, some companies use corporate training sessions to discuss the problems of applying their ethical standards. In difficult situations, judgment in making the leap from general policy statements to situationally specific action can be informed by discussion. Such discussion, if carefully conducted, can reveal the inadequacy or ambiguity of present policy, new areas in which the company must take a unified stand, and new ways to support individuals in making the right decisions.

As in all policy formulation and implementation, the deportment of the CEO, the development of relevant policy—and training in its meaning and application—are not enough. In companies determined to sustain or raise ethical standards, management expands the information system to illuminate pressure points—the rate of manufacturing defects, product returns and warranty claims, special instances of quality shortfalls, results of competitive benchmarking inquiries—whatever makes good sense in the special circumstances of the company.

Because trust is indispensable, ethical aspirations must be supported by information that serves not only to inform but also to control. Control need not be so much coercive as customary, representing not suspicion but a normal interest in the quality of operations. Experienced executives do not substitute trust for the awareness that policy is often distorted in practice. Ample information, like full visibility, is a powerful deterrent.

This is why purposely ethical organizations expand the traditional sphere of external and internal audits (which is wherever fraud may occur) to include compliance with corporate ethical standards. Even more important, such organizations pay attention to every kind of obstacle that limits performance and to problems needing ventilation so that help can be provided.

To obtain information that is deeply guarded to avoid penalty, internal auditors—long since taught not to prowl about as police or detectives—must be people with enough management experience to be sensitive to the manager's need for economically viable decisions. For example, they should have imagination enough to envision ethical outcomes from bread-and-butter profit and pricing decisions, equal opportunity and payoff dilemmas, or downsizing crunches. Establishing an audit and control climate that takes as a given an open exchange of information between the company's operating levels and policy-setting levels is not difficult—once, that is, the need to do so is recognized and persons of adequate experience and respect are assigned to the work.

But no matter how much empathy audit teams exhibit, discipline ultimately requires action. The secretary who steals petty cash, the successful salesman who falsifies his expense account, the accountant and her boss who alter cost records, and, more problematically, the chronically sleazy operator who never does anything actually illegal—all must be dealt with cleanly, with minimum attention to allegedly extenuating circumstances. It is true that hasty punishment may be unjust and absolve superiors improperly of their secondary responsibility for wrongdoing. But long delay or waffling in the effort to be humane obscures the message the organization requires whenever violations occur. Trying to conceal a major lapse or safeguarding the names of people who have been fired is kind to the offender but blunts the salutary impact of disclosure.

For the executive, the administration of discipline incurs one ethical dilemma after another: How do you weigh consideration for the offending individual, for example, and how do you weigh the future of the organization? A company dramatizes its uncompromising adherence to lawful and ethical behavior when it severs employees who commit offenses that were classified in advance as unforgivable. When such a decision is fair, the grapevine makes its equity clear even when more formal publicity is inappropriate. Tough decisions should not be postponed simply because they are painful. The steady support of corporate integrity is never without emotional cost.

In a large, decentralized organization, consistently ethical performance requires difficult decisions from not only the current CEO but also a succession of chief executives. Here the board of directors enters the scene. The board has the opportunity to provide for a succession of CEOs whose personal values and characters are consistently adequate for sustaining and developing established traditions for ethical conduct. Once in place, chief executives must rely on two resources for getting done what they cannot do personally: the character of their associates and the influence of policy and the measures that are taken to make policy effective.

An adequate corporate strategy must include noneconomic goals. An economic strategy is the optimal match of a company's product and market opportunities with its resources and distinctive competence. (That both are continually changing is of course true.) But economic strategy is humanized and made attainable by deciding what kind of organization the company will be—its character, the values it espouses, its relationships to customers, employees, communities, and shareholders. The personal values and ethical aspirations of the company's leaders, though probably not specifically stated, are implicit in all strategic decisions. They show through the choices management makes and reveal themselves as the company goes about its business. That is why this communication should be deliberate and purposeful rather than random.

Although codes of ethics, ethical policy for specific vulnerabilities, and disciplined enforcement are important, they do not contain in themselves the final emotional power of commitment. Commitment to quality objectives – among them compliance with law and high ethical standards – is an organizational achievement. It is inspired by pride more than by the profit that rightful pride produces. Once the scope of strategic decisions is thus enlarged, their ethical component is no longer at odds with a decision right for many reasons.

As former editor of HBR, I am acutely aware of how difficult it is to persuade businesspeople to write or speak about corporate ethics. I am not comfortable doing so myself. To generalize the ethical aspects of a business decision, leaving behind the concrete particulars that make it real, is too often to sermonize, to simplify, or to rationalize away the plain fact that many instances of competing ethical claims have no satisfactory solution. But we also hear little public comment from business leaders of integrity when incontestable breaches of conduct are made known – and silence suggests to cynics an absence of concern.

The impediments to explicit discussion of ethics in business are many, beginning with the chief executive's keen awareness that someday he or she may be betrayed by someone in his or her own organization. Moral exhortation and oral piety are offensive, especially when attended by hypocrisy or real vulnerability to criticism. Any successful or energetic individual will sometime encounter questions about his or her methods and motives, for even well-intentioned behavior may be judged unethical from some point of view. The need for cooperation among people with different beliefs diminishes discussion of religion and related ethical issues. That persons with management responsibility must find the principles to resolve conflicting ethical claims in their own minds and hearts is an unwelcome discovery. Most of us keep quiet about it.

In summary, my ideas are quite simple. Perhaps the most important is that management's total loyalty to the maximization of profit is the principal obstacle to achieving higher standards of ethical practice. Defining the purpose of the corporation as exclusively economic is a deadly oversimplification, which allows overemphasis on self-interest at the expense of consideration of others.

The practice of management requires a prolonged play of judgment. Executives must find in their own will, experience, and intelligence the principles they apply in balancing conflicting claims. Wise men and women will submit their views to others, for open discussion of problems reveals unsuspected ethical dimensions and develops alternative viewpoints that should be taken into account. Ultimately, however, executives must make a decision, relying on their own judgment to settle infinitely debatable issues. Inquiry into character should therefore be part of all executive selection – as well as all executive development within the corporation.

Ultimately, executives resolve conflicting claims in their own minds and hearts.

And so it goes. That much and that little. The encouraging outcome is that promulgating and institutionalizing ethical policy are not so difficult as, for example, escaping the compulsion of greed. Once undertaken, the process can be as straightforward as the articulation and implementation of policy in any sphere. Any company has the opportunity to develop a unique corporate strategy summarizing its chief purposes and policies. That strategy can encompass not only the economic role it will play in national and international markets but also the kind of company it will be as a human organization. It will embrace as well, though perhaps not publicly, the nature and scope of the leadership to which the company is to be entrusted.

To be implemented successfully over time, any strategy must command the creativity, energy, and desire of the company's members. Strategic decisions that are economically or ethically unsound will not long sustain such commitment.

Reprint 89501

Business men and women keep their word because they want to, not because honesty pays.

Why Be Honest if Honesty Doesn't Pay

by Amar Bhide and Howard H. Stevenson

We bet on the rational case for trust. Economists, ethicists, and business sages had persuaded us that honesty is the best policy, but their evidence seemed weak. Through extensive interviews we hoped to find data that would support their theories and thus, perhaps, encourage higher standards of business behavior.

To our surprise, our pet theories failed to stand up. Treachery, we found, can pay. There is no compelling economic reason to tell the truth or keep one's word—punishment for the treacherous in the real world is neither swift nor sure.

Honesty is, in fact, primarily a moral choice. Businesspeople do tell themselves that, in the long run,

Amar Bhide is an assistant professor of general management at the Harvard Business School. Howard H. Stevenson is the Sarofim-Rock Professor of Business Administration at the Harvard Business School.

they will do well by doing good. But there is little factual or logical basis for this conviction. Without values, without a basic preference for right over wrong, trust based on such self-delusion would crumble in the face of temptation.

Most of us choose virtue because we want to believe in ourselves and have others respect and believe in us. When push comes to shove, hardheaded businessfolk usually ignore (or fudge) their dollars-and-cents calculations in order to keep their word.

And for this, we should be happy. We can be proud of a system in which people are honest because they want to be, not because they have to be. Materially, too, trust based on morality provides great advantages. It allows us to join in great and exciting enterprises that we could never undertake if we relied on economic incentives alone.

Economists and game theorists tell us that trust is enforced in the marketplace through retaliation and reputation. If you violate a trust, your victim is apt to seek revenge and others are likely to stop doing business with you, at least under favorable terms. A man or woman with a reputation for fair dealing will prosper. Therefore, profit maximizers are honest.

This sounds plausible enough until you look for concrete examples. Cases that apparently demonstrate the awful consequences of abusing trust turn out to be few and weak, while evidence that treachery can pay seems compelling.

The moralists' standard tale recounts how E. F. Hutton was brought down by its check-kiting fraud.[1] Hutton, once the second largest broker in the nation, never recovered from the blow to its reputation and finances and was forced to sell out to Shearson.

Exxon's Valdez disaster is another celebrated example. Exxon and seven other oil companies persuaded the town of Valdez to accept a tanker terminal by claiming that a major spill was "highly unlikely." Their 1,800-page contingency plan ensured that any spill would be controlled within hours. In fact, when Exxon's supertanker spewed forth over 240,000 barrels of oil, the equipment promised in the cleanup plan was not available. The cost? According to recent (and still rising) estimates, Exxon's costs could exceed $2 billion, and the industry faces severe restrictions on its operations in Alaska.

But what do these fables prove? Check-kiting was only one manifestation of the widespread mismanagement that plagued Hutton and ultimately caused its demise. Incompetently run companies going under is not news. Exxon's underpreparedness was expensive, but many decisions turn out badly. Considering the low probability of a spill, was skimping on the promised cleanup equipment really a bad business decision at the time it was taken?

More damaging to the moralists' position is the wealth of evidence against trust. Compared with the few ambiguous tales of treachery punished, we can find numerous stories in which deceit was unquestionably rewarded.

Philippe Kahn, in an interview with *Inc.* magazine, described with apparent relish how his company, Borland International, got its start by deceiving an ad salesman for *BYTE* magazine.

Inc.: The story goes that Borland was launched by a single ad, without which we wouldn't be sitting here talking about the company. How much of that is apocryphal?

Kahn: It's true: one full-page ad in the November 1983 issue of *BYTE* magazine got the company running. If it had failed, I would have had nowhere else to go.

Inc.: If you were so broke, how did you pay for the ad?

Kahn: Let's put it that we convinced the salesman to give us terms. We wanted to appear only in *BYTE* — not any of the other microcomputer magazines — because *BYTE* is for programmers, and that's who we wanted to reach. But we couldn't afford it. We figured the only way was somehow to convince them to extend us credit terms.

Inc.: And they did?

Kahn: Well, they didn't *offer*. What we did was, before the ad salesman came in — we existed in two small rooms, but I had hired extra people so we would look like a busy, venture-backed company — we prepared a chart with what we pretended was our media plan for the computer magazines. On the chart we

Was E.F. Hutton really brought down by its check-kiting fraud?

had *BYTE* crossed out. When the salesman arrived, we made sure the phones were ringing and the extras were scurrying around. Here was this chart he thought he wasn't supposed to see, so I pushed it out of the way. He said, "Hold on, can we get you in *BYTE*?" I said, "We don't really want to be in your book, it's not the right audience for us." "You've got

1. The HBR Collection *Ethics in Practice* has six citations (Boston: Harvard Business School Press, 1989).

2. "Management by Necessity," *Inc.*, March 1989, p. 33. Reprinted with permission. Copyright © 1989 by Goldhirsh Group, Inc., 38 Commercial Wharf, Boston, Mass. 02110.

3. *The Discourses*, Chapter XIII, Book 2, Modern Library Edition, 1950.

to try," he pleaded. I said, "Frankly, our media plan is done, and we can't afford it." So he offered good terms, if only we'd let him run it just once. We expected we'd sell maybe $20,000 worth of software and at least pay for the ad. We sold $150,000 worth. Looking back now, it's a funny story; then it was a big risk.[2]

Further evidence comes from professional sports. In our study, one respondent cited the case of Rick Pitino, who had recently announced his decision to leave as coach of the New York Knicks basketball team with over three years left on his contract. Patino left, the respondent wrote, "to coach the University of Kentucky (a school of higher learning, that like many others, is a party in breaking contracts). Pitino was quoted in the *New York Times* the week before as saying that he never broke a contract. But he's 32 years old and has had five jobs. What he neglected to say is that he's never completed a contract. The schools always let him run out, as they don't want an unhappy coach.

"The same thing is done by professional athletes every year. They sign a long-term contract and after one good year, they threaten to quit unless the contract's renegotiated. The stupidity of it all is that they get their way."

Compared with the ambiguity of the Hutton and Exxon cases, the clear causality in the Kahn and Pitino cases is striking. Deceiving the *BYTE* salesman was crucial to Kahn's success. Without subterfuge, Borland International would almost certainly have folded. And there is a hard dollar number (with lots of zeros in it) that professional athletes and coaches gain when they shed a contract.

What of the long term? Does treachery eventually get punished? Nothing in the record suggests it does. Many of today's blue chip companies were put together at the turn of the century under circumstances approaching securities fraud. The robber barons who promoted them enjoyed great material rewards at the time – and their fortunes survived several generations. The Industrial Revolution did not make entirely obsolete Machiavelli's observation, "Men seldom rise from low condition to high rank without employing either force or fraud."[3]

Power can be an effective substitute for trust. In theory, Kahn and Coach Pitino should suffer the consequences of their deceits and incomplete contracts: scorned by its victims and a just society, Borland shouldn't be able to place an ad. Pitino shouldn't be able to blow a whistle. But they continue to prosper. Why do reputation and retaliation fail as mechanisms for enforcing trust?

Power – the ability to do others great harm or great good – can induce widespread amnesia, it appears. Borland International's large ad budget commands due respect. Its early deceit is remembered, if at all, as an amusing prank. Pitino's record for winning basketball games wipes out his record for abandoning teams in midstream.

Prestigious New York department stores, several of our respondents told us, cavalierly break promises to suppliers:

"You send the department store an invoice for $55,000 and they send you $38,000. If you question it

> "I've done transactions with horrible people. But the deal was so good, I just accepted it."

they say, 'Here is an $11,000 penalty for being two days late; here is the transportation tax and a dockage fee…you didn't follow our shipping instructions, Clause 42, Section 3C. You used the wrong carrier.' And half the time they call the order in and send the 600-page confirming document later, and they say you didn't follow our order."

"Department stores are horrible! Financial types have taken control, the merchants are out. The guy who keeps beating you down goes to his boss at the end of the year and says 'Look at the kind of rebates I got on freight reduction – $482,000. I delayed payments an average of 22 days from my predecessor at this kind of amount, and this is what I saved.'"

Nevertheless, suppliers still court their tormentors' orders.

"Don't tell me that department stores will go out of business because they treat their suppliers like that! I don't believe that at all. They have too much power – they screw one guy, and guys are waiting in line to take a shot at them again."

Heroic resistance to an oppressive power is the province of the students at Tiananmen Square, not the businessfolk in the capitalist societies the students risk their lives to emulate. Businesspeople do not stand on principle when it comes to dealing with abusers of power and trust. You have to adjust, we were told. If we dealt only with customers who share our ethical values, we would be out of business.

A real estate developer we interviewed was blunt:

"People are really whores. They will do business with someone they know they can't trust if it suits their convenience. They may tell their lawyers: 'Be careful, he's dishonest; he's not reliable and he will try to get out of the contract if something happens.'

But those two do business with each other....I've done transactions with people knowing that they were horrible and knowing that I'd never talk to them. But the deal was so good, I just accepted it, did the best I could, and had the lawyers make triply sure that everything was covered."

Sometimes the powerful leave others no choice. The auto parts supplier has to play ball with the Big Three, no matter how badly he or she has been treated in the past or expects to be treated in the future. Suppliers of fashion goods believe they absolutely have to take a chance on abusive department stores. Power here totally replaces trust.

Usually, though, power isn't quite that absolute, and some degree of trust is a necessary ingredient in business relationships. Pitino has demonstrated remarkable abilities in turning around basketball programs, but he isn't the only coach available for hire. Borland International's business is nice to have, but it can't make or break a computer magazine. Nevertheless, even those with limited power can live down a poor record of trustworthiness. Cognitive inertia – the tendency to search for data that confirm one's beliefs and to avoid facts that might refute them – is one reason why.

To illustrate, consider the angry letters the mail fraud unit of the U.S. Post Office gets every year from the victims of the fake charities it exposes. Appar-ently donors are annoyed that they can't keep sending contributions to a cause they believed in. They want to avoid information that says they have trusted a fraud.

When the expected reward is substantial and avoidance becomes really strong, reference checking goes out the window. In the eyes of people blinded by greed, the most tarnished reputations shine brightly.

Many a commodity broker's yacht has been financed by cleaning out one customer after another. Each new doctor or dentist who is promised the moon is unaware of and uninterested in his or her predecessor's fate. Such investors want to believe in the fabulous returns the broker has promised. They don't want references or other reality checks that would disturb the dreams they have built on sand. Thus can the retail commodity brokerage business flourish, even though knowledgeable sources maintain that it wipes out the capital of 70% of its customers every year.

The search for data that confirm wishful thinking is not restricted to naive medical practitioners dabbling in pork bellies. The *Wall Street Journal* recently detailed how a 32-year-old conglomerateur perpetrated a gigantic fraud on sophisticated financial institutions such as Citibank, the Bank of New England, and a host of Wall Street firms. A Salomon Brothers team that conducted due diligence on the wunderkind pronounced him highly moral and ethical. A few months later....

Even with a fully disclosed public record of bad faith, hard-nosed businesspeople will still try to find reasons to trust. Like the proverbial "other woman," they'll reason, "It's not his fault." And so it comes to pass that Oscar Wyatt's Coastal Corporation can walk away from its gas-supply contracts;[4] then, with the consequent lawsuits not yet settled, issue billions of dollars of junk bonds. Lured by high yields, junk bond investors choose to believe that their relationship will be different: Wyatt *had* to break his contracts when energy prices rose; and a junk bond is so much more, well, *binding* than a mere supply contract.

Similarly, we can imagine, every new Pitino employer believes the last has done Pitino wrong. Their relationship will last forever.

Ambiguity and complexity can also take the edge off reputational enforcement. When we trust others to keep their word, we simultaneously rely on their integrity, native ability, and favorable external circumstances. So when a trust appears to be breached, there can be so much ambiguity that even the aggrieved parties cannot apprehend what happened. Was the breach due to bad faith, incompetence, or circumstances that made it impossible to perform as promised? No one knows. Yet without such knowledge, we cannot determine in what respect someone has proved untrustworthy: basic integrity, susceptibility to temptation, or realism in making promises.

The following example, in which we hear the buyer of a company who was taken in by the seller's representations, is instructive:

"The seller said: 'We have a technology that is going to be here for a long time. We own the market.' We liked this guy so much, it was funny. He's in the local area, he knew my father. He's a great guy to talk to, with all sorts of stories.

Businesspeople learn not to get hung up about other people's pasts.

"He managed to fool us, our banks, and a mezzanine lender, and he ended up doing quite well on the deal. Then the company went on the skids. The funny thing is, afterwards he bought the business back from us, put a substantial amount of his own capital in, and still has not turned it around. I'm just not sure what was going on.

"I guess he believed his own story and believed it so much that he bought the business back. He was independently wealthy from another sale anyway, and I think he wanted to prove that he was a great businessman and that we just screwed the business up. If he was a charlatan, why would he have cared?"

Where even victims have difficulty assessing whether and to what extent someone has broken a trust, it is not surprising that it can be practically impossible for a third party to judge.

That difficulty is compounded by the ambiguity of communication. Aggrieved parties may underplay or hide past unpleasantnesses out of embarrassment or fear of lawsuits. Or they may exaggerate others' villainies and their own blamelessness. So unless the victims themselves can be trusted to be utterly honest and objective, judgments based on their experiences become unreliable and the accuracy of the alleged transgressor's reputation unknowable.

A final factor protecting the treacherous from their reputations is that it usually pays to take people at face value. Businesspeople learn over time that "innocent until proven guilty" is a good working rule and that it is really not worth getting hung up about other people's pasts.

Assuming that others are trustworthy, at least in their initial intentions, *is* a sensible policy. The average borrower does not plan million-dollar scams, most coaches do try to complete their contracts, and most buyers don't "forget" about their suppliers' bills or make up reasons for imposing penalties.

Even our cynical real estate developer told us:

"By and large, most people are intrinsically honest. It's just the tails, the ends of the bell-shaped curve, that are dishonest in any industry, in any area. So it's just a question of tolerating them."

Another respondent concurred:

"I tend to take people at face value until proven otherwise, and more often than not, that works. It doesn't work with a blackguard and a scoundrel, but how many total blackguards and scoundrels are there?"

Mistrust can be a self-fulfilling prophecy. People aren't exclusively saints or sinners; few adhere to an absolute moral code. Most respond to circumstances, and their integrity and trustworthiness can depend as much on how they are treated as on their basic character. Initiating a relationship assuming that the other party is going to try to get you may induce him or her to do exactly that.

Overlooking past lapses can make good business sense too. People and companies do change. It is more than likely that once Borland International got off the ground, Kahn never pulled a fast one on an ad salesman again. Today's model citizen may be yesterday's sharp trader or robber baron.

Trust breakers are not only unhindered by bad reputations, they are also usually spared retaliation by parties they injure. Many of the same factors apply. Power, for example: attacking a more powerful transgressor is considered foolhardy.

"It depends on the scale of the pecking order," we were told. "If you are a seller and your customer breaks promises, by and large you don't retaliate. And if you are an employee and your employer breaks promises, you usually don't retaliate either."

Where power doesn't protect against retaliation, convenience and cognitive inertia often do. Getting

---

4. "In the early 1970s," reports *Forbes* (Toni Mack, "Profitable if Not Popular," May 30, 1988, p. 34), "Wyatt found himself squeezed between rising natural gas prices and low-priced contracts to supply gas to cities like San Antonio and Austin. His solution? Renege. He simply refused to honor the contract."

even can be expensive; even thinking about broken trusts can be debilitating. "Forget and move on" seems to be the motto of the business world.

Businesspeople consider retaliation a wasteful distraction because they have a lot of projects in hand and constantly expect to find new opportunities to pursue. The loss suffered through any individual breach of trust is therefore relatively small, and revenge is regarded as a distraction from other, more promising activities.

Retaliation is a luxury you can't afford, respondents told us.

"You can't get obsessed with getting even. It will take away from everything else. You will take it out on the kids at home, and you will take it out on your wife. You will do lousy business."

"It's a realization that comes with age: retaliation is a double loss. First you lose your money; now you're losing time."

"Bite me once, it is your fault; bite me twice, my fault....But bite me twice, and I won't have anything to do with you, and I'm not going to bite back because I have better things to do with my life. I'm not going to litigate just for the pleasure of getting even with you."

Only those who have their best years behind them and see their life's work threatened actively seek to retaliate. In general, our interviews suggested, businesspeople would rather switch than fight. An employee caught cheating on expenses is quietly let go. Customers who are always cutting corners on payments are, if practicable, dropped. No fuss, no muss.

Our interviewees also seemed remarkably willing to forget injuries and to repair broken relationships. A supplier is dropped, an employee or sales rep is let go. Then months or years later the parties try again, invoking some real or imaginary change of circumstances or heart. "The employee was under great per-

"Retaliation is a double loss. First you lose your money; then you lose your time."

sonal strain." "The company's salesman exceeded his brief." "The company is under new management." Convenience and cognitive inertia seem to foster many second chances.

What about the supposed benefits of retaliation? Game theorists argue that retaliation sends a signal that you are not to be toyed with. This signal, we believe, has some value when harm is suffered outside a trusting relationship: in cases of patent infringement

or software piracy, for example. But when a close trusting relationship exists, as it does, say, with an employee, the inevitable ambiguity about who was at fault often distorts the signal retaliation sends. Without convincing proof of one-sided fault, the retaliator may get a reputation for vindictiveness and scare even honorable men and women away from establishing close relationships.

Even the cathartic satisfaction of getting even seems limited. Avenging lost honor is passé, at least in business dealings. Unlike Shakespeare's Venetian merchant, the modern businessperson isn't interested in exacting revenge for its own sake and, in fact, considers thirsting for retribution unprofessional and irresponsible.

"There is such a complete identification in my mind between my company's best interests and what I want to do that I am not going to permit anything official out of spite. If I can't rationalize [retaliation] and run it through my computer brain, it will be relegated to my diary and won't be a company action."

We would be guilty of gross exaggeration if we claimed that honesty has no value or that treachery is never punished. Trustworthy behavior does provide protection against the loss of power and against invisible sniping. But these protections are intangible, and their dollars-and-cents value does not make a compelling case for trustworthiness.

A good track record can protect against the loss of power. What if you stop being a winning coach or your software doesn't sell anymore? Long-suppressed memories of past abuses may then come to the fore, past victims may gang up to get you.

A deal maker cited the fate of an investment bank that was once the only source of financing for certain kinds of transactions.

"They always had a reputation for being people who would outline the terms of the deal and then change them when it got down to the closing. The industry knew that this is what you had to expect; our people had no choice. Now that the bank has run into legal problems and there are other sources of funds, people are flocking elsewhere. At the first opportunity to desert, people did—and with a certain amount of glee. They are getting no goodwill benefit from their client base because when they were holding all the cards they screwed everybody."

Another entrepreneur ascribed his longevity to his reputation for trustworthiness:

"The most important reason for our success is the quality of my [product] line. But we wouldn't have survived without my integrity because our lines weren't always very successful. There are parabola curves in all businesses, and people still supported me, even though we had a low, because they believed in me."

Trustworthiness may also provide immediate protection against invisible sniping. When the abuse of power banishes trust, the victims often try to get their own back in ways that are not visible to the abuser: "I'm not in business just to make a profit. If a client tries to jerk me around, I mark up my fees." "The way to get even with a large company is to sell more to them."

On occasion, sniping can threaten the power it rebels against. The high-handedness of department stores, for example, has created a new class of competitors, the deep discounter of designer apparel.

"Ordinarily, manufacturers don't like to sell their goods at throwaway prices to people like us," says one such discounter. "But our business has thrived because the department stores have been systematically screwing their suppliers, especially after all those leveraged buyouts. At the same time, the manufacturers have learned that we treat them right. We scrupulously keep our promises. We pay when we say we'll pay. If they ask us not to advertise a certain item in a certain area, we don't. If they make an honest mistake in a shipment, we won't penalize them.

"The department stores have tried to start subsidiaries to compete with us, but they don't understand the discount business. Anyone can set up an outlet. What really matters is the trust of the suppliers."

Neither of these benefits can be factored easily into a rational business analysis of whether to lie or keep

> How can you quantify the financial repercussions when suppliers you have abused ship hot items to your competitors first?

a promise. Sniping is invisible; the sniper will only take shots that you cannot measure or see. How could you possibly quantify the financial repercussions when suppliers you have abused refuse your telephone orders or ship hot items to your competitors first?

Assessing the value of protection against the loss of power is even more incalculable. It is almost as difficult to anticipate the nature of divine retribution as it is to assess the possibility that at some unknown time in the future your fortunes *may* turn, whereupon others *may* seek to cause you some unspecified harm. With all these unknowns and unknowables,

surely the murky future costs don't stand a chance against the certain and immediate financial benefits from breaking an inconvenient promise. The net present values, at any reasonable discount rate, must work against honoring obligations.

Given all this, we might expect breaches of trust to be rampant. In fact, although most businesspeople are not so principled as to boycott powerful trust breakers, they do try to keep their own word most of the time. Even allowing for convenient forgetfulness, we cannot help being swayed by comments like this:

"I've been in this business for 40 years. I've sold two companies; I've gone public myself and have done all kinds of dealings, so I'm not a babe in the woods, OK? But I can't think of one situation where people took advantage of me. I think that when I was young and naive about many things, I may have been underpaid for what my work was, but that was a learning experience."

One reason treachery doesn't swamp us is that people rationalize constancy by exaggerating its economic value.

"Costs have been going up, and it will cost me a million dollars to complete this job. But if I don't, my name will be mud and no one will do business with me again."

"If I sell this chemical at an extortionate price when there is a shortage, I will make a killing. But if I charge my customers the list price, they will do the right thing by me when there is a glut."

Just as those who trust find reasons for the risks they want to run, those who are called on to keep a difficult promise cast around for justification even when the hard numbers point the other way. Trustworthiness has attained the status of "strategic focus" and "sustainable competitive advantage" in business folklore—a plausible (if undocumented) touchstone of long-term economic value.

But why has it taken root? Why do business men and women want to believe that trustworthiness pays, disregarding considerable evidence to the contrary? The answer lies firmly in the realm of social and moral behavior, not in finance.

The businesspeople we interviewed set great store on the regard of their family, friends, and the community at large. They valued their reputations, not for some nebulous financial gain but because they took pride in their good names. Even more important, since outsiders cannot easily judge trustworthiness, businesspeople seem guided by their inner voices, by their consciences. When we cited examples to our interviewees in which treachery had apparently paid, we heard responses like:

"It doesn't matter how much money they made. Right is right and wrong is wrong."

"Is that important? They may be rich in dollars and very poor in their own sense of values and what life is about. I cannot judge anybody by the dollars; I judge them by their deeds and how they react."

"I can only really speak for myself, and to me, my word is the most important thing in my life and my credibility as an individual is paramount. All the other success we have had is secondary."

The importance of moral and social motives in business cannot be overemphasized. A selective memory, a careful screening of the facts may help sustain the fiction of profitable virtue, but the fundamental basis of trust is moral. We keep promises because we believe it is right to do so, not because it is good business. Cynics may dismiss the sentiments we heard as posturing, and it is true that performance often falls short of aspiration. But we can find no other way than conscience to explain why trust is the basis for so many relationships.

At first, these findings distressed us. A world in which treachery pays because the average businessperson won't fight abusive power and tolerates dishonesty? Surely that wasn't right or efficient, and the system needed to be fixed! On further reflection, however, we concluded that this system was fine, both from a moral and a material point of view.

The moral advantages are simple. Concepts of trust and, more broadly, of virtue would be empty if bad faith and wickedness were not financially rewarding. If wealth naturally followed straight dealing, we would only need to speak about conflicts between the long term and the short, stupidity and wisdom, high discount rates and low. We would worry only about others' good sense, not about their integrity. It is the very absence of predictable financial reward that makes honesty a moral quality we hold dear.

Trust based on morality rather than self-interest also provides a great economic benefit. Consider the alternative, where trust is maintained by fear.

A world in which the untrustworthy face certain retribution is a small world where every one knows (and keeps a close eye on!) everyone else. A village, really, deeply suspicious not only of commodities brokers but also of all strangers, immigrants, and innovators.

No shades or ambiguities exist here. The inhabitants trust each other only in transactions in which responsibilities are fully specified — "deliver the diamonds to Point A, bring back cash" — and breaches of trust are clear. They do not take chances on schemes that might fail through the tangled strands of bad faith, incompetence, overoptimism, or plain bad luck.

A dark pessimism pervades this world. Opportunities look scarce and setbacks final. "You can't afford to be taken in even once" is the operating principle. "So when in doubt, don't."

In this world, there are no second chances either. A convicted felon like Thomas Watson, Sr. would

> **Fortunately, our world is full of trusting optimists — a Steve Jobs with no track record to speak of can start an Apple.**

never be permitted to create an IBM. A Federal Express would never again be extended credit after an early default on its loan agreements. The rules are clear: an eye for an eye and a tooth for a tooth. Kill or be killed.

Little, closed, tit-for-tat worlds do exist. Trust is self-reinforcing because punishment for broken promises is swift — in price-fixing rings, loan-sharking operations, legislative log rolling, and the mutually assured destruction of nuclear deterrence. Exceed your quota and suffer a price war. Don't pay on time and your arm gets broken. Block my pork barrel project and I'll kill yours. Attack our cities and we'll obliterate yours.

At best such a world is stable and predictable. Contracts are honored and a man's word really does become his bond. In outcome, if not intent, moral standards are high, since no one enters into relationships of convenience with the untrustworthy. On the other hand, such a world resists all change, new ideas, and innovations. It is utterly inimical to entrepreneurship.

Fortunately, the larger world in which we live is less rigid. It is populated with trusting optimists who readily do business with strangers and innovators. A 26-year-old Steve Jobs with no track record to speak of or a 52-year-old Ray Kroc with nearly ten failures behind him can get support to start an Apple or a McDonald's. People are allowed to move from Maine to Montana or from plastics to baked goods without a lot of whys and wherefores.

Projects that require the integrity and ability of a large team and are subject to many market and technological risks can nonetheless attract enthusiastic support. Optimists focus more on the pot of gold at the end of the rainbow than on their ability to find and punish the guilty in case a failure occurs.

Our tolerance for broken promises encourages risk taking. Absent the fear of debtors' prison and the stigma of bankruptcy, entrepreneurs readily borrow the funds they need to grow.

Tolerance also allows resources to move out of enterprises that have outlived their functions. When the buggy whip manufacturer is forced out of business, we understand that some promises will have to be broken—promises that perhaps ought not to have been made. But adjustments to the automobile age are more easily accomplished if we don't demand full retribution for every breach of implicit and explicit contract.

Even unreconstructed scoundrels are tolerated in our world as long as they have something else to offer. The genius inventors, the visionary organizers, and the intrepid pioneers are not cast away merely because they cannot be trusted on all dimensions. We "adjust"—and allow great talent to offset moral frailty—because we know deep down that knaves and blackguards have contributed much to our progress.

And this, perhaps unprincipled, tolerance facilitates a dynamic entrepreneurial economy.

Since ancient times, philosophers have contrasted a barbaric "state of nature" with a perfect, well-ordered society that has somehow tamed humankind's propensity toward force and fraud. Fortunately, we have created something that is neither Beirut nor Bucharest. We don't require honesty, but we honor and celebrate it. Like a kaleidoscope, we have order and change. We make beautiful, well-fitting relationships that we break and reform at every turn.

We should remember, however, that this third way works only as long as most of us live by an honorable moral compass. Since our trust isn't grounded in self-interest, it is fragile. And, indeed, we all know of organizations, industries, and even whole societies in which trust has given way either to a destructive free-for-all or to inflexible rules and bureaucracy. Only our individual wills, our determination to do what is right, whether or not it is profitable, save us from choosing between chaos and stagnation.

Reprint 90501

*At Levi Strauss, the company's most important
asset is its people's "aspirations."*

Values Make the Company:
An Interview with Robert Haas

by Robert Howard

As chairman and CEO of Levi Strauss & Co., Robert D. Haas has inherited a dual legacy. Ever since its founding in 1850, the San Francisco-based apparel manufacturer has been famous for combining strong commercial success with a commitment to social values and to its work force.

Achieving both goals was relatively easy throughout much of the postwar era, when the company's main product – Levi's jeans – became an icon of American pop culture and sales surged on the demographic wave of the expanding baby boom. But in the uncertain economic climate of the 1980s, Haas and his management team have had to rethink every facet of the business – including its underlying values.

Since his appointment as CEO in 1984, Haas has redefined the company's business strategy; created a flatter organization, including the painful step of cutting the work force by one-third; and invested heavily in new-product development, marketing, and technology. In 1985, he and his team took the company private in one of the most successful management-led LBOs of the 1980s. And in 1987, he oversaw the development of the Levi Strauss Aspirations Statement, a major initiative to define the shared values that will guide both management and the work force. (See the insert "Aspirations Statement.")

Many CEOs talk about values, but few have gone to the lengths Haas has to bring them to the very center of how he runs the business. The Aspirations Statement is shaping how the company defines occupational roles and responsibilities, conducts performance evaluations, trains new employees, organizes work, and makes business decisions.

The result is a remarkably flexible and innovative company, despite its age and size. Levi is a pioneer in using electronic networks to link the company more closely to its suppliers and retailers. The Dockers line of clothing, introduced in 1986, has been one of the fastest growing new products in apparel industry history. And the company has made a successful major push into global markets. In 1989, international operations accounted for 34% of Levi's total sales and 45% of pretax operating profit.

Levi's financial results have also been extraordinary. From 1985 to 1989, sales increased 31% to $3.6 billion. And profits have risen fivefold to $272 million.

Meanwhile, the company has stayed true to its traditional commitment to social issues even as it has updated that commitment to reflect the economic and social realities of a new era. Levi Strauss has an exemplary record on issues ranging from work force diversity to benefits for workers dislocated by plant closings and technological change. Haas himself is the foremost corporate spokesperson on the responsibilities of business in the AIDS crisis.

Reinventing the Levi Strauss heritage has a special meaning for Haas. He is the great-great-grandnephew of the company founder, and his uncle, father, and grandfather all led the company before him. He joined Levi Strauss in 1973 and has served in a variety of leadership positions, including senior vice president of corporate planning and policy, president of the operating groups, and executive vice president and chief operating officer. He has also worked as an associate at McKinsey & Co. and spent two years as a Peace Corps volunteer in the Ivory Coast.

The interview was conducted at Levi's San Francisco headquarters by HBR associate editor Robert Howard.

HBR: *Levi Strauss has long had a reputation for its social responsibility. Why are you placing so much emphasis on defining the company's values now?*

Robert Haas: Levi has always treated people fairly and cared about their welfare. The usual term is "paternalism." But it is more than paternalism, really—a genuine concern for people and a recognition that people make this business successful.

In the past, however, that tradition was viewed as something separate from how we ran the business. We always talked about the "hard stuff" and the "soft

---

> ## "A company's values—what it stands for, what its people believe in—are crucial to its competitive success."

---

stuff." The soft stuff was the company's commitment to our work force. And the hard stuff was what really mattered: getting pants out the door.

What we've learned is that the soft stuff and the hard stuff are becoming increasingly intertwined. A company's values—what it stands for, what its people believe in—are crucial to its competitive success. Indeed, values drive the business.

What is happening in your environment to bring you to that conclusion?

Traditionally, the business world had clear boundaries. Geographical or regional borders defined the marketplace. Distinctions between suppliers and customers, workers and managers, were well defined. Once you had a strong market position, you could go on for a long time just on inertia. You could have a traditional, hierarchical, command-and-control organization, because change happened so slowly.

People's expectations for work were also narrowly defined. They gave their loyalty and their efforts in exchange for being taken care of. They expected information and commands to come down from on high, and they did what they were told.

As a result of all the tumult of the 1980s—increased competition, corporate restructurings, the globalization of enterprises, a new generation entering the work force—those traditional boundaries and expectations are breaking down.

What do those changes mean for leadership?

There is an enormous diffusion of power. If companies are going to react quickly to changes in the marketplace, they have to put more and more accountability, authority, and information into the hands of the people who are closest to the products and the customers. That requires new business strategies and different organizational structures. But structure and strategy aren't enough.

This is where values come in. In a more volatile and dynamic business environment, the controls have to be conceptual. They can't be human anymore: Bob Haas telling people what to do. It's the *ideas* of a business that are controlling, not some manager with authority. Values provide a common language for aligning a company's leadership and its people.

Why isn't a sound business strategy enough to create that alignment?

A strategy is no good if people don't fundamentally believe in it. We had a strategy in the late 1970s and early 1980s that emphasized diversification. We acquired companies, created new brands, and applied our traditional brand to different kinds of apparel. Our people did what they were asked to do, but the problem was, they didn't believe in it.

The big change at Levi is that we have worked hard to listen to our suppliers, our customers, and our own people. We have redefined our business strategy to focus on core products, and we have articulated the values that the company stands for—what we call our Aspirations. We've reshaped our business around this strategy and these values, and people have started marching behind this new banner. In fact, they are running to grab it and take it on ahead of senior management. Because it's what they *want* to do.

At Levi, we talk about creating an "empowered" organization. By that, we mean a company where the people who are closest to the product and the customer take the initiative without having to check with anyone. Because in an organization of 31,000 people, there's no way that any one of us in management can be around all the time to tell people what to do. It has to be the strategy and the values that guide them.

What is the role of a manager in an empowered company?

If the people on the front line really are the keys to our success, then the manager's job is to help those people and the people that they serve. That goes against the traditional assumption that the manager is in control. In the past, a manager was expected to know everything that was going on and to be deeply involved in subordinates' activities.

I can speak from experience. It has been difficult for me to accept the fact that I don't have to be the smartest guy on the block – reading every memo and signing off on every decision. In reality, the more

> ### "It's the *ideas* of a business that are controlling, not some manager with authority."

you establish parameters and encourage people to take initiatives within those boundaries, the more you multiply your own effectiveness by the effectiveness of other people.

So in a business world without boundaries, the chief role of managers is to establish some?

To set parameters. Those parameters are going to be different for different individuals. And for the same individual, they're going to be different for different tasks. Some people are going to be very inexperienced in certain things, so you need to be careful about setting the parameters of where they have authority and where they need to stop to seek clarification. Other people have experience, skills, and a track record, and within certain areas you want to give them a lot of latitude.

How does that compare with the traditional manager's job?

In many ways, it's a much tougher role because you can't rely on your title or unquestioning loyalty and obedience to get things done. You have to be thoughtful about what you want. You have to be clear about

---

ASPIRATIONS STATEMENT

We all want a company that our people are proud of and committed to, where all employees have an opportunity to contribute, learn, grow, and advance based on merit, not politics or background. We want our people to feel respected, treated fairly, listened to, and involved. Above all, we want satisfaction from accomplishments and friendships, balanced personal and professional lives, and to have fun in our endeavors.

When we describe the kind of Levi Strauss & Co. we want in the future, what we are talking about is building on the foundation we have inherited: affirming the best of our company's traditions, closing gaps that may exist between principles and practices, and updating some of our values to reflect contemporary circumstances.

What type of leadership is necessary to make our Aspirations a Reality?

New Behaviors: Leadership that exemplifies directness, openness to influence, commitment to the success of others, willingness to acknowledge our own contributions to problems, personal accountability, teamwork, and trust. Not only must we model these behaviors but we must coach others to adopt them.

Diversity: Leadership that values a diverse work force (age, sex, ethnic group, etc.) at all levels of the organization, diversity in experience, and diversity in perspectives. We have committed to taking full advantage of the rich backgrounds and abilities of all our people and to promoting a greater diversity in positions of influence. Differing points of view will be sought; diversity will be valued and honesty rewarded, not suppressed.

Recognition: Leadership that provides greater recognition – both financial and psychic – for individuals

and teams that contribute to our success. Recognition must be given to all who contribute: those who create and innovate and also those who continually support the day-to-day business requirements.

Ethical Management Practices: Leadership that epitomizes the stated standards of ethical behavior. We must provide clarity about our expectations and must enforce these standards through the corporation.

Communications: Leadership that is clear about company, unit, and individual goals and performance. People must know what is expected of them and receive timely, honest feedback on their performance and career aspirations.

Empowerment: Leadership that increases the authority and responsibility of those closest to our products and customers. By actively pushing responsibility, trust, and recognition into the organization, we can harness and release the capabilities of all our people.

the standards that you're setting. You have to negotiate goals with your work group rather than just set them yourself. You have to interact personally with individuals whom you're dealing with, understand their strengths and shortcomings, and be clear about what you want them to do.

You also have to accept the fact that decisions or recommendations may be different from what you would do. They could very well be better, but they're going to be different. You have to be willing to take your ego out of it.

That doesn't mean abdication. Managers still have to make decisions, serve as counselors and coaches, be there when things get sticky, and help sort out all the tangles.

What else do managers in an empowered organization need to do?

They can clear away the obstacles to effective action that exist in any large organization. In most companies, including ours, there is a gap between what the organization says it wants and what it feels like to work there. Those gaps between what you say and what you do erode trust in the enterprise and in the leadership, and they inhibit action. The more you can narrow that gap, the more people's energies can be released toward company purposes.

Most people want to make a contribution and be proud of what they do. But organizations typically teach us bad habits—to cut corners, protect our own turf, be political. We've discovered that when people talk about what they want for themselves and for their company, it's very idealistic and deeply emotional. This company tells people that idealism is OK. And the power that releases is just unbelievable. Liberating those forces, getting the impediments out of the way, that's what we as managers are supposed to be doing.

What is happening in the apparel business that makes managing by values so important?

The same things that are happening in most businesses. For decades, apparel has been a very fragmented industry. Most producers were small. Typically, changes in manufacturing technology, the use of computers, and the application of marketing techniques came slowly if at all. Our customers were also highly fragmented. In the old days, we had some 18,000 domestic accounts of all sizes and in every town in the country.

In this environment, we considered ourselves a manufacturer. Our job was to design products, manufacture them, deliver them in accordance with our re-

tailers' orders, and support the retailers with some consumer advertising to help the products sell. But the rest was up to the individual retailer.

Now all that is changing very rapidly. Today the top 50 accounts make up a large part of our domestic business. Style changes happen more rapidly because of innovations in fabric finishes and also because customers adopt new fashions more quickly. Technology is transforming sewing work and our relationships with our suppliers and customers. And we are operating in a global marketplace against international competition. As a result, the way we see our business has also changed.

What's the new vision?

First, we are a marketer rather than a manufacturer. And second, we are at the center of a seamless web of mutual responsibility and collaboration.

Take our relationships with our retailers: to secure the availability of a product, apparel retailers have traditionally had to order it as much as four to five months in advance. That's crazy. It forces retail buyers to guess four and five months down the road what a consumer who is 15 years old is going to want in jeans. During that time, a new movie can come out, and the trend goes from blue denim to black denim. And suddenly that inventory commitment is obsolete, causing costly markdowns.

One answer to this new circumstance is technology. Our electronic data-interchange system, LeviLink, was a pioneering effort in apparel to communicate with our customers and manage the order-replenishment cycle faster and more accurately than conventional systems could. [See the insert "How Values Shape Technology."] As a result, we have customers operating with 20% to 30% less inventory and achieving 20% to 30% increased sales. Their return on their investment with us is much greater than it was in the past. And these retailers also serve their customers better because the desired product is in stock when the consumer goes to purchase it.

We're also forming closer relationships with our suppliers. We used to have ten or twelve U.S. denim suppliers. Now we're down to four or five. There is a seamless partnership, with interrelationships and mutual commitments, straight through the chain that would've been unimaginable ten years ago. You can't be responsive to the end-consumer today unless you can count on those kinds of collaborations at each step along the way.

What are the implications of that seamless partnership for your work force?

Our employees have many new responsibilities. For example, because of our computer linkages to our customers, our account representatives have more information on what's selling at the store level than the retailer does – not only products but sizes, fabrics, and styles. The rep has to know how to analyze that information and interpret it for the customer. What's more, since the computer does all the mundane record-keeping now, the rep can concentrate on planning and projecting the store's needs and being a marketing consultant.

What our employees do for the retailers is also much broader. In addition to the account representative, we have merchandising coordinators who make sure the stock is replenished and train salesclerks so they know how to sell our products more effectively. We have specialists in "visual merchandising" who work with our accounts to improve the ways they display our products. We have promotions experts who help stores tailor promotions to their clientele. And we run consumer hot lines to help customers find the products they want.

The work is much more creative, more entrepreneurial. It's as if these people are in business for themselves. They're doing what human beings do best – think, plan, interact, see trends, humanize the business to make it more successful.

What does that have to do with values?

To do that kind of work effectively requires a whole new set of attitudes and behaviors. The passivity and dependence of traditional paternalism – doing what you're told – doesn't work anymore. People have to take responsibility, exercise initiative, be accountable for their own success and for that of the

How Values Shape Technology

According to Chief Information Officer Bill Eaton, the Levi Strauss & Co. technology strategy is a direct reflection of the company's Aspirations Statement. "Empowerment is meaningless unless people have access to information," says Eaton. "The goal of our technology strategy is to make sure that the information is available on the desktop of the person who is doing the job."

To that end, Levi Strauss has embarked on a three-part program for the global integration of its business through information technology. The most visible part of this strategy is LeviLink, the electronic data-interchange system that ties retailers to the company's distribution network. The system collects point-of-sale information from cash registers at the company's major accounts, then uses the information to generate reorders, invoices, packing slips, and advance notifications to retailers of future shipments. It also provides company sales representatives with far more information on the activity of individual retailers than was available in the past. Currently, about 40% of the company's business comes through LeviLink – a figure that the company hopes to double over the next five years.

Although less visible, Levi Strauss has also made major strides in computerizing its manufacturing operations. In 10 of the company's 32 factories worldwide, every sewing station now comes equipped with a hand-sized computer terminal. As a bundle of fabric moves through the plant, each employee who works on it passes the bundle's bar-coded label through a scanner built into the terminal. The result is a "real-time production control" system that allows the company to track work-in-process as it moves through the factory. The system also provides workers with information on their own performance, which they can use to increase productivity.

The ultimate goal is to link these two systems, allowing the company to issue production orders for new products immediately as existing products are sold in retailers' stores. This capacity will be provided by the Levi's Advanced Business System (LABS), which the company will be implementing over the next three years. LABS will be able to track a product from its conception – including orders, inventory, and financial information. Based on a new "relational database" software architecture, LABS will allow employees to perform more powerful and more flexible searches of company databases and to get rapid access to information typically limited in the past to managers.

The way Levi Strauss manages the development of new systems also reflects its commitment to using technology to support people. CIO Eaton serves on the company's executive management committee, ensuring the integration of technology and business strategies. And close ties between the information systems and human resources departments – one HR staff member now works in information systems – help connect the development of the company's new information technology platform to the creation of new business processes, organization designs, and people skills.

company as a whole. They have to communicate more frequently and more effectively with their colleagues and their customers.

In a traditional command-and-control organization, acting in this way is difficult, even risky. The Aspirations encourage and support the new behaviors that we need. For example, in an empowered organization there are bound to be a lot more disagreements. Because we value open and direct com-

> ## "Because we value open and direct communication, we give people permission to disagree."

munication, we give people permission to disagree. They can tell a manager, "It doesn't seem aspirational to be working with that contractor because from what we've seen, that company really mistreats its workers." Or they can say, "It may help us conserve cash to be slow in paying our bills, but that company has been a supplier for a long time, and it's struggling right now. Wouldn't it be better in terms of the partnership we're trying to create with our suppliers to pay our bills on time?"

Those are very challenging discussions for peers to have—let alone for somebody to have with his or her boss. But if we can "sanctify" it by reference to commonly held standards that we all share, it makes it all right to disagree.

So the values help bring about the kind of business behavior you need to stay competitive.

Values are where the hard stuff and the soft stuff come together. Let me give another example: in the new, more dynamic business environment, a company has to understand the relationship between work and family. It used to be that what happened to your employees when they went home at the end of the day was their business. But today that worker's sick child *is* your business, because if she's worrying about her child or calling in sick when she isn't—and probably feeling resentful because she's had to lie—she isn't going to be productive.

By contrast, if employees aren't worrying about things outside the workplace, if they feel supported—not just financially but "psychically"—then they are going to be more responsive to the needs of customers and of the business. That support needs to come in a whole set of managerial areas: supervisory practices, peer relations, training, work organization, access to information, and the like.

What is Levi doing about this particular issue?

We've established a companywide task force that's looking at how to balance work and family commitments. In itself, that's no big deal. A lot of companies are studying the issue. But even the way we manage the task force reflects our values. For instance, I'm on the task force, but I don't run it. We have everyone from secretaries and sewing machine operators to senior managers on the task force—as part of our commitment to diversity.

And that too makes perfect business sense. After all, my family situation is about as traditional as it gets. I have a wife at home who looks after our daughter. What do I know about the problems of a sewing machine operator—expected to punch in at a certain time and punch out at another and with a half-hour lunch break—whose child's day-care arrangements fall through that morning? Obviously, a better result is going to come out of a broad task force that represents a diversity of opinions, family situations, and points of view. [See the insert "The Making of an Aspiration."]

How does a CEO manage for values?

The first responsibility for me and for my team is to examine critically our own behaviors and manage-

ANDY
WARHOL
LEVI'S
501
JEANS

ment styles in relation to the behaviors and values that we profess and to work to become more consistent with the values that we are articulating. It's tough work. We all fall off the wagon. But you can't be one thing and say another. People have unerring detection systems for fakes, and they won't put up with them. They won't put values into practice if you're not.

You said it's tough. What are the common kinds of breakdowns?

It's difficult to unlearn behaviors that made us successful in the past. Speaking rather than listening. Valuing people like yourself over people of different genders or from different cultures or parts of the organization. Doing things on your own rather than collaborating. Making the decision yourself instead of asking different people for their perspectives. There's a whole range of behaviors that were highly functional in the old hierarchical organization that are dead wrong in the flatter, more responsive, empowered organization that we're seeking to become.

Once your own behavior is in line with the new values, how do you communicate the values to others?

One way is to model the new behaviors we are looking for. For example, senior managers try to be explicit about our vulnerability and failings. We talk to people about the *bad* decisions we've made. It demystifies senior management and removes the stigma traditionally associated with taking risks. We also talk about the limitations of our own knowledge, mostly by inviting other people's perspectives.

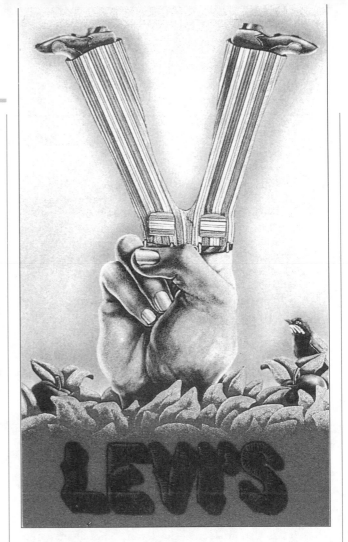

> "Senior managers try to be explicit about our vulnerability and failings. We talk to people about the *bad* decisions we've made."

When I talk to employees about the development of the Aspirations Statement, I describe the stark terror I felt when I took over this company, just having turned 43 years old. We were a company in crisis. Our sales were dropping, our international business was heading for a loss, our domestic business had an eroding profit base, our diversification wasn't working, and we had too much production capacity. I had no bold plan of action. I knew that values were important but didn't have the two granite tablets that I could bring down from Mount Sinai to deliver to the organization. I talk about how alone I felt as a senior manager and how tough it is to be held up as a paragon to the organization. It helps people realize that senior management is human, that we can't be expected to know everything, and that we're inviting them in as partners in the organization.

Another important way to communicate values is through training. We've developed a comprehensive training program that we call the core curriculum. The centerpiece is a week-long course known as "leadership week" that helps managers practice the behavior outlined in the Aspirations Statement. We run about 20 sessions a year for a small group of about 20 people at a time. By the end of this year, the top 700 people in the company will have been through it. And at least one member of the executive management committee—the top 8 people in the company—or some other senior manager participates in every week-long session, just to send a signal of how important this is to us.

Can you really train people in new values?

You can't train anybody to do anything that he or she doesn't fundamentally believe in. That's why we've designed leadership week to give people an opportunity to reflect on their own values and to allow

The Making of an Aspiration

In 1985, a small group of minority and women managers asked for a private meeting with Levi Strauss & Co. CEO Robert Haas. The company had always been committed to equal employment opportunity; compared with other corporations, its numbers were good. But the managers felt strongly that they had reached a plateau. There were invisible barriers keeping women and minorities from advancing in the organization.

In response to their concerns, Haas organized an off-site retreat. Ten senior managers, all white men, were paired with either a woman or minority manager from their work group. The senior managers believed the company had been doing a good job hiring and promoting women and minorities. They were surprised to discover the depth of frustration and anger their subordinates felt. After two-and-a-half days of often painful discussion, the group concluded that equal employment opportunity was not just a matter of numbers but of attitudes, and that considerable unconscious discrimination still existed at the company. Something more needed to be done.

Since that 1985 meeting, Levi Strauss has renewed its commitment to full diversity at all levels. It has also broadened the definition of diversity beyond equal employment opportunity to the active encouragement of different points of view and their inclusion in company decision making.

Between 1985 and 1988, 16 more off-site sessions paired white, male managers with women or minorities who work for them to reflect on unexamined assumptions about diversity and stereotypes about particular groups. In 1987, diversity became one of the six Aspirations defined in the company's Aspirations Statement. That same year, members of the company's executive management committee – the top 8 people in the company – began holding monthly forums for small groups of 15 to 20 employees. By 1989, 20 ongoing forums were taking place. And while the original focus of the meetings was on questions of race and gender, the forums have expanded to consider a broad range of workplace issues.

The forums have been the catalyst for a number of new initiatives:

□ Recognizing that women and minority employees often have special problems and needs, the company has inaugurated four new career-development courses – one each for women, blacks, Hispanics, and Asians.

□ These courses have led to the creation of ethnic support networks for blacks, Asians, and Hispanics. Representatives of these networks have direct feedback to top management through quarterly meetings with the senior personnel committee.

□ In 1989, Levi Strauss established a companywide task force to recommend new policies to support a more effective balance between work and family life. Its 18 members are drawn from all levels of management and the work force – from sewing operators and secretaries to a division president and the CEO. This past summer, the task force sent a 25-page questionnaire to 15,000 of Levi's 21,000 U.S. employees to survey their family needs.

□ In 1989, the company also inaugurated a three-day course on "Valuing Diversity." About 240 top managers will have taken the course by the end of 1990. Eventually, all Levi Strauss employees will take diversity training.

them to say what they want to get from work. In most cases, people learn that their personal values are aligned with those of the company. Of course, not everybody will buy into it. We've had some very honest discussions where managers say, "Look, I'm 53 years old, I've managed one way all my life and been successful, and now the company wants me to change. I don't know if I can do it."

But two things happen during leadership week. Because the groups are small, people build up a support network. They realize that others have the same problems that they have. Suddenly, they don't feel so alone.

Second, the training makes clear what's expected of them and what the consequences of succeeding or failing to adapt will be. It gives people the freedom to opt out. The real success of our core curriculum will be if it convinces some people that our environment is simply not right for them.

We also try to make sure that the core curriculum isn't just some nice experience that stops as soon as people get back to their jobs. For instance, there is a section of leadership week called "unanswered questions" where people voice concerns inspired by the course. Our human resources people collect these unanswered questions and report on them every quarter to the executive management committee. Sometimes, these questions can be handled by a particular individual. In other cases, we've set up a companywide task force to study the issue and come back with suggestions for changes in the way we do things. This creates a dialogue within the company among the people who have to make things happen.

Do the company's values influence the way you evaluate managers?

One-third of a manager's raise, bonus, and other financial rewards depends on his or her ability to manage aspirationally – the "how" of management rather than the "what." That goes for decisions about succession planning as well.

In some areas of the company, they're weighting it even more strongly. The point is, it's big enough to get people's attention. It's real. There's money attached to it. Giving people tough feedback and a low rating on aspirational management means improvement is necessary no matter how many pants they got out the door. Promotion is not in the future unless you improve.

How important is pay for pushing the company's values through the organization?

It's an influence but not the most important one. The key factors determining whether the values take or not will be individual commitment and desire and the peer pressure in the environment that we create. To me, the idea of a person as a marionette whose arms and legs start moving whenever you pull the pay string is too simplistic a notion of what motivates people in organizations.

That goes against the trend in recent years to fine-tune compensation incentives and tie them more closely to performance.

What happens there is you end up using pay to manage your company. But pay shouldn't manage your company; managers should. Managers should set the example, create the expectations, and provide the feedback. Managers should create an environment where people want to move in a constructive direction – not because there's money tied to the end of it, but because they feel it's right and they want to do it. That's why the way we conduct performance evaluations is probably more important than the pay we attach to aspirational management.

What's the process?

The typical performance evaluation in business has a manager set goals for a subordinate at the start of the year, and then at the end of the year make a subjective judgment about how well he or she has fulfilled them. That tends to create rabid "upward serving" behavior. People play to the person who's buttering their bread.

But what constitutes effective performance for a manager, anyway? Not necessarily pleasing your boss. Rather, good managers mobilize the talents of subordinates, peers, and clients to further the group's goals.

So what I started doing years ago – long before we developed the Aspirations Statement – was to talk with the direct reports of the people I manage, as well as with their peers and others they interact with. To evaluate one individual, I might interview anywhere from 10 to 16 people. The discussions are anonymous and confidential. And I report only trends, not isolated incidences.

This is an extremely powerful process that promotes ongoing feedback. The quotes may be anonymous, but they are very direct. "Here's what a group of people who work for you feel: You're much too controlling. You don't give them the latitude they need to show you how much they could do. People feel scared to take risks with you or to say controversial things because you act like you don't believe them."

I also ask the people who contribute to somebody's evaluation to say the same things to the person's face. If we can encourage regular dialogue among people so that they give their bosses or peers feedback on their

performance, managers begin to realize that they have to pay attention to their people. If they create an

> ## "Suddenly, this $4 billion company feels like an owner-operated company, which is the goal."

unwholesome, unproductive environment and can't change it, we're not going to tolerate it.

Has the Aspirations Statement had any impact yet on the quality of major business decisions?

I'm the first to say our journey is incomplete. But compared with, say, five years ago, there definitely is a change. Suddenly, this $4 billion company feels like an owner-operated company, which is the goal.

Take the example of our Dockers product line. Dockers was like a new invention—a brand new segment in the casual pants market. The concept started in Argentina. Our Japanese affiliate picked it up under another name. Our menswear division adapted the idea to the U.S. market under the name of Dockers. Then the other domestic divisions saw its potential, and now it's in womenswear and kidswear. We also have a Shirts Dockers line and in selected international markets, we're seeing the startup of a Dockers product. In 1986, we sold 35,000 units. This year, we'll be doing a half-a-billion-dollar business in the United States.

We didn't have a business plan for Dockers. We had managers who saw an opportunity. They created a product and went out and made commitments for production that were greater than the orders they had in hand, because they believed in the product and its momentum. They got corporate support for an investment in advertising that was not justified on a cost-per-unit basis and created a product that anybody else in the market could have done. And five years later, it's a staple in the American wardrobe. None of this would have happened before this more collaborative, open style of management.

We've talked about getting managers to accept and live the company's values. But more than 75% of Levi's work force consists of operators in your sewing and finishing plants. Isn't the real challenge to make the company's values meaningful for them?

Empowerment isn't limited to just white-collar workers. By utilizing our people more fully than the apparel industry traditionally has, we can organize

sewing work in ways that are much more in keeping with our Aspirations. About a year ago, we initiated an experiment at our Blue Ridge, Georgia plant, where we set up a gain-sharing program. We said to the employees, "You are the experts. If you meet predetermined production goals and predetermined absenteeism and safety standards, we'll split 50-50 with you any savings that result from economies or productivity improvements."

Sewing machine operators are now running the plant. They're making the rules and in some cases changing them because they understand why the rules are there and which rules make sense and which don't. They're taking initiatives and making things work better because it's in their interest and they don't have to be told.

This was not an unproductive plant. It was among the top 10% in the company. Today it's one of the top two plants—after only nine months in the new program. The financial payoff has been considerable, and there's certainly more potential there. But to me, the most exciting thing is to see the transformation in the workplace. People who felt that they weren't valued despite maybe 20 years of work for the company have a completely different attitude about their work.

In my judgment, we can restructure the workplace far beyond what we've done in Blue Ridge. I see us moving to a team-oriented, multiskilled environment in which the team itself takes on many of the supervisor's and trainer's tasks. If you combine that with some form of gain sharing, you probably will have a much more productive plant with higher employee satisfaction and commitment.

> ## "You can't promise employment security and be honest. The best you can do is not play games with people."

During the same period in which Levi has been defining its values, you've also been downsizing the company. Is it possible to get a high-commitment work force without offering some kind of employment security?

You can't promise employment security and be honest. The best you can do is not play games with people. You can't make any guarantees.

Through the 1950s, 1960s, and 1970s, Levi was growing so dramatically that unless you committed a felony, you weren't going to lose your job. But that

was a special era stimulated by economic expansion and tremendous demographic growth. Now we're in a real-world situation where market forces are less favorable, external competitive pressures are more intense, and change is more rapid. You have to help people appreciate the need to deal constructively with the changing environment. If we're doing our job, we need to understand the rapidity and magnitude of the changes taking place and provide people with all the tools we can to cope with change.

But isn't it disingenuous to be championing values like empowerment in an environment where workers are worried about losing their jobs?

There is an apparent contradiction but not a real one, because our most basic value is honesty. If we have too much capacity, it's a problem that affects the entire company. Sometimes, the only solution is to close a plant, and if we don't have the guts to face that decision, then we risk hurting a lot of people—not just those in one plant. We need to be honest about that.

We tie it to Aspirations by asking, "How are we going to treat people who are displaced by technology, by changes in production sources, or by market changes?" We are committed to making the transition as successful as possible and to minimizing the uprooting and dislocation. We give more advance notice than is required by law. We provide more severance than is typical in our industry, so the effect of displacement is cushioned. We extend health care benefits. We also support job-training programs and other local initiatives to help our former employees find new jobs. And in the community itself, which has been depending on us as a major employer, we continue for a period of time to fund community organizations and social causes that we've been involved with, so that our withdrawal isn't a double hit—a loss of employment and also a loss of philanthropic support.

But has the Aspirations Statement changed the way you make decisions about capacity and plant closings in the first place?

The Aspirations make us slow down decisions. We challenge ourselves more explicitly to give some factors more weight than we did before—especially the impact of a plant closing on the community. There have been plants we have decided not to close, even though their costs were higher than other plants we did close. The reason was the community impact.

The Aspirations also provide a way to talk about these difficult trade-offs inside the company. People now have the freedom and authority to say, "Is it aspirational to be closing a plant when we're having a good year?" Or, "If we must close this plant, are we meeting our responsibilities to the employees and their community?" That forces us to be explicit about all the factors involved. It causes us to slow up, reflect, and be direct with one another about what's happening.

If the company's values cause you to slow up, doesn't that make it more difficult to respond to fast-changing markets?

Only if you assume it's still possible to separate the hard stuff from the soft stuff. Most managers say they want to optimize their business decisions. My personal philosophy is to suboptimize business decisions. Too often, optimizing really means taking only one dimension of a problem into account. Suboptimizing means looking at more than one factor and taking into account the interests and the needs of all the constituents. When you do that, suddenly the traditional hard values of business success and the nontraditional soft values relating to people start blending. The result is a better business decision—and it can still be done quickly if your employees understand the company's values and are empowered to take action without layers of review.

You mentioned collecting "unanswered questions" from employees about the role of values in the business. What's the most difficult for you to answer?

One of the most frequent things I hear is: "When the next downturn in the business happens, is top management going to remain committed to Aspirations?" The only answer to that one is, "Test us." We hope we won't have a downturn, but even if we do, I have no doubts about what management's commitment is. Only the experience of going through that kind of a situation, however, will convincingly demonstrate that commitment.

Where is that commitment to let values drive the business leading?

We've launched an irreversible process. Now we have to support the commitment that the Aspirations Statement is creating and be willing to deal with the tough issues that it raises.

Two years ago, I gave a speech about the Aspirations at one of our worldwide management meetings. At the end, I held up the Aspirations Statement and ripped it to shreds. And I said, "I want each of you to throw away the Aspirations Statement and think about what you want for the company and what kind of person you want to be in the workplace and what kind of a legacy you want to leave behind. If the result happens to be the Aspirations, that's fine. But if it happens to be something else, the important thing is that you think deeply about who you are and what you stand for. I have enough confidence in your judgment and motivations that I'll go with whatever you come up with."

The point is, the Levi Strauss of the future is not going to be shaped by me or even by the Aspirations Statement. It's going to be shaped by our people and their actions, by the questions they ask and the responses we give, and by how this feeds into the way we run our business. ⊟

Reprint 90504

Moral mazes: bureaucracy and managerial work

Robert Jackall

With moral choices tied to personal fates, how does bureaucracy shape managerial morality?

Generations of Americans have been taught that the way to move up in corporate management is to work hard and make sound decisions. Has the bureaucratic world changed all that? Has the connection between work and reward become more capricious? The author of this study believes that the answer to both questions is yes. Interviewing more than 100 managers, he sought answers to such questions as: What kind of ethic does bureaucracy produce in middle and upper middle managers? Why does one person rise to the top while another doesn't? The managers interviewed offer many provocative answers to questions like these. They describe the experiences of themselves and their acquaintances. They speak freely—and sometimes humorously—of how they see credit for accomplishments being awarded, the role of loyalties and alliances, the meaning of team play, the significance of patrons, the ambiguities of "hitting your numbers," the part played by luck, "blame time," outrunning one's mistakes, the subtleties of bureaucratic language, and other elements of their work. While the impressions reported are unlikely to gratify top management, they may lead the HBR reader to rethink the unintended consequences of working for large-scale enterprises and to see the problems of executive development in a new light.

Mr. Jackall is associate professor of sociology at Williams College. He is the author of Workers in a Labyrinth: Jobs and Survival in a Bank Bureaucracy *(Allanheld, Osmun and Co., 1978), and the co-editor (with Henry M. Levin) of* Worker Cooperatives in America *(Univeristy of California Press, 1984). He is also working on a book about managerial work to be published by Oxford University Press.*
Illustrations by Christopher Bing.

Corporate leaders often tell their charges that hard work will lead to success. Indeed, this theory of reward being commensurate with effort has been an enduring belief in our society, one central to our self-image as a people where the "main chance" is available to anyone of ability who has the gumption and the persistence to seize it. Hard work, it is also frequently asserted, builds character. This notion carries less conviction because businessmen, and our society as a whole, have little patience with those who make a habit of finishing out of the money. In the end, it is success that matters, that legitimates striving, and that makes work worthwhile.

What if, however, men and women in the big corporation no longer see success as necessarily connected to hard work? What becomes of the social morality of the corporation—I mean the everyday rules in use that people play by—when there is thought to be no "objective" standard of excellence to explain how and why winners are separated from also-rans, how and why some people succeed and others fail?

This is the puzzle that confronted me while doing a great many extensive interviews with managers and executives in several large corporations, particularly in a large chemical company and a large textile firm. (See the insert for more details.) I went into these corporations to study how bureaucracy—the prevailing organizational form of our society and economy—shapes moral consciousness. I came to see that managers' rules for success are at the heart of what may be called the bureaucratic ethic.

This article suggests no changes and offers no programs for reform. It is, rather, simply an

Author's note: I presented an earlier version of this paper in the Faculty Lecture Series at Williams College on March 18, 1982. The intensive field work done during 1980 and 1981 was made possible by a Fellowship for Independent Research from the National Endowment for the Humanities and by a Junior Faculty Leave and small research grant from Williams College.

Editor's note: All references are listed at the end of the article.

interpretive sociological analysis of the moral dimensions of managers' work. Some readers may find the essay sharp-edged, others familiar. For both groups, it is important to note at the outset that my materials are managers' own descriptions of their experiences.[1] In listening to managers, I have had the decided advantages of being unencumbered with business responsibilities and also of being free from the taken-for-granted views and vocabularies of the business world. As it happens, my own research in a variety of other settings suggests that managers' experiences are by no means unique; indeed they have a deep resonance with those of other occupational groups.

What happened to the Protestant Ethic?

To grasp managers' experiences and the more general implications they contain, one must see them against the background of the great historical transformations, both social and cultural, that produced managers as an occupational group. Since the concern here is with the moral significance of work in business, it is important to begin with an understanding of the original Protestant Ethic, the world view of the rising bourgeois class that spearheaded the emergence of capitalism.

The Protestant Ethic was a set of beliefs that counseled "secular asceticism" – the methodical, rational subjection of human impulse and desire to God's will through "restless, continuous, systematic work in a worldly calling."[2] This ethic of ceaseless work and ceaseless renunciation of the fruits of one's toil provided both the economic and the moral foundations for modern capitalism.

On one hand, secular asceticism was a ready-made prescription for building economic capital; on the other, it became for the upward-moving bourgeois class – self-made industrialists, farmers, and enterprising artisans – the ideology that justified their attention to this world, their accumulation of wealth, and indeed the social inequities that inevitably followed such accumulation. This bourgeois ethic, with its imperatives for self-reliance, hard work, frugality, and rational planning, and its clear definition of success and failure, came to dominate a whole historical epoch in the West.

But the ethic came under assault from two directions. First, the very accumulation of wealth that the old Protestant Ethic made possible gradually stripped away the religious basis of the ethic, especially among the rising middle class that benefited from it. There were, of course, periodic reassertions of

the religious context of the ethic, as in the case of John D. Rockefeller and his turn toward Baptism. But on the whole, by the late 1800s the religious roots of the ethic survived principally among independent farmers and proprietors of small businesses in rural areas and towns across America.

In the mainstream of an emerging urban America, the ethic had become secularized into the "work ethic," "rugged individualism," and especially the "success ethic." By the beginning of this century, among most of the economically successful, frugality had become an aberration, conspicuous consumption the norm. And with the shaping of the mass consumer society later in this century, the sanctification of consumption became widespread, indeed crucial to the maintenance of the economic order.

Affluence and the emergence of the consumer society were responsible, however, for the demise of only aspects of the old ethic – namely, the imperatives for saving and investment. The core of the ethic, even in its later, secularized form – self-reliance, unremitting devotion to work, and a morality that postulated just rewards for work well done – was undermined by the complete transformation of the organizational form of work itself. The hallmarks of the emerging modern production and distribution systems were administrative hierarchies, standardized work procedures, regularized timetables, uniform policies, and centralized control – in a word, the bureaucratization of the economy.

This bureaucratization was heralded at first by a very small class of salaried managers, who were later joined by legions of clerks and still later by technicians and professionals of every stripe. In this century, the process spilled over from the private to the public sector and government bureaucracies came to rival those of industry. This great transformation produced the decline of the old middle class of entrepreneurs, free professionals, independent farmers, and small independent businessmen – the traditional carriers of the old Protestant Ethic – and the ascendance of a new middle class of salaried employees whose chief common characteristic was and is their dependence on the big organization.

Any understanding of what happened to the original Protestant Ethic and to the old morality and social character it embodied – and therefore any understanding of the moral significance of work today – is inextricably tied to an analysis of bureaucracy. More specifically, it is, in my view, tied to an analysis of the work and occupational cultures of managerial groups within bureaucracies. Managers are the quintessential bureaucratic work group; they not only fashion bureaucratic rules, but they are also bound by them. Typically, they are not just *in* the organization; they are *of* the organization. As such, managers represent the prototype of the white-collar salaried employee. By analyzing the kind of ethic bureaucracy produces in managers, one can begin to understand how bureaucracy shapes morality in our society as a whole.

Pyramidal politics

American businesses typically both centralize and decentralize authority. Power is concentrated at the top in the person of the chief executive officer and is simultaneously decentralized; that is, responsibility for decisions and profits is pushed as far down the organizational line as possible. For example, the chemical company that I studied—and its structure is typical of other organizations I examined—is one of several operating companies of a large and growing conglomerate. Like the other operating companies, the chemical concern has its own president, executive vice presidents, vice presidents, other executive officers, business area managers, entire staff divisions, and operating plants. Each company is, in effect, a self-sufficient organization, though they are all coordinated by the corporation, and each president reports directly to the corporate CEO.

Now, the key interlocking mechanism of this structure is its reporting system. Each manager gathers up the profit targets or other objectives of his or her subordinates, and with these formulates his commitments to his boss; this boss takes these commitments, and those of his other subordinates, and in turn makes a commitment to *his* boss. (Note: henceforth only "he" or "his" will be used to allow for easier reading.) At the top of the line, the president of each company makes his commitment to the CEO of the corporation, based on the stated objectives given to him by his vice presidents. There is always pressure from the top to set higher goals.

This management-by-objectives system, as it is usually called, creates a chain of commitments from the CEO down to the lowliest product manager. In practice, it also shapes a patrimonial authority arrangement which is crucial to defining both the immediate experiences and the long-run career chances of individual managers. In this world, a subordinate owes fealty principally to his immediate boss. A subordinate must not overcommit his boss; he must keep the boss from making mistakes, particularly public ones; he must not circumvent the boss. On a social level, even though an easy, breezy informality is the prevalent style of American business, the subordinate must extend to the boss a certain ritual deference: for instance, he must follow the boss's lead in conversation, must not speak out of turn at meetings, and must laugh at the boss's jokes while not making jokes of his own.

In short, the subordinate must not exhibit any behavior which symbolizes parity. In return, he can hope to be elevated when and if the boss is elevated, although other important criteria also intervene here. He can also expect protection for mistakes made up to a point. However, that point is never exactly defined and always depends on the complicated politics of each situation.

Who gets credit?

It is characteristic of this authority system that details are pushed down and credit is pushed up. Superiors do not like to give detailed instructions to subordinates. The official reason for this is to maximize subordinates' autonomy; the underlying reason seems to be to get rid of tedious details and to protect the privilege of authority to declare that a mistake has been made.

It is not at all uncommon for very bald and extremely general edicts to emerge from on high. For example, "Sell the plant in St. Louis. Let me know when you've struck a deal." This pushing down of details has important consequences:

1 Because they are unfamiliar with entangling details, corporate higher echelons tend to expect highly successful results without complications. This is central to top executives' well-known aversion to bad news and to the resulting tendency to "kill the messenger" who bears that news.

2 The pushing down of detail creates great pressure on middle managers not only to transmit good news but to protect their corporations, their bosses, and themselves in the process. They become the "point men" of a given strategy and the potential "fall guys" when things go wrong.

Credit flows up in this structure and usually is appropriated by the highest ranking officer involved in a decision. This person redistributes credit as he chooses, bound essentially by a sensitivity to public perceptions of his fairness. At the middle level, credit for a particular success is always a type of refracted social honor; one cannot claim credit even if it is earned. Credit has to be given, and acceptance of the gift implicitly involves a reaffirmation and strengthening of fealty. A superior may share some credit with subordinates in order to deepen fealty relationships and induce greater future efforts on his behalf. Of course, a different system is involved in the allocation of blame, a point I shall discuss later.

Fealty to the 'king'

Because of the interlocking character of the commitment system, a CEO carries enormous influence in his corporation. If, for a moment, one thinks of the presidents of individual operating companies as barons, then the CEO of the parent company is the king. His word is law; even the CEO's wishes and whims are taken as commands by close subordinates on the corporate staff, who zealously turn them into policies and directives.

A typical example occurred in the textile company last year when the CEO, new at the time, expressed mild concern about the rising operating costs of the company's fleet of rented cars. The following day, a stringent system for monitoring mileage replaced the previous casual practice.

Great efforts are made to please the CEO. For example, when the CEO of the large conglomerate that includes the chemical company visits a plant, the most important order of business for local management is a fresh paint job, even when, as in several cases last year, the cost of paint alone exceeds $100,000. I am told that similar anecdotes from other organizations have been in circulation since 1910; this suggests a certain historical continuity of behavior toward top bosses.

The second order of business for the plant management is to produce a complete book describing the plant and its operations, replete with photographs and illustrations, for presentation to the CEO; such a book costs about $10,000 for the single copy. By any standards of budgetary stringency, such expenditures are irrational. But by the social standards of the corportion, they make perfect sense. It is far more important to please the king today than to worry about the future economic state of one's fief, since if one does not please the king, there may not be a fief to worry about or indeed any vassals to do the worrying.

By the same token, all of this leads to an intense interest in everything the CEO does and says. In both the chemical and the textile companies, the most common topic of conversation among managers up and down the line is speculation about their respective CEOs' plans, intentions, strategies, actions, styles, and public images.

Such speculation is more than idle gossip. Because he stands at the apex of the corporation's bureaucratic and patrimonial structures and locks the intricate system of commitments between bosses and subordinates into place, it is the CEO who ultimately decides whether those commitments have been satisfactorily met. Moreover, the CEO and his trusted associates determine the fate of whole business areas of a corporation.

Field work details

The field work during 1980 to 1981 encompassed four companies—a large chemical company, one of several operating companies of a diversified conglomerate; a large textile company; a medium-sized chemical company; and a large defense contractor. My access to the latter two businesses was limited to a series of interviews with top executive officers, some observation, and some access to internal company documents. Although many of the themes treated in this article emerged in my work in these two companies, I have for the most part treated these materials as preliminary data.

It is also important to note that I was denied access to 36 companies, an instructive experience in itself. In about half these cases, access was denied after lengthy negotiations involving interviews with various company officials; these materials are also treated as preliminary. In this article, when I claim that something occurs in all the companies that I studied, I mean to include these preliminary materials as well as the more substantive data described here.

I concentrated most of my substantive work in the two companies where my access was broadest—in the large textile company and particularly in the large chemical company. I pursued the research in these companies until mid-1982 and mid-1983, respectively. I draw my analysis principally from these two organizations. My materials from both are rich and detailed; moreover, their size and complexity make them representative of important sectors of American industry. Further, the kinds of problems managers face in these companies—organizational, regulatory, and personal—are, I think, typical of those confronted more generally.

My methodology in this research was intensive semi-structured interviews with managers and executives at every level of management. The interviews usually lasted between two and three hours but, sometimes, especially with reinterviews, went much longer. I interviewed more than 100 people in these two companies alone.

In addition, I gathered material in a number of more informal ways—for example, through nonparticipant observation, over meals, and in attendance at various management seminars. I also had extensive access to internal company documents and publications.

Shake-ups & contingency

One must appreciate the simultaneously monocratic and patrimonial character of business bureaucracies in order to grasp what we might call their contingency. One has only to read the *Wall Street Journal* or the *New York Times* to realize that, despite their carefully constructed "eternal" public image, corporations are quite unstable organizations. Mergers, buy-outs, divestitures, and especially "organizational restructuring" are commonplace aspects of business life. I shall discuss only organizational shake-ups here.

Usually, shake-ups occur because of the appointment of a new CEO and/or division president, or because of some failure that is adjudged to demand retribution; sometimes these occurrences work together. The first action of most new CEOs is some form of organizational change. On the one hand, this prevents the inheritance of blame for past mistakes; on the other, it projects an image of bareknuckled aggressiveness much appreciated on Wall Street. Perhaps most important, a shake-up rearranges the fealty structure of the corporation, placing in power those barons whose style and public image mesh closely with that of the new CEO.

A shake-up has reverberations throughout an organization. Shortly after the new CEO of the conglomerate was named, he reorganized the whole business and selected new presidents to head each of the five newly formed companies of the corporation. He mandated that the presidents carry out a thorough reorganization of their separate companies complete with extensive "census reduction" – that is, firing as many people as possible.

The new president of the chemical company, one of these five, had risen from a small but important specialty chemicals division in the former company. Upon promotion to president, he reached back into his former division, indeed back to his own past work in a particular product line, and systematically elevated many of his former colleagues, friends, and allies. Powerful managers in other divisions, particularly in a rival process chemicals division, were: (1) forced to take big demotions in the new power structure; (2) put on "special assignment" – the corporate euphemism for Siberia (the saying is: "No one ever comes back from special assignment"); (3) fired; or (4) given "early retirement," a graceful way of doing the same thing.

Up and down the chemical company, former associates of the president now hold virtually every important position. Managers in the company view all of this as an inevitable fact of life. In their view, the whole reorganization could easily have gone in a completely different direction had another CEO been named or had the one selected picked a different president for the chemical company, or had the president come from a different work group in the old organization. Similarly, there is the abiding feeling that another significant change in top management could trigger yet another sweeping reorganization.

Fealty is the mortar of the corporate hierarchy, but the removal of one well-placed stone loosens the mortar throughout the pyramid and can cause things to fall apart. And no one is ever quite sure, until after the fact, just how the pyramid will be put back together.

Success & failure

It is within this complicated and ambiguous authority structure, always subject to upheaval, that success and failure are meted out to those in the middle and upper middle managerial ranks. Managers rarely spoke to me of objective criteria for achieving success because once certain crucial points in one's career are passed, success and failure seem to have little to do with one's accomplishments. Rather, success is socially defined and distributed. Corporations do demand, of course, a basic competence and sometimes specified training and experience; hiring patterns usually ensure these. A weeding-out process takes place, however, among the lower ranks of managers during the first several years of their experience. By the time a manager reaches a certain numbered grade in the ordered hierarchy – in the chemical company this is Grade 13 out of 25, defining the top 8 1/2% of management in the company – managerial competence as such is taken for granted and assumed not to differ greatly from one manager to the next. The focus then switches to social factors, which are determined by authority and political alignments – the fealty structure – and by the ethos and style of the corporation.

Moving to the top

In the chemical and textile companies as well as the other concerns I studied, five criteria seem to control a person's ability to rise in middle and upper middle management. In ascending order they are:

1   **Appearance and dress.** This criterion is so familiar that I shall mention it only briefly. Managers have to look the part, and it is sufficient to say that corporations are filled with attractive, well-groomed, and conventionally well-dressed men and women.

2   **Self-control.** Managers stress the need to exercise iron self-control and to have the ability to mask all emotion and intention behind bland, smiling, and agreeable public faces. They believe it is a fatal weakness to lose control of oneself, in any way, in a public forum. Similarly, to betray valuable secret knowledge (for instance, a confidential reorganization plan) or intentions through some relaxation of self-control – for example, an indiscreet comment or a lack of adroitness in turning aside a query – can not only jeopardize a manager's immediate position but can undermine others' trust in him.

3   **Perception as a team player.** While being a team player has many meanings, one of the most important is to appear to be interchangeable with other managers near one's level. Corporations discourage narrow specialization more strongly as one goes higher. They also discourage the expression of moral or political qualms. One might object, for example, to working with chemicals used in nuclear power, and most corporations today would honor that objection. The public statement of such objections, however, would end any realistic aspirations for higher posts because one's usefulness to the organization depends on versatility. As one manager in the chemical company commented: "Well, we'd go along with his request but we'd always wonder about the guy. And in the back of our minds, we'd be thinking that he'll soon object to working in the soda ash division because he doesn't like glass."

Another important meaning of team play is putting in long hours at the office. This requires a certain amount of sheer physical energy, even though a great deal of this time is spent not in actual work but in social rituals—like reading and discussing newspaper articles, taking coffee breaks, or having informal conversations. These rituals, readily observable in every corporation that I studied, forge the social bonds that make real managerial work—that is, group work of various sorts—possible. One must participate in the rituals to be considered effective in the work.

4   **Style.** Managers emphasize the importance of "being fast on your feet"; always being well organized; giving slick presentations complete with color slides; giving the appearance of knowledge even in its absence; and possessing a subtle, almost indefinable sophistication, marked especially by an urbane, witty, graceful, engaging, and friendly demeanor.

I want to pause for a moment to note that some observers have interpreted such conformity, team playing, affability, and urbanity as evidence of the decline of the individualism of the old Protestant Ethic.[3] To the extent that commentators take the public images that managers project at face value, I think they miss the main point. Managers up and down the corporate ladder adopt the public faces that they wear quite consciously; they are, in fact, the masks behind which the real struggles and moral issues of the corporation can be found.

Karl Mannheim's conception of self-rationalization or self-streamlining is useful in understanding what is one of the central social psychological processes of organizational life.[4] In a world where appearances—in the broadest sense—mean everything, the wise and ambitious person learns to cultivate assiduously the proper, prescribed modes of appearing. He dispassionately takes stock of himself, treating himself as an object. He analyzes his strengths and weaknesses, and decides what he needs to change in order to survive and flourish in his organization. And then he systematically undertakes a program to reconstruct his image. Self-rationalization curiously parallels the methodical subjection of self to God's will that the old Protestant Ethic counseled; the difference, of course, is that one acquires not moral virtues but a masterful ability to manipulate personae.

5　**Patron power.** To advance, a manager must have a patron, also called a mentor, a sponsor, a rabbi, or a godfather. Without a powerful patron in the higher echelons of management, one's prospects are poor in most corporations. The patron might be the manager's immediate boss or someone several levels higher in the chain of command. In either case the manager is still bound by the immediate, formal authority and fealty patterns of his position; the new—although more ambiguous—fealty relationships with the patron are added.

A patron provides his "client" with opportunities to get visibility, to showcase his abilities, to make connections with those of high status. A patron cues his client to crucial political developments in the corporation, helps arrange lateral moves if the client's upward progress is thwarted by a particular job or a particular boss, applauds his presentations or suggestions at meetings, and promotes the client during an organizational shake-up. One must, of course, be lucky in one's patron. If the patron gets caught in a political crossfire, the arrows are likely to find his clients as well.

motable" by belonging to central political networks. Patrons protect those already selected as rising stars from the negative judgments of others; and only the foolhardy point out even egregious errors of those in power or those destined for it.

Failure is also socially defined. The most damaging failure is, as one middle manager in the chemical company puts it, "when your boss or someone who has the power to determine your fate says: 'You failed.'" Such a godlike pronouncement means, of course, out-and-out personal ruin; one must, at any cost, arrange matters to prevent such an occurrence.

As it happens, things rarely come to such a dramatic point even in the midst of an organizational crisis. The same judgment may be made but it is usually called "nonpromotability." The difference is that those who are publicly labeled as failures normally have no choice but to leave the organization; those adjudged nonpromotable can remain, provided they are willing to accept being shelved or, more colorfully, "mushroomed"—that is, kept in a dark place, fed manure, and left to do nothing but grow fat. Usually, seniors do not tell juniors they are nonpromotable (though the verdict may be common knowledge among senior peer groups). Rather, subordinates are expected to get the message after they have been repeatedly overlooked for promotions. In fact, middle managers interpret staying in the same job for more than two or three years as evidence of a negative judgment. This leads to a mobility panic at the middle levels which, in turn, has crucial consequences for pinpointing responsibility in the organization.

Social definitions of performance

Surely, one might argue, there must be more to success in the corporation than style, personality, team play, chameleonic adaptability, and fortunate connections. What about the bottom line—profits, performance?

Unquestionably, "hitting your numbers"—that is, meeting the profit commitments already discussed—is important, but only within the social context I have described. There are several rules here. First, no one in a line position—that is, with responsibility for profit and loss—who regularly "misses his numbers" will survive, let alone rise. Second, a person who always hits his numbers but who lacks some or all of the required social skills will not rise. Third, a person who sometimes misses his numbers but who has all the desirable social traits will rise.

Performance is thus always subject to a myriad of interpretations. Profits matter, but it is much more important in the long run to be perceived as "pro-

Capriciousness of success

Finally, managers think that there is a tremendous amount of plain luck involved in advancement. It is striking how often managers who pride themselves on being hardheaded rationalists explain their own career patterns and those of others in terms of luck. Various uncertainties shape this perception. One is the sense of organizational contingency. One change at the top can create profound upheaval throughout the entire corporate structure, producing startling reversals of fortune, good or bad, depending on one's connections. Another is the uncertainty of the markets that often makes managerial planning simply elaborate guesswork, causing real economic outcome to depend on factors totally beyond organizational and personal control.

It is interesting to note in this context that a line manager's credibility suffers just as much from missing his numbers on the up side (that is, achieving profits higher than predicted) as from missing them on the down side. Both outcomes undercut the ideology of managerial planning and control, perhaps the only bulwark managers have against market irrationality.

Even managers in staff positions, often quite removed from the market, face uncertainty. Occupational safety specialists, for instance, know that the bad publicity from one serious accident in the workplace can jeopardize years of work and scores of safety awards. As one high-ranking executive in the chemical company says, "In the corporate world, 1,000 'Attaboys!' are wiped away by one 'Oh, shit!'"

Because of such uncertainties, managers in all the companies I studied speak continually of the great importance of being in the right place at the right time and of the catastrophe of being in the wrong place at the wrong time. My interview materials are filled with stories of people who were transferred immediately before a big shake-up and, as a result, found themselves riding the crest of a wave to power; of people in a promising business area who were terminated because top management suddenly decided that the area no longer fit the corporate image desired; of others caught in an unpredictable and fatal political battle among their patrons; of a product manager whose plant accidentally produced an odd color batch of chemicals, who sold them as a premium version of the old product, and who is now thought to be a marketing genius.

The point is that managers have a sharply defined sense of the *capriciousness* of organizational life. Luck seems to be as good an explanation as any of why, after a certain point, some people succeed and others fail. The upshot is that many managers decide that they can do little to influence external events in their favor. One can, however, shamelessly streamline oneself, learn to wear all the right masks, and get to know all the right people. And then sit tight and wait for things to happen.

'Gut decisions'

Authority and advancement patterns come together in the decision-making process. The core of the managerial mystique is decision-making prowess, and the real test of such prowess is what managers call "gut decisions," that is, important decisions involving big money, public exposure, or significant effects on the organization. At all but the highest levels of the chemical and textile companies, the rules for making gut decisions are, in the words of one upper middle manager: "(1) Avoid making any decisions if at all possible; and (2) if a decision has to be made, involve as many people as you can so that, if things go

south, you're able to point in as many directions as possible."

Consider the case of a large coking plant of the chemical company. Coke making requires a gigantic battery to cook the coke slowly and evenly for long periods; the battery is the most important piece of capital equipment in a coking plant. In 1975, the plant's battery showed signs of weakening and certain managers at corporate headquarters had to decide whether to invest $6 million to restore the battery to top form. Clearly, because of the amount of money involved, this was a gut decision.

No decision was made. The CEO had sent the word out to defer all unnecessary capital expenditures to give the corporation cash reserves for other investments. So the managers allocated small amounts of money to patch the battery up until 1979, when it collapsed entirely. This brought the company into a breach of contract with a steel producer and into violation of various Environmental Protection Agency pollution regulations. The total bill, including lawsuits and now federally mandated repairs to the battery, exceeded $100 million. I have heard figures as high as $150 million, but because of "creative accounting," no one is sure of the exact amount.

This simple but very typical example gets to the heart of how decision making is intertwined with a company's authority structure and advancement patterns. As the chemical company managers see it, the decisions facing them in 1975 and 1979 were crucially different. Had they acted decisively in 1975—in hindsight, the only rational course—they would have salvaged the battery and saved their corporation millions of dollars in the long run.

In the short run, however, since even seemingly rational decisions are subject to widely varying interpretations, particularly decisions which run counter to a CEO's stated objectives, they would have been taking a serious risk in restoring the battery. What is more, their political networks might have unraveled, leaving them vulnerable to attack. They chose short-term safety over long-term gain because they felt they were judged, both by higher authority and by their peers, on their short-term performances. Managers feel that if they do not survive the short run, the long run hardly matters. Even correct decisions can shorten promising careers.

By contrast, in 1979 the decision was simple and posed little risk. The corporation had to meet its legal obligations; also it had to either repair the battery the way the EPA demanded or shut down the plant and lose several hundred million dollars. Since there were no real choices, everyone could agree on a course of action because everyone could appeal to inevitability. Diffusion of responsibility, in this case by procrastinating until total crisis, is intrinsic to organizational life because the real issue in most gut decisions is: Who is going to get blamed if things go wrong?

'Blame time'

There is no more feared hour in the corporate world than "blame time." Blame is quite different from responsibility. There is a cartoon of Richard Nixon declaring: "I accept all of the responsibility, but none of the blame." To blame someone is to injure him verbally in public; in large organizations, where one's image is crucial, this poses the most serious sort of threat. For managers, blame—like failure—has nothing to do with the merits of a case; it is a matter of social definition. As a general rule, it is those who are or who become politically vulnerable or expendable who get "set up" and become blamable. The most feared situation of all is to end up inadvertently in the wrong place at the wrong time and get blamed.

Yet this is exactly what often happens in a structure that systematically diffuses responsibility. It is because managers fear blame time that they diffuse responsibility; however, such diffusion inevitably means that someone, somewhere is going to become a scapegoat when things go wrong. Big corporations encourage this process by their complete lack of any tracking system. Whoever is currently in charge of an area is responsible—that is, potentially blamable—for whatever goes wrong in the area, even if he has inherited others' mistakes. An example from the chemical company illustrates this process.

When the CEO of the large conglomerate took office, he wanted to rid his capital accounts of all serious financial drags. The corporation had been operating a storage depot for natural gas which it bought, stored, and then resold. Some years before the energy crisis, the company had entered into a long-term contract to supply gas to a buyer—call him Jones. At the time, this was a sound deal because it provided a steady market for a stably priced commodity.

When gas prices soared, the corporation was still bound to deliver gas to Jones at 20¢ per unit instead of the going market price of $2. The CEO ordered one of his subordinates to get rid of this albatross as expeditiously as possible. This was done by selling the operation to another party—call him Brown—with the agreement that Brown would continue to meet the contractual obligations to Jones. In return for Brown's assumption of these costly contracts, the corporation agreed to buy gas from Brown at grossly inflated prices to meet some of its own energy needs.

In effect, the CEO transferred the drag on his capital accounts to the company's operating expenses. This enabled him to project an aggressive, asset-reducing image to Wall Street. Several levels down the ladder, however, a new vice president for a particular business found himself saddled with exorbitant operating costs when, during a reorganization, those plants purchasing gas from Brown at inflated prices came under his purview. The high costs helped to undercut the vice president's division earnings and thus to erode his position in the hierarchy. The origin of the situation did not matter. All that counted was that the vice president's division was steadily losing big money. In the end, he resigned to "pursue new opportunities."

One might ask why top management does not institute codes or systems for tracking responsibility. This example provides the clue. An explicit system of accountability for subordinates would probably have to apply to top executives as well and would restrict their freedom. Bureaucracy expands the freedom of those on top by giving them the power to restrict the freedom of those beneath.

On the fast track

Managers see what happened to the vice president as completely capricious, but completely understandable. They take for granted the absence of any tracking of responsibility. If anything, they blame the vice president for not recognizing soon enough the dangers of the situation into which he was being drawn and for not preparing a defense – even perhaps finding a substitute scapegoat. At the same time, they realize that this sort of thing could easily happen to them. They see few defenses against being caught in the wrong place at the wrong time except constant wariness, the diffusion of responsibility, and perhaps being shrewd enough to declare the ineptitude of one's predecessor on first taking a job.

What about avoiding the consequences of their own errors? Here they enjoy more control. They can "outrun" their mistakes so that when blame time arrives, the burden will fall on someone else. The ideal situation, of course, is to be in a position to fire one's successors for one's own previous mistakes.

Some managers, in fact, argue that outrunning mistakes is the real key to managerial success. One way to do this is by manipulating the numbers. Both the chemical and the textile companies place a great premium on a division's or a subsidiary's return on assets. A good way for business managers to increase their ROA is to reduce their assets while maintaining sales. Usually they will do everything they can to hold down expenditures in order to decrease the asset base, particularly at the end of the fiscal year. The most common way of doing this is by deferring capital expenditures, from maintenance to

innovative investments, as long as possible. Done for a short time, this is called "starving" a plant; done over a longer period, it is called "milking" a plant.

Some managers become very adept at milking businesses and showing a consistent record of high returns. They move from one job to another in a company, always upward, rarely staying more than two years in any post. They may leave behind them deteriorating plants and unsafe working conditions, but they know that if they move quickly enough, the blame will fall on others. In this sense, bureaucracies may be thought of as vast systems of organized irresponsibility.

Flexibility & dexterity with symbols

The intense competition among managers takes place not only behind the agreeable public faces I have described but within an extraordinarily indirect and ambiguous linguistic framework. Except at blame time, managers do not publicly criticize or disagree with one another or with company policy. The sanction against such criticism or disagreement is so strong that it constitutes, in managers' view, a suppression of professional debate. The sanction seems to be rooted principally in their acute sense of organizational contingency; the person one criticizes or argues with today could be one's boss tomorrow.

This leads to the use of an elaborate linguistic code marked by emotional neutrality, especially in group settings. The code communicates the meaning one might wish to convey to other managers, but since it is devoid of any significant emotional sentiment, it can be reinterpreted should social relationships or attitudes change. Here, for example, are some typical phrases describing performance appraisals followed by their probable intended meanings:

Stock phrase	Probable intended meaning
Exceptionally well qualified	Has committed no major blunders to date
Tactful in dealing with superiors	Knows when to keep his mouth shut
Quick thinking	Offers plausible excuses for errors
Meticulous attention to detail	A nitpicker
Slightly below average	Stupid
Unusually loyal	Wanted by no one else

For the most part, such neutered language is not used with the intent to deceive; rather, its purpose is to communicate certain meanings within specific contexts with the implicit understanding that, should the context change, a new, more appropriate meaning can be attached to the language already used. In effect, the corporation is a setting where people are not held to their word because it is generally understood that their word is always provisional.

The higher one goes in the corporate world, the more this seems to be the case; in fact, advancement beyond the upper middle level depends greatly on one's ability to manipulate a variety of symbols without becoming tied to or identified with any of them. For example, an amazing variety of organizational improvement programs marks practically every corporation. I am referring here to the myriad ideas generated by corporate staff, business consultants, academics, and a host of others to improve corporate structure; sharpen decision making; raise morale; create a more humanistic workplace; adopt Theory X, Theory Y, or, more recently, Theory Z of management; and so on. These programs become important when they are pushed from the top.

The watchword in the large conglomerate at the moment is productivity and, since this is a pet project of the CEO himself, it is said that no one goes into his presence without wearing a blue *Productivity!* button and talking about "quality circles" and "feedback sessions." The president of another company pushes a series of managerial seminars that endlessly repeats the basic functions of management: (1) planning, (2) organizing, (3) motivating, and (4) controlling. Aspiring young managers attend these sessions and with a seemingly dutiful eagerness learn to repeat the formulas under the watchful eyes of senior officials.

Privately, managers characterize such programs as the "CEO's incantations over the assembled multitude," as "elaborate rituals with no practical effect," or as "waving a magic wand to make things wonderful again." Publicly, of course, managers on the way up adopt the programs with great enthusiasm, participate in or run them very effectively, and then quietly drop them when the time is right.

Playing the game

Such flexibility, as it is called, can be confusing even to those in the inner circles. I was told the following by a highly placed staff member whose work requires him to interact daily with the top figures of his company:

"I get faked out all the time and I'm part of the system. I come from a very different culture.

Where I come from, if you give someone your *word*, no one ever questions it. It's the old hard-work-will-lead-to-success ideology. Small community, Protestant, agrarian, small business, merchant-type values. I'm disadvantaged in a system like this."

He goes on to characterize the system more fully and what it takes to succeed within it:

"It's the ability to play this system that determines whether you will rise....And part of the adeptness [required] is determined by how much it bothers people. One thing you have to be able to do is to play the game, but you can't be disturbed by the game. What's the game? It's bringing troops home from Vietnam and declaring peace with honor. It's saying one thing and meaning another.

"It's characterizing the reality of a situation with *any* description that is necessary to make that situation more palatable to some group that matters. It means that you have to come up with a culturally accepted verbalization to explain why you are *not* doing what you are doing....[Or] you say that we had to do what we did because it was inevitable; or because the guys at the [regulatory] agencies were dumb; [you] say we won when we really lost; [you] say we saved money when we squandered it; [you] say something's safe when it's potentially or actually dangerous....Everyone knows that it's bullshit, but it's *accepted.* This is the game."

In addition, then, to the other characteristics that I have described, it seems that a prerequisite for big success in the corporation is a certain adeptness at inconsistency. This premium on inconsistency is particularly evident in the many areas of public controversy that face top-ranking managers. Two things come together to produce this situation. The first is managers' sense of beleaguerment from a wide array of adversaries who, it is thought, want to disrupt or impede management's attempts to further the economic interests of their companies. In every company that I studied, managers see themselves and their traditional prerogatives as being under siege, and they respond with a set of caricatures of their perceived principal adversaries.

For example, government regulators are brash, young, unkempt hippies in blue jeans who know nothing about the businesses for which they make rules; environmental activists—the bird and bunny people—are softheaded idealists who want everybody to live in tents, burn candles, ride horses, and eat berries; workers' compensation lawyers are out-and-out crooks who prey on corporations to appropriate exorbitant fees from unwary clients; labor activists are radical troublemakers who want to disrupt harmonious industrial communities; and the news media consist of rabble-rousers who propagate sensational antibusiness stories to sell papers or advertising time on shows like "60 Minutes."

Second, within this context of perceived harassment, managers must address a multiplicity of audiences, some of whom are considered adversaries. These audiences are the internal corporate hierarchy with its intricate and shifting power and status cliques, key regulators, key local and federal legislators, special publics that vary according to the issues, and the public at large, whose goodwill and favorable opinion are considered essential for a company's free operation.

Managerial adeptness at inconsistency becomes evident in the widely discrepant perspectives, reasons for action, and presentations of fact that explain, excuse, or justify corporate behavior to these diverse audiences.

Adeptness at inconsistency

The cotton dust issue in the textile industry provides a fine illustration of what I mean. Prolonged exposure to cotton dust produces in many textile workers a chronic and eventually disabling pulmonary disease called byssinosis or, colloquially, brown lung. In the early 1970s, the Occupational Safety and Health Administration proposed a ruling to cut workers' exposure to cotton dust sharply by requiring textile companies to invest large amounts of money in cleaning up their plants. The industry fought the regulation fiercely but a final OSHA ruling was made in 1978 requiring full compliance by 1984.

The industry took the case to court. Despite an attempt by Reagan appointees in OSHA to have the case removed from judicial consideration and remanded to the agency they controlled for further cost/benefit analysis, the Supreme Court ruled in 1981 that the 1978 OSHA ruling was fully within the agency's mandate, namely, to protect workers' health and safety as the primary benefit exceeding all cost considerations.

During these proceedings, the textile company was engaged on a variety of fronts and was pursuing a number of actions. For instance, it intensively lobbied regulators and legislators and it prepared court materials for the industry's defense, arguing that the proposed standard would crush the industry and that the problem, if it existed, should be met by increasing workers' use of respirators.

The company also aimed a public relations barrage at special-interest groups as well as at the general public. It argued that there is probably no such thing as byssinosis; workers suffering from pulmonary problems are all heavy smokers and the real culprit is the government-subsidized tobacco industry. How can cotton cause brown lung when cotton is white? Further, if there is a problem, only some workers are afflicted, and therefore the solution is more careful screening of the work force to detect susceptible people and prevent them from ever reaching the workplace. Finally, the company claimed that if the regulation were imposed, most of the textile industry would move overseas where regulations are less harsh.[5]

In the meantime, the company was actually addressing the problem but in a characteristically indirect way. It invested $20 million in a few plants where it knew such an investment would make money; this investment automated the early stages of handling cotton, traditionally a very slow procedure, and greatly increased productivity. The investment had the side benefit of reducing cotton dust levels to the new standard in precisely those areas of the work process where the dust problem is greatest. Publicly, of course, the company claims that the money was spent entirely to eliminate dust, evidence of its corporate good citizenship. (Privately, executives admit that, without the productive return, they would not have spent the money and they have not done so in several other plants.)

Indeed, the productive return is the only rationale that carries weight within the corporate hierarchy. Executives also admit, somewhat ruefully and only when their office doors are closed, that OSHA's regulation on cotton dust has been the main factor in forcing technological innovation in a centuries-old and somewhat stagnant industry.

Such adeptness at inconsistency, without moral uneasiness, is essential for executive success. It means being able to say, as a very high-ranking official of the textile company said to me without batting an eye, that the industry has never caused the slightest problem in any worker's breathing capacity. It means, in the chemical company, propagating an elaborate hazard/benefit calculus for appraisal of dangerous chemicals while internally conceptualizing "hazards" as business risks. It means publicly extolling the carefulness of testing procedures on toxic chemicals while privately ridiculing animal tests as inapplicable to humans.

It means lobbying intensively in the present to shape government regulations to one's immediate advantage and, ten years later, in the event of a catastrophe, arguing that the company acted strictly in accordance with the standards of the time. It means claiming that the real problem of our society is its unwillingness to take risks, while in the thickets of one's bureaucracy avoiding risks at every turn; it means as well making every effort to socialize the risks of industrial activity while privatizing the benefits.

The bureaucratic ethic

The bureaucratic ethic contrasts sharply with the original Protestant Ethic. The Protestant Ethic was the ideology of a self-confident and independent propertied social class. It was an ideology that extolled the virtues of accumulating wealth in a society organized around property and that accepted the stewardship responsibilities entailed by property. It was an ideology where a person's word was his bond and where the integrity of the handshake was seen as crucial to the maintenance of good business relationships. Perhaps most important, it was connected to a predictable economy of salvation—that is, hard work will lead to success, which is a sign of one's election by God—a notion also containing its own theodicy to explain the misery of those who do not make it in this world.

Bureaucracy, however, breaks apart substance from appearances, action from responsibility, and language from meaning. Most important, it breaks apart the older connection between the meaning of work and salvation. In the bureaucratic world, one's success, one's sign of election, no longer depends on one's own efforts and on an inscrutable God but on the capriciousness of one's superiors and the market; and one achieves economic salvation to the extent that one pleases and submits to one's employer and meets the exigencies of an impersonal market.

In this way, because moral choices are inextricably tied to personal fates, bureaucracy erodes internal and even external standards of morality, not only in matters of individual success and failure but also in all the issues that managers face in their daily work. Bureaucracy makes its own internal rules and social context the principal moral gauges for action. Men and women in bureaucracies turn to each other for moral cues for behavior and come to fashion specific situational moralities for specific significant people in their worlds.

As it happens, the guidance they receive from each other is profoundly ambiguous because what matters in the bureaucratic world is not what a person is but how closely his many personae mesh with the organizational ideal; not his willingness to stand by his actions but his agility in avoiding blame; not what he believes or says but how well he has mastered the ideologies that serve his corporation; not what he stands for but whom he stands with in the labyrinths of his organization.

In short, bureaucracy structures for managers an intricate series of moral mazes. Even the inviting paths out of the puzzle often turn out to be invitations to jeopardy.

Reprint 83507

References

1 There is a long sociological tradition of work on managers and I am, of course, indebted to that literature. I am particularly indebted to the work, both joint and separate, of Joseph Bensman and Arthur J. Vidich, two of the keenest observers of the new middle class. See especially their *The New American Society: The Revolution of the Middle Class* (Chicago: Quadrangle Books, 1971).

2 See Max Weber, *The Protestant Ethic and the Spirit of Capitalism,* translated by Talcott Parsons (New York: Charles Scribner's Sons, 1958), p. 172.

3 See William H. Whyte, *The Organization Man* (New York: Simon & Schuster, 1956), and David Riesman, in collaboration with Reuel Denney and Nathan Glazer, *The Lonely Crowd: A Study of the Changing American Character* (New Haven: Yale University Press, 1950).

4 Karl Mannheim, *Man and Society in an Age of Reconstruction* (London: Paul (Kegan), Trench, Trubner Ltd. 1940), p. 55.

5 On February 9, 1982, the Occupational Safety and Health Administration issued a notice that it was once again reviewing its 1978 standard on cotton dust for "cost-effectiveness." See *Federal Register,* vol. 47, p. 5906. As of this writing (May 1983), this review has still not been officially completed.

Joseph Auerbach

The Poletown dilemma

A disturbing case raises some questions about a corporation's responsibility to the community in which it operates

Whether the company left the city or stayed, one group of people would lose all that their lives depended on. If General Motors moved its manufacturing operations to the suburbs or the Sunbelt, the autoworkers and suppliers would lose their jobs. If the company built the new assembly plant it needed in Detroit, the elderly residents of Poletown would lose their homes. Unemployment was already high throughout Detroit, but the immigrants who had settled in this one community in the city were looking forward to retirement there after years of hard work. These were the circumstances GM faced when it decided to accept the Detroit city council's terms for acquiring the Poletown property as a site for an assembly plant. The residents of Poletown fought the terms in court but lost their case and everything they had hoped for when it ruled that the city council's action was a legitimate use of eminent domain. Two of the judges disputed the city's action, however. Their dissenting opinions raise serious questions about the degree of a company's responsibility for the social consequences of its decisions and serve as the basis for the author's recommendations in this article. What a company can do to resolve dilemmas that plant sitings and other business decisions raise, he says, is to give the affected community a voice in considering the options. He presents a six-step process that helps a company think through an issue and determine its most responsible course.

Mr. Auerbach is the Class of 1957 Professor of Business Administration at the Harvard Business School, where he specializes in the relationships between law and business. An attorney since 1941, he often serves as outside counsel to industry.

Illustration by Bob Ziering.

"The evidence then," wrote Justice James L. Ryan of the Michigan Supreme Court in a dissenting opinion, "is that what General Motors wanted, General Motors got." What it wanted, why it wanted it, and why the court determined that GM should keep what it got are the subject of *Poletown Neighborhood Council* v. *City of Detroit*, 410 Mich. 616 (1981).

At issue was a parcel of land in Poletown, a section of Detroit largely inhabited by first- and second-generation homeowners of Polish descent. GM required land for a new automobile assembly plant, so the city government of Detroit selected and took the parcel by eminent domain and sold it to the company.

Financial and economic reasons compelled GM to modernize its manufacturing. To stay competitive with foreign automakers, it needed a type of plant that would require more land than traditional operations. To find enough land, it began considering sites out of the city and the state. With its high rate of unemployment, Detroit could not afford to lose the jobs that GM offered. The parcel of 300 acres adjoined another 165 acres available in Hamtramck and formed a rectangle that was the only site Detroit possessed that the company found feasible for its new plant. But the homeowners were mostly elderly and retired. To them, Justice Ryan wrote, their homes were their "single most valuable and cherished assets and their stable ethnic neighborhood the unchanging symbol of the security and quality of their lives."

What was the fair thing to do? Whatever the court decided would mean sacrifice for some group.

Finding the predominant interest

When Detroit determined to take the property, the Poletown Neighborhood Council brought a suit against the city. The residents of Poletown tried to protect their homes by asserting that a condemnation would be for a private rather than a public use and therefore in violation of Michigan's state constitution. Furthermore, they argued, giving up the parcel of land would destroy the cultural and social institutions of Poletown and thus contravene Michigan's environmental protection law.

The court's decision

Nevertheless, by a 5-2 vote, the state's supreme court denied Poletown's suit. The court agreed that the Michigan constitution permitted the exercise of the right of eminent domain for a public use or purpose only. It considered that *use* and *purpose* were legally interchangeable concepts, however, and that, properly interpreted, they would describe the city's objective of allowing the taking of the land parcel for the public's benefit.

In reaching this decision, the court stressed that the interpretation of *public use* changed along with social conditions and that the right of the public to enjoy the benefits of the use would determine whether that use was public or private. In the circumstances surrounding the exercise of eminent domain in this case, the court found a "need for new industrial development to revitalize local industries." The "significance for the people of Detroit and the state," the court said, "has been demonstrated."

It was not simply a matter of providing jobs but of determining whether the public rather than the private interest "is the predominant interest being advanced," the court said. It found the transfer of private property from the people of Poletown to General Motors for the purpose of constructing and operating a private industrial plant to be a valid public use.

The court held, further, that the state's environmental protection act was designed to protect only air, water, and other natural resources from pollution, impairment, or destruction. It concluded that the "natural resources" referred to in the act did not encompass the adverse impact on the social and cultural environment of the people of Poletown that the taking would have.

The company's needs

In 1980 Chrysler, Ford, American Motors, and General Motors all reported the largest financial losses in their histories. Keeping costs down and competing effectively with foreign producers was vital to the future of these U.S. companies. They concluded that to be competitive they must redesign their products and manufacture lighter, more fuel-efficient automobiles. To do so meant making production design changes and constructing new manufacturing facilities.

The design changes needed were so fundamental that remodeling old factories was out of the question—not only because the costs would be prohibitively high but also because the assembly process would be so different from what it had been. A "new generation" automobile assembly plant would have an overhead conveyor system in which automobile engines could be installed from the bottom rather than from the top, as was then being done. The plant would be designed to meet hydrocarbon emission controls.

Instead of several stories, which existing plants had, the new plant would need only one long floor in a single story. Horizontal movement, GM had concluded, would be more efficient than the vertical movement of auto bodies through several levels.

GM determined that its new-generation plant would take up an area of 3 million square feet. It would need a site of about 500 cleared acres with access to a freeway stem, to rail marshaling yards, and to long-haul rail lines.

Detroit had no adequate "green field" sites, and the only areas fitting this description it did have entailed the demolition of populated neighborhoods. Even if it were possible to find a site in Detroit, the cost of building a plant there would be at least $500 million.

GM decided that it would be most economical for it to remove its Cadillac and Fisher Body operations from Detroit and to relocate them in the suburbs or in the Sunbelt.

The city's problems

To the city, the removal of the Cadillac and Fisher Body plants would mean the loss of 6,150 jobs plus thousands of others in allied activities such as design, manufacturing, and sales.

Unemployment at that time was 18% in Detroit (30% among black persons) and in Michigan, 14%. GM's withdrawal would also mean the loss of millions of dollars of real estate and income tax revenues to the city and possibly the state. Detroit could not afford to lose this major industry.

The mayor of Detroit, Coleman Young, was well aware of the industry's problems and of how important remaining a principal home for the automotive industry was to Detroit. He had requested all the automobile manufacturers to give Detroit an opportunity to participate in their decision making if they were planning to expand or build new plants, so when GM reached its decision to move, its chairman, Thomas Murphy, called on Mayor Young. Murphy told him that General Motors might be interested in remaining in Detroit and building a new plant within the city limits if a site could be found within a year. It was essential to its competitiveness that GM get started on its new designs soon, he told Mayor Young, and that it obtain title to an appropriate site by May 1, 1981.

The mayor and the city went to work on the problem and, by the summer of 1980, had found nine possible locations. Of these, GM found only the Poletown site adequate for its needs. By July 1980, the matter of taking the site by eminent domain was before the Detroit city council. The initial submissions to the city were followed by filing required materials, including environmental impact analyses, with the government agencies involved.

Under a Michigan statute, municipalities are permitted to form economic development corporations. These are empowered to acquire property for a "project," to finance it, and to lease or sell it. The municipalities alone, however, retain the power of eminent domain. It is they who transfer property rights for industrial and commercial use to the economic development corporations.

During the summer General Motors and the city worked out the terms for such a transfer and presented them in a letter on October 8, 1980 from Murphy to Detroit. In it, he said, "We know how difficult it is to accomplish a project of this magnitude without inconveniencing some individuals. However, we know that this site presents the fewest such problems of any location in the city. I also know you will address the concerns of the individuals in the area with great care and concern."

The costs to the community

The "inconveniencing" proved to be immense. It represented an extraordinary social problem: 3,438 persons were displaced from their homes, and 1,176 houses were destroyed. Psychological turmoil and deterioration of ethnic identity would result.

The cost to General Motors for acquiring the Poletown site was $8 million (the purchase price the company agreed to pay the city) plus plant construction costs (expected to be about $500 million).

The cost to the public of providing the site was estimated to exceed $200 million. That included compensation of $62 million to the people of Poletown for their property, $25 million for their relocation, $35 million for the demolition of homes on the land, and another $74 million for site preparation. The city also agreed to give the corporation tax concessions over a 12-year period.

Justice Ryan noted that, as the project planning progressed "a crescendo of supportive applause sustained the city and General Motors and their purpose. Labor leaders, bankers, and businessmen... were joined by radio, television, newspapers, and political opinion makers in extolling the virtues of the bold and innovative fashion in which, almost overnight, a new and modern plant would rise from a little-known inner-city neighborhood of minimal tax base significance.... It was in such an atmosphere that the plaintiffs sued to enjoin the condemnation of their homes."

Considering the consequences

Justice John W. Fitzgerald, who joined Justice Ryan in dissenting from the court's decision, stated, "Any business enterprise produces benefits to society at large. Now that we have authorized local legislative bodies to decide that a different...use of property will produce greater public benefits,...no...property, however productive or valuable to its owner, is immune from condemnation for the benefit of other private interests...."

Two "compelling considerations," Justice Ryan wrote, make this interpretation of "public use" by the majority of the court unacceptable in future cases:

1   The exercise of the power of eminent domain is "far more intrusive than the taxing power, although both deprive the person of property." In this case, the use of eminent domain produced "intangible losses, such as the severance of personal attachments to one's domicile and neighborhood and the destruction of an organic community of a most unique and irreplaceable character."

2   Where the private corporation is the beneficiary and is "large and influential," it is the corporation and not the municipality that has the practical power of eminent domain. "When individual citizens are forced to suffer great social dislocation to permit private corporations to construct plants where they deem it most profitable, one is left to wonder who the sovereign is."

The company's conduct

What did General Motors do that impelled Justice Ryan to treat the issue as one in which the corporation had been permitted to act as a sovereign for the benefit of its private purse? Was its appraisal of the situation at fault?

There can be little dispute that General Motors had tremendous business problems in 1979-1980. To remain viable, it had to produce a new competitive product.

The company faced two choices. It could either build a new plant in Detroit, which would cost more for GM and demolish the homes of an ethnic minority but provide jobs and tax revenues for the city, or it could build a new plant elsewhere, which would cost less for the company but worsen economic conditions for the city as a whole.

Locating the plant in the Sunbelt might have been of most economic benefit to the company, but GM thought it had to consider the benefit to the city of preventing still higher unemployment. It also thought that the city and its people should have the chance to demonstrate that continuing to operate in Detroit might be feasible. The adverse effect of unemployment in Detroit might be greater than any benefit the company could take to the people in the Sunbelt.

In choosing to accept Detroit's terms, GM had clearly considered more than its own welfare. And it had looked to the city for guidance. Still, an immense social problem loomed—the effect of the decision on Poletown. Was the company at fault for ending its accountability to the public with its decision to prevent the loss of jobs in the city? Should it have handled the situation differently?

If General Motors was at fault in any way in its attempt to be socially accountable, it was that the company failed to recognize that others in the community often play the social responsibility game with a stacked deck. Distinctions between accountability and responsibility are apt to blur and what is commonly accepted is likely to be equated with objectivity—in this case, the interdependence of GM and Detroit.

As Justice Ryan said, the objectivity of General Motors was not an issue: "It is a corporation having a history, especially in recent years, of a responsible, even admirable 'social conscience'. In fact, this project may well entail compromises of sound business dictates...."

The community's voice

All during the search for a way out of the dilemma, who in the city appeared on the part of Poletown? Who listened to its needs? Since it had no strong representation while the social issues were being determined, its subsequent suit on purely legal issues was futile.

However admirable the corporation's "responsible" conscience may have been, Poletown could not win the responsibility game. Detroit had stacked the deck. It had "set the scene," as Justice Ryan said—a scene "in which...broad-based support for the project was orchestrated in the state, fostering a sense of inevitability and dire consequences if the plan was not approved by all concerned. General Motors is not the villain of the piece," he concluded.

Defining corporate responsibility

In considering how to deal with a Poletown situation, a company must find a way to determine what the critical social problems are. It should call for a demonstration of need and an evaluation of proposed solutions from all factions concerned.

The company's board of directors can direct the corporation to participate in the demonstration process or refrain from it entirely. Since it may raise public doubt about the objectivity of the final conclusion, active corporate participation is only rarely desirable. The corporation's input is often extremely valuable, however. Better than anyone, the company knows the dimensions of the economic problem as well as the compromises possible.

If it decides that the corporation should not be part of the demonstration process, the board can still make a genuine effort to be socially accountable by offering senior personnel who have no preconceived positions for consultation, assistance, and compromise with those who have responsibility for making social decisions.

Representative groups

The public agencies and instrumentalities available for making the determination are the community's political leaders, its social welfare organizations, the corporation's employees, and their labor organizations. One course of action would be to put the problems and proposals for solution before all these groups collectively. This would support a corporation's "hands-off" policy in the determination process and would not establish as a selected instrument a favored public group with whom the company could conduct authoritative communication.

The corporation is sure to find that the political leaders of the community want the task and are more generally accepted as representatives of the social interests of the community than the leaders of other groups.

The pressure to arrive at satisfactory political solutions, however, usually overshadows the objectivity of political leaders. No matter their good faith, the consequences of economic decisions to their careers cannot be distant from their thinking. Leaders look for acceptable trade-offs between the impact of the proposed solutions on many persons and their impact on lesser numbers. As politicians, they count bodies but try to avoid counting scars. They compute direct and indirect revenue losses—losses of wages and taxes—and weigh their impact in relation to the health, welfare, and culture of the entire community.

The social agencies ostensibly disdain the political emphasis implicit in the thinking of other groups and genuinely attempt to concern themselves with individuals. Agencies may find it difficult in a case like Poletown's, however, to evaluate losses of jobs with losses of domicile and culture, but they will try to count scars as well as bodies.

The employees and their organizations are the most subjective in their approach to solving social problems. It is their own jobs and concern for their families' welfare that they measure against losses of other individuals in the community if jobs are saved. Adequate substitutes for the losses of other persons, they assume, are readily available and, because of the payment for the taking in a case like Poletown, without financial hardship. Employees are unlikely to accept the idea of curing economic problems for a corporation until they become convinced that changes are necessary.

No one is there to represent a group like the Poletown residents—not even the social agencies, who are not unsympathetic but who ease their qualms by retreating to a comparison of numbers of affected persons.

Corporate social accountability

Does a corporation have an obligation to search for the views of a Poletown champion? That would mean being somewhat subjective. Or is it enough for a corporation to recognize, as General Motors did, that one consequence of corporate change is the "inconveniencing of some individuals" and to make it clear that remedying the problem is up to the political authorities?

In 1837, in a case tried in England at the Tralee assizes, Howel Walsh said that the corporation had "a throat to swallow the rights of the community, and a stomach to digest them! But whoever has yet discovered, in the anatomy of any corporation, either bowels, or a heart?" The American publicly owned corporation has long since, even without the pressure of legislation, been concerned that in its business decisions it demonstrate both bowels and heart.

The recognition of corporate social accountability may be found early in American history in the formation of planned corporate communities fostering various social mores—in the Oneida Community, for example, which was established in 1847—and in the practices of companies like Hershey Chocolate Company and Endicott Johnson Corporation. For decades in this century, Johnson & Johnson has had a published credo stating that it has responsibilities to the communities in which it functions, including the world community and involving support for good works and charities, acceptance of a fair share of taxes, encouragement of civic improvements and benefits, and maintenance of its property in a way that will protect the environment and national resources.

Corporations match public contributions and sponsor United Fund campaigns, library and hospital drives, blood bank programs, civic benefit groups, cultural and sports events, scholarships, and summer job programs, but these efforts are often merely ritualistic.

The most significant responsibilities companies take on concern the effects of adverse corporate financial circumstances on employee job security, the impact of intended corporate business on the natural environment, and the implications of closing down a business or one of its operations. Of these, the maintenance or change of location of a plant or operation is invariably an extremely important decision for the corporation and consequently of tantamount importance to a community.

To be socially accountable in these situations, a corporation must look for solutions to the social problems it causes by going beyond corporate-political dialogue. Certainly an agreement between the corporation and the majority's elected leadership of the community to cooperate in finding a solution to a problem is a step toward fruitful negotiation. But this kind of agreement can miss the target and, notwithstanding goodwill and candor, may never produce a responsible solution.

A definitive process

What the community and the corporation need in addition to an atmosphere of negotiation is a definitive process by which to settle the following issues:

Under what terms the corporation should meet its responsibilities.

Who is to participate in determining how the terms are to be met.

What part the corporation is to play in that determination.

Whether the corporation has an obligation to try to make the process work.

For the corporation, the process for settling these issues would have six steps:

1   After using all its available tools to reach a business decision it considered sensible, the corporation would appraise the consequences of the decision for the affected social communities and determine its social obligations.

General Motors took this step in the Poletown case when it determined that its ability to compete in its principal business operations depended on constructing a new-generation assembly plant, that remodeling its existing plants would not suffice, and that the impact of removal on the host communities would be so drastic as to raise a question of social accountability.

2   The corporation would then define the terms it deemed tolerable from a business standpoint to lessen the harm to the community. In an income statement problem, for example, the curative terms might involve such matters as changed employee compensation, benefits, or tax concessions. An environmental problem might suggest corporate terms embodying a municipal issue of industrial revenue bonds. An employee stock ownership plan might offset the effects of liquidation.

In each case, the corporation must determine the trade-off between the business decision and the terms of social accountability it can tolerate. It must not devise the terms as a negotiating position, since in carving social concessions out of its business decision, the corporation's good faith must be unquestioned and the terms more or less final. That is not to say, however, that the corporation should not be prepared to discuss, negotiate, and agree on how to implement the terms fairly.

In Poletown, General Motors took this step by formulating its site specifications and time limits.

3   The corporation must then disclose the terms to all the social communities involved and to their representatives. There may be many host communities involved from a social standpoint, in both number and political sovereignty.

In this case, General Motors singled out the city for disclosure of terms and establishment of communication and thus effectively foreclosed the significant participation of other affected social communities.

4   The corporation would solicit the participation of all groups concerned.

In Poletown, General Motors dealt only with the city of Detroit. Apparently, it secured the approval of its proposal from the political representatives and thus avoided the participation of all the other affected groups. To be heard, the residents of Poletown had to take an adversary stance. Elected staff of the city, with paid assistance, used public assets to generate media support, prepare environmental statements, and start eminent domain proceedings. This frustrated Poletown's participation in determinations whose costs its residents had to share with other taxpayers.

5   Once a corporation had identified the affected interests, it would negotiate with them. Affected groups vary widely, not only in who their members are but also in their financial status and their ability to accept the terms of the business decision. The corporation will be fortunate if the mere act of communication encompassed by Step 3 brings an end to its social accountability.

It is more likely, as would have been true in the Poletown situation if General Motors had looked, that the corporation will find unprotected interests that should be brought into the determination process.

6   The corporation would provide these interests with a means of protection. Although it cannot become the proxy for an unprotected interest and must remain aloof from the determination of what is socially responsible in the circumstances, it can find a champion to speak for the weaker group and listen to its recommendations. The need to remain distant from the determination is the corollary of the corporation's interest in preventing the process from taking on the taint of subjectivity.

In the Poletown case, General Motors might have done so by appointing a public committee. Its members could have been respected citizens of the community such as university professors, sociologists, psychologists, and economists. GM could have paid for the services and expenses of the committee without conflict since the question of what the corporation should do would not be the issue. The answer to the question of how the community should respond to the business terms would not affect General Motors, which would be seeking only to permit the affected social interests to meet the terms.

With this six-step process, a corporation could meet its objective of being socially accountable for a business decision that its board has determined warrants giving protection to a community.

Unlike the outcome of *Poletown* v. *Detroit,* this kind of process would have precluded the dilemma that nagged Justice Ryan and the social accountability problem that faced General Motors. Whether the consequences for the people of Poletown would have been favorable we cannot know. But a process based on a search for the least unfavorable solution might have brought them an outcome that was less bitter. ▽

Reprint 85302

Literature and ideas are forever strolling through the marketplace with business.

Reading Fiction to the Bottom Line

by Benjamin DeMott

A short story entitled "The Other Margaret" by Lionel Trilling appeared in the *Partisan Review* in 1945. The story follows a businessman named Stephen Elwin, a publisher, through a routine day marked by encounters with misbehavior on the part of several representatives of the underclass. The encounters direct the hero's inner reflections and prepare him for the story's crisis, which is brought on by the misbehavior of the Elwin family's new black maid, the "other Margaret" of the title. (Elwin's daughter, a schoolgirl, is also named Margaret.)

The approach to the crisis begins at drinks time when Elwin's wife, patience gone, tells her husband and daughter that Margaret, the new maid, is a "nasty, mean person." The daughter objects, having learned at her progressive school that Negro domestic servants have a "slave psychology" that families like her own exploit. When she proceeds to argue, further, that the poor can't be held responsible for their acts, Elwin – to his own moderate surprise – interrupts. "Why not?" he asks, and his daughter explains that "...society didn't give her a chance....She bears a handicap. Because she's colored. She has to struggle hard – against prejudice. It's so hard for her."

Cautiously, nonrhetorically, Elwin draws young Margaret's attention to family experiences – happy experiences – with an earlier black maid, proposing that handicaps are borne differently by different people and that moral behavior depends heavily on each individual human being's self-conception. The previous black maid had had to borrow money from the Elwins and was still repaying it; Elwin's daughter in-

> The Great Crash of '29 put business in the doghouse. Neither World War II nor the Cold War could get it out again.

sists that "she can't afford it." Elwin, agreeing, adds that "she can't afford not to" either, because "she needs to think of herself...as a responsible person."

A few moments later comes an eruption: the new maid, Margaret, abruptly gives notice to her employers and then smashes, seemingly on purpose, a bit of

Benjamin DeMott teaches humanities at Amherst College. This article is adapted from the Philip Morris Foundation lectures on business and culture he recently delivered at Baruch College (City University of New York).

pottery that Margaret the daughter had made for her mother as a birthday present. This event, together with Elwin's previous criticism of the talk of "prejudice" and "handicaps," begins young Margaret's advance from cant.

Much-commented on at the time of its publication, "The Other Margaret" is a shade solemn in execution and (for us) outdated in idiom; it is no masterwork as fiction. It is, however, a suggestive portrait of the liberal wrestling with himself. Like much of Trilling's best literary criticism, it shows us a mind determined not to dodge the difficulties inherent in any restricted concept of either societal or personal responsibility. Frustrated by those difficulties, Elwin has been sorting them out for himself during most of the day and takes no satisfaction in his effort to do the same for his daughter. When in the end he declares himself, his tone is rueful: "Had he been truly the wise man he wanted to be, he would have been able to explain, to Margaret and himself, the nature of the double truth. As much as Margaret, he believed that 'society is responsible.' He believed the other truth too [the truth of personal responsibility]."

This declaration is commensurate with the events of Elwin's day. Those events—ranging from a bus conductor's harshness to a child, to a patch of Jew-baiting—bring pointed reminders that the failure of individual members of the underclass to achieve standards of personal responsibility is in part a function of lack of advantage (the "gentle rearing and the good education that made a man like Stephen Elwin answerable for all his actions"). The same events confirm that mean deeds are committed by whites and blacks alike and demand to be considered in the light of the circumstances that generate acts of resistance and rebellion, the circumstance that counts most being that the underclass is, in the main, bullied and powerless. As "The Other Margaret" closes in on the conduct of one member of the underclass—and on one kind of liberal platitude—none of these reminders is forgotten. As a result, the final unflamboyant assertion of belief in a "double truth" has strength and weight. It does justice not only to the decencies—the awareness of inequity, the desire for reform—that breathe within many liberal pieties, but also to the intractable realities that the pieties tend to veil.

Which realities exactly? One is that respectful attitudes toward money and debt can be a badge of moral worth. Another is that invoking "capitalism" and wealth as causes of moral turpitude in others is absurd. Still another is that a businessperson, because of exposure to the daily world of practical affairs, can be better situated than a schoolteacher to comprehend the complex relationships between personal and societal responsibility.

The public image of business in 1945 was considerably dimmer than at present. The Depression had been an experience of radical captivity for the business community, a kind of dark night of the soul. Abuse of business entered so fully into the national psyche via the popular arts that many a subsequent political leader, conservative and liberal alike, had difficulty squeezing it out of his or her veins. (President Kennedy, for instance, was quoted as remarking, at a moment of frustration with a dispute involving U.S. Steel, that his father "always said businessmen were sons of bitches.") The return of

> The sacred cows of the Great Depression were simply wrong: poverty is not saintly, and wealth is not immoral.

prosperity after World War II was widely attributed to governmental action (the war itself), not to business initiatives, and the onset of Cold War anticommunism didn't in itself reshape the business image.

Looking back on this moment, we can see quite clearly what kind of changes were needed to rehabilitate business in the public mind. One change concerned moral understanding and involved a correction of sentimentally inflated estimates of the saintliness of poverty. Feelings of solidarity with "the little people" are much in the democratic grain in any season; in times of mass unemployment and suffering these natural inclinations are intensified by the vanity of self-laceration. The Depression had been marked by the ascendancy of an absolutist moral calculus in which poverty invariably equaled virtue and economic means invariably equaled vice. Getting business out of the doghouse clearly required some kind of effective challenge to this calculus: a dispelling of moral illusion.

A second change essential to effect rehabilitation amounted to an end to the deification of government—especially of government planning. Implicit in the notion that centralized planning held the key to the prevention of socioeconomic disaster was the proposition that the business of America was no longer business but planning itself. There would be no refurbishing the business image until idolatry of the planners was moderated.

More important than any of these changes was a philosophical turn. The thirties had taken an un-American swerve toward determinism, and that philosophy, with its assumption of individual human impotence in the face of social conditioning and fate, was plainly out of key with a business ethos. Getting business out of the doghouse unquestionably required some kind of successful protest against the conventional wisdom of determinism, along with an

> ## Social determinism was the enemy of social responsibility, initiative, and optimism.

effort to restore a measure of vitality to themes of optimistic self-reliance, private initiative, and personal responsibility. I would argue that this reinvigoration of antideterminism was the intellectual change most vital to the recovery, by business, of the grip on the public imagination it had possessed before the Great Crash.

I would also argue, farfetched as it may seem, that this reinvigoration began in 1945 with the publication of "The Other Margaret." In this short story, Lionel Trilling was working on an ambitious cultural project, nothing less than the emancipation of American liberalism from naïveté. In literary essays, a novel, and a study of novelist E.M. Forster, he set himself against the kind of liberal mind that believes that "good is good and bad is bad," the mind that understands the "moods of optimism and pessimism" but can neither name nor understand "the mood that is the response to good-and-bad."

Trilling was sailing against the wind in those years—but he did have readers, some of whom later pressed the critique of liberalism beyond the limits he himself set. Some of them were to become shapers, publicists, and theorists of the movement called neoconservatism—Irving Kristol, for one, Edward Banfield, Pat Moynihan, Robert Nisbet, Norman Podhoretz, Hilton Kramer, for others. Over the years an impressive number of significant contributors to the movement have cited Trilling's work as powerfully influential. Many have singled out "The Other Margaret" for its dramatization of a sensitive hero, a businessman, trying to exorcise the demon of social determinism from his daughter's mind.

Imagine Trilling, if you will, having lunch in 1945 with one or two business friends. During the meal he's asked what he's working on. "Actually, I've been fiddling lately with a story," says the professor. "A piece of fiction. A girl accuses her mother of racism. Her father tries to answer back. It's really about—I *think*—personal responsibility. About the problems people seem to be having these days believing that anybody is responsible for anything. For themselves, for their behavior, their fate....Want to hear more?"

The business listeners might or might not have wanted to hear more; might or might not have been able to make a connection between the themes of a literary short story and the current status of business itself; might or might not have been drawn to reflect on the tie between the health of the idea of personal responsibility and the health of individualistic, entrepreneurial drive. Certainly it would have been dif-

DRAWING BY CHUCK MORRIS

ficult to have recognized "The Other Margaret" as a potential key text of cultural and economic history. Only retrospectively can we ourselves see it in those terms—as an important instrument of transformation, a means by which negative stereotypes of business were challenged and a fresh assessment of capitalism begun.

But it's undeniable that the subjects alive in this particular English professor's mind were by no means remote from the marketplace—were in fact intimately related to it. Communication between Trilling and his business friends should have been easy—and should be easy today. Yet business tends to believe that business, enjoying the distinction of rigorous practicality, is somehow sealed off from the world of art and ideas. Happenings in the land of the intellect are no doubt interesting, perhaps important, in their way. But business finds that such happenings are, generally speaking, irrelevant to what it is and does. Business believes, in short, that business occupies a world apart.

In my view, this is a wrongheaded belief. Granted, the movement of ideas between any two or more sectors of human endeavor—not just between a campus and a corporate headquarters—isn't easy to track. Crossovers often take place in a no-man's-land of popularization and jargon borrowings wherein the real substance of the exchange can't be precisely named or documented. Even when a sharply defined concept in philosophical discourse—"existential" in existentialism—suddenly dislodges itself from the woodwork of an academic discipline and begins whirling in the general culture, the best speculation about how and why this happens, and what it signifies, is necessarily tentative and diffident.

But it's one thing to acknowledge and another to accept this imprisonment of business in its sealed-off world—to behave as though rigid compartmentalization was inevitable—to assume that iron separation of the intellectual from the practical, of culture from business, is somehow ordained. We need to remind ourselves now and then of the fundamental interdependencies of *all* the sectors of human endeavor. We need also to reacquaint ourselves with the way in which the influence of powerful *general* ideas works to erase barriers between businesspeople and academic and creative thinkers, revealing the unities hidden by occupational screens.

All well and good, says a carper, but 1945 was a long time ago. Stories were more straightforward in those days. Your interdependence of literature and commerce, of academics and businesspeople, may have made some sense when art spoke to everyone. But creative thinking—academic

thinking—doesn't have that reach any more. Writers are immersed in weird experiments today. When you pick up a piece of fiction you're lucky to make any sense of it at all.

This attitude is as wrongheaded now as it was 40 years ago. The interdependence of contemporary business and ideas may not be quite as obvious as hindsight has rendered the connection between "The Other Margaret" and the rehabilitation of business morale at the end of the Depression, but the interdependence exists.

Let me try a contemporary example, a short story called "The Emerald," by Donald Barthelme. On its face, "The Emerald" is a perfect example of far-out postmodernist writing in which logic and convention are defied, the ridiculous takes command, and finding and maintaining your bearings as an ordinary thinker is possible only if you enter into a state of exceptionally acute consciousness of your activity as a reader.

All the elements of a conventional narrative are present, to be sure. There's a heroine, a plot, several dramatic confrontations, two dozen or so short scenes in which one character talks with another (or to himself), a resolution, and even a moral, of a sort, at the end. In addition, there's some wonderfully exact miming of several familiar contemporary voices—a

Healthy entrepreneurialism springs from a healthy view of personal responsibility.

hard-nosed newspaper editor, a bouncer-bodyguard, various minor crooks and con artists—and much amusing banter between (among other folks) a newspaper reporter and her source:

"Look kid," [says the source] "this is going to cost you. Sixty dollars."

"Sixty dollars for what?"

"For the interview."

"That's checkbook journalism!"

"Sho nuff."

"It's against the highest traditions of the profession!"

"You get paid, your boss gets paid, the stockholders get their slice, why not us members of the raw material? Why shouldn't the raw material get paid?"

Everywhere in "The Emerald" we hear realistic accents and idioms—the kind of talk that usually gives readers a sense of at-homeness, a feeling they're in a comfortable, negotiable spot.

But the story nevertheless is, on its surface, a wild and crazy piece of work. The heroine, Mad Moll, is a witch. She's given birth to a 7,000 carat talking emerald, after being raped by the man in the moon. A figure named Vandermaster who hungers to live twice (he was poor in youth and hasn't yet experienced "love") wants to do a deal with Moll for the emerald; he believes a carat a day of powdered emerald will guarantee him eternal life. He proposes a straight swap of Moll's jewel for the Foot of Mary Magdalene, a relic Vandermaster has stolen from a Carthusian monastery. (The Foot is famous for injuries it has inflicted on witches in the past.) The action of the tale involves various forced entries to Moll's premises, culminating in an emerald kidnapping. The moral climax, so to speak, occurs when the talking jewel chides Vandermaster ("It is wrong to want to live twice") and points him in the direction of a pretty reporter named Lily.

Silly stuff, funny stuff. But, astonishingly, never merely silly for longer than a few moments at a time. Barthelme keeps mixing his pitches, changing his tone, obliging his reader to double back and reconsider decisions about whether the piece is a joke or a parody or some kind of parable—or is it actually a mystery? Snippets of mystical wisdom mingle with city room sleaze. Coarse, side-of-the-mouth cynicism abuts allusions to yesteryear's spiritual questers. Time and again, Mad Moll's overtly hilarious musings fall into sudden gravity ("memories of God who held me up and sustained me until I fell from His hands into the world..."). Repeatedly you find you are watching yourself as you read, noting the way

Extracting a thread of order out of confusion is a standard human labor.

you closed off as absurd a possibility or a reflective response that now seems right. The story's wild, weird moves bring a new subject into view—the subject of how we sift evidence and data, how we decide what is and isn't relevant, how we distinguish a significant clue from a "trivial detail," how, in sum, we perform our standard human labor of running a thread of order through chaos, extracting meaning from the hum and buzz around us.

We'll come in a moment to the pertinence of all this to business thinking. First, a word or two more on short story form—and on related developments in a field of scientific research. In recent decades, stories like "The Emerald" have become favored instruments for the moment-to-moment destabilization of readers' expectations. A fiction mainstream still exists where characters inhabit recognizable hu-

man situations (like Stephen Elwin in "The Other Margaret") and pass through a logically connected series of events, objective and subjective, toward a resolution that gives readers a sense of closure and confirms their powers of comprehension.

But the new, stranger current also flows strongly, and the world of letters finds it increasingly pleasing and provocative. The story ceases to be a single consecutive narration in which, at any given moment, readers know their location and direction, and can state (if asked) the nature of the characters and problem confronting them. Instead a story becomes 20 or 30 run-on versions of a single narrative, each compressed into a single paragraph, each unpredictably changing the preceding narrative by subtle variation. Or a story becomes a numbered list of 100 sentences, apparently disconnected, related only as miscellany; or an array of commentaries on visual illustrations; or a swiftly changing series of geographical scenes over which the mind is allowed to pause no longer than a sentence or so; or an eruption in which figures from the past as remote as Vercingetorix make sudden unexplained appearances on contemporary turf....

The two leading practitioners of this form, Donald Barthelme and Robert Coover, are teaching readers to relish a new kind of mental operation in the process of reading—a new alertness to and wariness of the trap of expectation, a readiness to live along the nerves of a narrative in a condition of unprecedented, self-mocking self-consciousness, a willingness to abandon feelings of confident mastery and to reject the conventional aesthetic hunger to transform a messy, unsettled world into a place of fixed, rational continuities. Yet these contemporary fictionists are not the only people engaged in what Alan Wilde calls—in a study of the school of Barthelme and related writers—"a dismantling of assurances of the stability of reality." Something very similar is occurring in science.

Like many others with general interests, I turn the pages of works on science written for nonscientists. One highly praised recent work of this kind is James Gleick's *Chaos: Making a New Science*, which reports on a movement now centered in physics and mathematics but beginning to enter biology via epidemiology and related fields. The movement represents a departure from "the reductionist program in science" that refuses attention to "unmanageable" data—material that's unresponsive to efforts to organize, synthesize, or order it by formula. The movement is absorbed with so-called "erratic data." Mr. Gleick's most affecting pages treat the question, "Why are snowflakes different?"—formerly a nonquestion. The author holds that "the heart of the new

"I think I can shed light on that question since I know diddley squat about thermographers."

snowflake model is the essence of chaos: a delicate balance between forces of stability and forces of instability; a powerful interplay of forces on atomic scales and forces on everyday scales."

Reading Gleick, we realize that scientists in many fields have arrived at a state of mind in which science need no longer be terrified by the destabilizing and erratic, and can face full into chaos and search for new modes of order. William M. Schaffer, a leader in the field of research called, simply, "chaos," finds that "ecology based on a sense of equilibrium seems doomed to fail. The traditional models are betrayed by their linear basis. Nature is more complicated...." Gleick quoted Schaffer as declaring that chaos is "both exhilarating and a bit threatening."

Readers of a Donald Barthelme story have an intuition of what it means, in the context of short fiction, to say that literary expectation "based on a sense of equilibrium seems doomed to fail"; there's a by no means negligible resonance between the themes of Mr. Gleick's *Chaos* and the themes of an art teaching "acceptance...of a disorder beyond human control."

The resonance goes further still, beyond art and science into business. Readers of business theory can have a similar intuition about the way traditional eco-

nomic and market expectations are doomed to fail; among those who think about business, a similar language of disequilibrium seems in the process of emerging. It, too, lies somewhat outside the mainstream. Capitalism depends on predictability and equilibrium, at least as understood by its elder theorists; Max Weber thought that only in cultures where predictability, objective impersonality, and rational control rank as paramount values could capitalistic development go forward. Yet, oddly, the language of many academic specialists and consultants on business organization has begun to reveal a remarkable emphasis on the destabilizing impulse as a positive force. A number of specialists seem almost prepared to claim that the "dismantling of assurances of the stability of reality" amounts to something close to the duty of effective corporate leaders.

Edgar Schein of MIT takes as a key metaphor that of "unfreezing." The manager with a problem of productivity and competitiveness wants knowledge of his corporate culture so that he can begin the project of destabilizing the cultural norms: "The organizational culture must be unfrozen....If necessary, managers use coercive persuasion to produce the unfreezing."

Hazel Henderson defines inflation as "the sum of all variables that economists have left out of their models." (Chaos, James Gleick might say, is the sum of all the variables scientists have left out of their models. An antinarrative, Donald Barthelme might say, is a way of focusing attention on all the experience conventional story writing excludes from its models, and on all the fakery those models include.)

Another theorist, Ralph Kilmann, asserts in *Beyond the Quick Fix* that "what we need...is a fundamental change in our thoughts, perceptions, and values," and contends that the "beginnings of this change are already visible in all fields....The gravity and global extent of our crisis indicate that the current changes are likely to result in a transformation of unprecedented dimensions, a turning point for the planet as a whole."

Heady talk. And when these concepts move from academic business discourse into the unbuttoned, gunslinging prose of Tom Peters, they take shape as flat-out endorsements of chaos as a value. Some key passages from Peters's *Thriving On Chaos*:

"The world today is uniquely 'messy,' with a host of new variables surfacing at lightning speed.... The madness of thousands of simultaneous experiments...is the only plausible path to survival. What once amounted to being 'in control'...is a design for disaster today.

"The true objective is to take chaos as given and learn to thrive *on* it. The winners of tomorrow will

> All of us belong to the whole of the age we inhabit— not just to science, or to art, or to business.

deal *proactively* with chaos, will look at the chaos per se as the source of market advantage, not as a problem to be got around.

"*Constant change by everyone requires a dramatic increase in the capacity to accept disruption.*"

Barthelme and the scientists Gleick writes about are probably unaware of the use of the language of chaos in the newer business discourse. All parties would surely agree, moreover, that chaos does not mean the same thing in each of the three sectors, art, science, and business. We cannot understand the connections among the three sectors in terms of simple stimulus-response models of "influence." We need a more flexible concept: cultural paradigm, for example, which acknowledges the elements of autonomy in separate branches of human endeavor while simultaneously observing links, interdependencies, broad unifying themes.

What matters is that people who think, regardless of their discipline or occupation, participate in a culture that has powerful, overarching, all-embracing tides, and that creative thought, particularly as it surfaces in the literary arts, is an exceptionally valuable guide to the direction of those tides. Decades before the return to general public favor of antideterminist themes of personal responsibility, the story writer Lionel Trilling was developing these themes for himself and a small, thoughtful audience of venturesome readers. Decades before the general culture began to appreciate chaos, story writer Donald Barthelme was deeply engaged in exploring its value as awakener, educator, inducer of pointed scrutiny both of self and methods. When business announces that what happens "over there" in the arts and humanities isn't relevant, it's shutting its ears to priceless early warning systems, squandering information utterly unavailable elsewhere. The truth is that all of us belong to the whole of the age we inhabit, not alone to the special sector called work, production, investment; none of us *can* live in a world apart. ▽

Reprint 89304

Case Studies

Problems in Review

David W. Ewing

Case of the disputed dismissal

'In nature there are neither rewards nor punishments— there are consequences'*

Scene

The office of Alf Jarvis, chairman of the voluntary, elected board of the Public Health Department of Marshall City (pop. 61,215).

Characters

Board members:
Alf Jarvis,
vice president of a local food company.
Elaine Crawley,
personnel director of a local pharmaceutical concern.
Ted Nordhoff,
vice president of a local bank.
Polly Nimmo,
attorney.
"Doc" Hartle,
internist at the community hospital.

Adviser:
Cy Ellsworth,
office of the state public health department.

Those discussed:
Adrian Reese,
superintendent of health.
Gus Griffith,
former city manager.
Andy Melville,
garage owner.
Chuck Sands,
current city manager.
Sid Scott,
attorney for Adrian Reese.
Judge Belanger,
U.S. District Court in Saint Carl.

Managers in the United States, acting in anger, indignation, frustration, or even error, fire many capable employees every year. In some of these cases, the managers act unfairly. Perplexing questions arise when the story of an unjustified discharge catches the public's eye. Does an organization have an obligation to manage equitably as well as efficiently? Is it conceivable that every man and woman has a right to a job, and, if so, is this right a factor that managers must weigh in deciding to lay off an employee who doesn't "fit in"?

The employee in this case, "Adrian Reese," is an outspoken health official who irritates the city manager and members of the "Marshall City" board of health. Like most HBR cases, this is based on a real situation. As the problem unfolds, readers may find the circumstances and the characters familiar. And yet they may be surprised at the outcome, as truth is stranger than fiction.

HBR invited three executives to give their views on this case: Jenifer Renzel, senior vice president, Bank of America; Edward J. Mandt, vice president and director of personnel, Maccabees Mutual Life Insurance Company; and David L. Nye, a human resources manager with a major energy company and vice president of the Western Reserve Group, a consulting firm in Solon, Ohio. We invite readers to see if they agree with these commentators' views.

Mr. Ewing is managing editor of HBR. He is the author of 'Do It My Way or You're Fired!' (John Wiley & Sons, 1983) and of numerous HBR articles, including "Your Right to Fire" (March-April 1983).

---

*Robert Green Ingersoll

Jenifer Renzel

Edward J. Mandt

David L. Nye

Jarvis: We've got to make up our minds what to do about Adrian. This saga is getting a little weird, and, frankly, as a businessman, I find it damned embarrassing. Just in the past week a dozen people at the food company asked me what was happening. I don't mind 'em asking, but the way they raise their eyebrows—

Crawley: Like they're saying, "I hope you don't run the company that way!"

Nordhoff: A customer came up to my desk and asked, "Hey, what's going on over there?" Adrian's beating on every drum he can get hold of.

Ellsworth: How did this rhubarb start, anyway?

Jarvis: Cy, when we first brought Adrian here as acting superintendent of health four years ago, we couldn't have asked for more. Bachelor of science degree from my old alma mater, two years in the army, a couple of years in business, a dozen years in municipal public health—a fine track record, good references.

Ellsworth: I remember asking around when you gave me a call

about 'im, Alf. They liked 'im a lot in Pennsburgh, they hated to see 'im go.

Jarvis: Things went OK the first year. Oh, Adrian had a tiff or two with Griff—that's Gus Griffith, the former city manager, Cy. But who didn't strike sparks with Griff? So two years ago we appointed him permanent superintendent of health—

Nordhoff: Over my objections.

Ellsworth: Was that in writing?

Nimmo: No, just at a board meeting. But it's in the minutes—and was reported in the *Sentinel*.

Jarvis: Your objections weren't all that loud, Ted. Not all that loud at all. You kind of grumbled but you went along. You agreed that giving the job to Adrian on a permanent basis would assure him, help him along. But instead the sparks between him and Griff got worse. That's a long answer to your question, Cy, but the real trouble seemed to start after Adrian dug in.

Ellsworth: If you made 'im permanent health commissioner, you

must've had good reasons. A lot of others would've fit the bill.

Jarvis: Well, he worked hard, he always returned a telephone call, people liked his family.

Nimmo: He got the well-baby clinic started here, Cy. He was effective in getting state aid.

Hartle: However, he didn't in my opinion ever get it clear in his mind what that well-baby clinic is supposed to do.

Crawley: Lots of young mothers like it, Doc—

Jarvis: Not everybody can afford your prices, Doc.

Hartle: You get what you pay for.

Crawley: And Adrian improved morale in the department, Cy. When he came, morale was poor. It's much better now.

Hartle: How could it help but get better? The department of health didn't have a chief for a whole year before Adrian came.

Crawley: Cy, what about Adrian's work here? I know Alf asked you to do an expert evaluation. What do you think?

Ellsworth: Well, I went over Adrian's work, I went back to what was in the pipeline when he came and what's happened since. I guess I'd say there's not much doubt that he knows his communicable diseases pretty good and he's got a handle on immunization programs. It wasn't easy to wangle state aid to get that well-baby clinic started, I don't have to tell you that.

Crawley: So you would give him good marks.

Ellsworth: In that respect of proficiency, yes.

Jarvis: Well, as I was saying, the sparks flew between Adrian and Griff. But then Griff left for a job in Kentucky and we all sighed with relief. We figured we'd have some peace and quiet. And so we did—for a while. Then, the next thing we knew, Adrian sent that damned questionnaire out, and that was when things busted open.

Crawley: I'd like to comment on that questionnaire, Alf.

Ellsworth: Hold on a bit, there's something that puzzles me—the nature of what Griffith was sore about. Adrian didn't report to him in any way, did he?

Jarvis: No, he reports just to us. But Griff was a hands-on manager, Cy, and there wasn't very much he didn't want to get his hands on. Before Adrian got here, Griff ran that health department. Marshall City's a small town, you know. All the town offices are here under this one roof. Griff and Adrian, being full time, couldn't avoid coming together. But the members of the board here, we're all voluntary. We've got jobs of our own and we only meet once a week. Sometimes every two weeks around Christmas and the like.

Nordhoff: What Alf is saying, Cy—and this is the bottom line of it all—is that we expect the superintendent of health to work productively with the city manager. He's got to.

Ellsworth: And Adrian knew that, did he? Was he clear on that?

Jarvis: Well, we told him how important it was when we first sat down with him.

Hartle: It was mentioned to him at board meetings, which he always attended, but he was such a stubborn idiot—

Crawley: But Doc, *nobody* hit it off well with Griff!

Hartle: He was the worst. Nobody else had so much trouble.

Ellsworth: But I still don't understand. Was it a personality clash, or did they cross wires, or what?

Nimmo: There was the plaque incident. Tell him about the plaque incident, Alf.

Jarvis: Griff had a plaque on his desk with the figure "1" on it, Cy. Most of us thought it was kind of funny, and we laughed and made jokes about it. But not our friend Adrian. He got hot under the collar every time he thought about it! "Well," I remember telling Adrian one time, tongue in cheek, "he was first in his class, maybe, and number one with his wife, and he is, after all, number one in the town hall." But Adrian couldn't see the humor of it.

Nordhoff: He couldn't stand the thought of Griff getting satisfaction in that manner.

Jarvis: Then one day Griff came to his office in the morning, and his plaque was gone from the desk but in its place was another plaque that looked just like it, only with a "0" on it instead of a "1." Griff made a bee line for Adrian's office, hot as a pistol, and he stormed in accusing Adrian. It wasn't his idea of a joke, Griff yelled, but Adrian denied any involvement.

Nimmo: In all fairness, pinning that one on Adrian is unwarranted. The evidence is all circumstantial, and piece by piece nothing holds up.

Crawley: It was Griff's abrasiveness more than anything else, his early Gulag management style. He treated Adrian like a subordinate. Of course Adrian got riled. Who wouldn't? One time Adrian sent a memo to Griff with a proposal for solving the sewer problem. Griff sent back a memo saying that the proposal was written in Adrian's inimitable style combining bad taste with ignorance of the facts.

Hartle: It was a suppurating reply but Adrian had it coming.

Crawley: Griff sent copies of his reply, Cy, to all of us. That was the back of the hand that stung Adrian.

Nimmo: Adrian came to me asking what he should do.

Ellsworth: What'd you say?

Nimmo: I told him he had to work it out by himself and I gave him a little background on Griff.

Ellsworth: Is that all?

Nimmo: What else could I tell him?

Jarvis: Then there was the time, Cy, that Adrian sent a letter to the Marshall *Sentinel*, and unfortunately they ran it—I say "unfortunately" because it was in poor taste, as practically everybody agreed. It not only gored the ox of President Reagan for cutting back on welfare but it also slammed the editor for quoting Reagan at length in an editorial. Griff called Adrian on the carpet for that, and Adrian, well, he got mad as a hornet; he didn't calm down for a long time.

Hartle: Somebody had to tell him. I'm glad Griff did. It was a putrid letter.

Nordhoff: Griff called Adrian in again for insulting Andy Melville on his auto service department. What happened is that the health department car had a carburetor problem or something, and after Adrian took it in for service, it got worse instead of better. This happened on two occasions. Adrian told Andy his service department was the pits, and Andy, you know, isn't used to being addressed in that manner. He's a pretty powerful man in this city, a factor to be dealt with. When you put your foot in your mouth with Andy, he makes you chew it off. Andy got on the phone with Griff and burned his ear off, and Griff called Adrian in and gave him the treatment.

Crawley: Adrian wasn't the only one on Griff's hit list. There were lots of people on it.

Ellsworth: Well, what'd the board say to Adrian about this?

Nordhoff: We tried to get Adrian to see the big picture, how we're elected officials responsible for public health, and how one thing led to another, and how Griff was a force to be respected even if he was abrasive—

Crawley: But every time, Ted, we ended up arguing among ourselves.

Jarvis: Then came the questionnaire incident. A few months after Griff leaves, Adrian sends out a questionnaire to a couple of dozen city employees. He was going to make it part of his master's thesis in public administration at State, and he'd talked it over with his thesis adviser—but he sent it out without consulting us in advance.

Ellsworth: Not a word to anybody?

Jarvis: Not a word. And it was mostly about Griff, how he was regarded and how he got on in this way and that.

Nordhoff: We couldn't even get a copy of it at first. I couldn't believe it. "Why didn't you consult us?" I asked him. "*Why?*"

Hartle: Because he's a sulphurous idiot.

Jarvis: In his covering letter he promised everyone anonymity, and so far as I know, he respected that pledge. He described the questionnaire as a scholarly effort to assess reaction to a departed public official they all knew.

Crawley: He went over every question with his thesis adviser.

Nordhoff: But it was loaded, Elaine! There was one place where he asked, "How would you describe the city manager?" and he had a long list of words to circle, and there was the word *liar* in that list, and the word *unjust.* Now, let me ask you: How would *you* like someone, your associate no less, to send out a questionnaire after you left town—after you left and couldn't defend yourself—asking people what they thought of your management style?

Crawley: Ted, there were almost a *hundred* words in the list. You make it sound like they were all critical. A hundred words and more of them complimentary, I think, than critical. *Articulate, forceful, farsighted, strong leader*—all sorts of praise to choose from.

Hartle: In my opinion it was a pejorative list, I don't care how long.

Crawley: But he couldn't have all nice adjectives, Doc, don't you see? It wouldn't have given the respondents any choice.

Hartle: The list was pejorative, and the tone of the thing was dyspeptic.

Jarvis: You're in rare form tonight, Doc.

Crawley: The list of descriptive adjectives was only one part of it. Adrian also asked for specific incidents from the respondent's experience with the city manager, and opinions on the city manager's achievements and failures—

Hartle: There, you said it. *Failures.* The word stuck out like a broken bone.

Crawley: And still another part of the questionnaire offered a series of statements about the city manager, like "He is a good leader."

Hartle: Don't forget the statement about the city manager blaming others for his own mistakes.

Crawley: It was only one of a couple of dozen choices. Now, really, Doc, that's not so unfair, is it?

Hartle: If it's part of a personal vendetta, yes.

Ellsworth: Did they all fill out the questionnaire? Did Adrian get what he wanted?

Nimmo: Only 11 did. Eleven of two dozen or more.

Jarvis: Adrian thinks pressure was put on them not to reply.

Ellsworth: This new city manager, Sykes—

Jarvis: Chuck Sands.

Ellsworth: What does he think about all this?

Jarvis: Well, I don't know exactly. He hasn't said an awful lot. But he's friendly to Griff, and when Griff was here, Chuck worked under him. But Chuck hasn't said much about it.

Hartle: If you ask me, Chuck is practically apoplectic wondering when Adrian is going to send out a questionnaire about *him.*

Ellsworth: Is Adrian rubbing Sands against the grain too?

Nordhoff: Chuck's a different type, Cy. He doesn't make nearly so much noise. He's the kind to keep his head below the grass if he can. If Adrian bothers him, he won't show it. That's the debit side. But if you turn it around and ask, does he seem to *like* Adrian, well, there's not much to go on on the credit side, either.

Jarvis: But we're not to the end of the story yet. Polly's got some important news to tell us.

Nimmo: As you all know, on May 16 the board voted to terminate Adrian—

Hartle: Benignly, I thought, as we allowed him an extra month with pay to hunt for a new position. We didn't have to be so generous.

Nimmo: Nevertheless, he got an attorney, Sid Scott—he's a member of the American Civil Liberties Union—and took us to the U.S. district court in Saint Carl to sue to get his job back. At the trial our letter to Adrian listing the reasons for terminating him – his poor communications with the city manager, his tactlessness over the car repairs, etcetera etcetera – was produced in evidence, but Judge Belanger would not allow argument on the merits of those reasons. The only thing Judge Belanger wanted argued was the role of the questionnaire in our decision to terminate Adrian.

Hartle: The most emetic day I ever wasted in a courtroom.

Nimmo: And Judge Belanger ruled, as everyone in Marshall now knows –

Jarvis: Thanks to the *Sentinel*, which is following this business like a horsefly. Their reporter sat in on the termination decision and has talked to Adrian a lot since.

Nimmo: Judge Belanger ruled that the questionnaire was the motivating reason for the termination and therefore an infringement of Adrian's right to constitutionally protected free speech. He found that any mistakes Adrian made, and I quote, "were insubstantial."

Hartle: Inexpiable. The most inexpiable decision possible.

Ellsworth: Let me tell you, even the top law firm of Saint Carl takes extreme care when dealing with old Judge Belanger or when speaking of 'im in public. He is an intimidating man, and thin-skinned to boot, and even at the *Pennsburgh News* they're a little afraid of 'im, hesitant to criticize.

Nimmo: I have just talked with Judge Belanger. First he inquired whether Adrian was working again as health superintendent. I answered yes. Then he said, "Well, when are you going to let him go for the right reason?" And I said to him, "Do you mean by the right reason, no reason?" And he nodded.

Hartle: This Homeric tale isn't over yet, then.

Nordhoff: You're getting ahead of me, Polly. You mean the judge

is assuming we *are* going to fire Adrian? I'm not sure I heard you right.

Nimmo: You heard me right.

Nordhoff: But last month he ruled that the questionnaire was why we fired Adrian, and if that's the way he feels –

Nimmo: You see, the common law rule is that an employee at will – that's Adrian, because he's not covered by civil service –

Hartle: *Uncivil* service, I call it. A device to protect government deadwood.

Nimmo: The common law rule is that an employee at will can be terminated for no reason. Our mistake was that we gave a reason, or, at least, an impermissible reason. Now, if we don't give any reason...

Nordhoff: Why are we just sitting here? I hereby move that we terminate Adrian Reese as health superintendent of Marshall City as of tomorrow at five P.M. Period.

Jarvis: Hold it, Ted –

Hartle: Mr. Chairman, "To see the salve doth make the wound ache more." I second Mr. Nordhoff's motion.

Jarvis: Now look here! There are going to be some repercussions from this, and as a businessman I don't think we should go ahead until we've thought it through and looked at all the angles. We better not decide anything till we know exactly what we're doing.

Query to readers: Putting yourself in Alf Jarvis's shoes, what questions would you ask the board members to consider? What course of action would you urge on the board? What might the board do to prevent a recurrence of this?

Judging from experience, many executives in Jarvis's place

would go along with Nordhoff and Hartle and fire Reese again. Their rationalizations would be brief and blunt. "Managing is hard enough without having a troublemaker to contend with," some would say. "The chemistry isn't right," others would explain. "We don't have to have a reason," still others would point out.

But our three commentators all believe that Reese should be kept on. Although their reasons vary, they feel that the board is at least partly to blame for the situation and, more important, they think that it is not too late for the board to work constructively with Reese to iron out most difficulties. They also object to letting Reese go on the grounds that it is not *fair* to do so. They contend that an organization has a responsibility to govern equitably as well as to manage efficiently.

Case for Reese?

Jenifer Renzel succinctly states her view. "If I were Alf Jarvis, I would not agree to fire Reese as proposed at the end." She then itemizes her reasons for retaining Reese:

"**Impropriety of discharge.** Firing Reese again, without reason, would be foolish in light of all that has transpired earlier, including his rehire. It would only alienate others on the staff as well as raise questions in the public's mind regarding the competence of the board. Firing him now would appear retaliatory, arbitrary, and unjust.

"**Effect on employee relations.** Refiring Reese for no reason would create employee relations problems as it might signal that others could also be terminated capriciously for no reason. Such an employment practice would certainly result in lowered morale, increased insecurity, and decreased loyalty to a management that appears insensitive and unjust. Employees would ask, 'If they did it to Reese, when will they do it to me?' Ultimately, firing Reese might lead other employees to consider organizing for protection.

"**Insecurity of successors.** Future superintendents of health would be justifiably nervous about their jobs and might hesitate to take decisive action for fear of being instantly terminated for no reason. Some qualified candidates may decide they prefer organizations that offer more due process to employees."

Edward J. Mandt is equally critical:

"Reese should not have been fired in the first place. He most certainly should not be refired on the basis of an anachronistic terminable-at-will doctrine. This common law concept is a relic of an agrarian economy, which few questioned when most people lived off the land and there were few permanent employees. Then, whenever a farmer or a merchant wanted to hire someone, it was for a specific or limited term—until the harvest was in, for example, or until the boats were unloaded."

Right to a job

Mandt continues:

"Such is no longer the case. Today, as Peter F. Drucker has pointed out, 'A job is the employee's means of access to social status, to personal opportunity, to achievement, and to power.' In industrialized countries, making a living generally means having a job. If we accept the thesis that everyone has a right to live, then it must follow that everyone also has a right to a job.

"This right is not unqualified, however; it has to be subordinate to the rights of other interested parties. No organization, be it profit, nonprofit, or governmental, should be required— or even expected—to retain superfluous, incompetent, or problem workers. On the other hand, employers have a moral obligation to think through any decision to terminate anyone. Although many still have the legal right to terminate at will, arbitrary discharge is a clear violation of social justice because it unfairly interferes with a person's right to earn a living.

"To deal fairly with an employee, managers should clearly define at the outset the organization's purpose; explain how the employee fits in terms of job objectives, duties, and relationships; and set down expected results, including how and when performance will be measured. Managers should then regularly evaluate performance and give feedback; give direction and assistance; and provide rewards along with, if necessary, punishments.

"If a manager conscientiously follows these steps and fails to get satisfactory results, he or she may have to resort to discharge. And even then demotion or reassignment may be preferable."

Case against Reese

Mandt reasons:

"Presumably, in the case of Adrian Reese, the board did define the organization. Jarvis states that they told Reese it was important for him to work productively with the city manager when they first sat down with him. Beyond this, there seems to have been no constructive counsel or feedback. In fact, the actual reason for the firing is not at all clear. Jarvis and Ellsworth report that Reese's credentials were first-rate. His performance during his first year as acting superintendent was acceptable except for 'a tiff or two' with Griffith. Reese then served two years as superintendent.

"Jarvis, Nimmo, and Crawley are complimentary about his performance: he worked hard and returned phone calls; department morale improved; a well-baby clinic was started; state aid was secured. Ellsworth attests that Reese 'knows his communicable diseases pretty good' and has 'a handle on immunization programs.'

"On the debit side, there's little of substance. Reese did not get along with Griffith, but others had similar problems and Griffith appears to have been the aggressor anyway. It is Griffith who writes what Hartle (no supporter of Reese) terms a 'suppurating' reply to Reese's memo on the sewer problem. It is Griffith who calls Reese on the carpet for his letter to the local paper and who burns his ear off for his complaint about the service at Melville's garage.

"Reese's letter to the editor may have been unwise but the city manager had no authority to chastise him over this. And in the other two situations, Reese was clearly acting well within his job. If the tone of Reese's communications was inappropriate, it was the board's duty to correct him. Finally, there's the matter of the questionnaire. (I ignore the incident of the plaque because there is no proof of his involvement.)

"The questionnaire—part of a graduate thesis reviewed by his adviser—seems to have been a legitimate but possibly ill-considered project, since it referred to Griffith. But even if it caused problems, this is hardly grounds for dismissal.

"The underlying problem is not Reese or Griffith but the board itself, which, with its laissez-faire attitude, seems to have forgotten what its role is. Board members permitted Griffith to treat Reese as a subordinate. Instead of supporting their appointee, they urged him to work things out. If Reese exceeded his authority, exercised poor judgment, or acted abrasively in any of the incidents mentioned, it was the board members' duty to step in and counsel him. They did not. The letter and the questionnaire both caught them by surprise. Eventually, apparently as a result of political pressure or sheer exasperation, they terminated him peremptorily.

"My advice to the board is to sit down and think through its role, issue a written position paper on the responsibilities of the department of public health, and finally, create a subgroup to advise and support Reese. Termination is indefensible from every point of view; it would probably lower department morale; it would cost the city the services of a productive professional for no good reason; and it could probably be successfully challenged in the courts."

David L. Nye summarizes his thoughts on the dismissal:

"This case is especially challenging because of the setting. In most corporations a manager would hear the arguments advanced by his staff and legal counsel and then decide how to deal with the employee in question. At that point, the staff goes back to work. Not so in Marshall City. Here the managers, volunteer board members, are influential citizens who have been personally embarrassed by the Reese incident. If alienated further, they could resign and oppose the city administration. Nevertheless, the basic considerations for a proper decision on employee discharge would apply here just as they do in the private sector.

"A second termination of Reese would be unjust and inappropriate. It would not likely stand up in court; more important, there is reason for optimism about Reese's performance. His main personal problem is political naiveté. With Griffith gone, that problem can be largely cured without killing the patient. The board members contributed to the unhappy situation facing them and can help turn it around."

What should Jarvis do?

Nye puts himself in Jarvis's shoes:

"As Jarvis, I would first seek the board's agreement that having a second discharge decision reversed would be a debilitating blow to the board, the city administration, and the community. At the least, Newman, the new city manager, should be consulted. Nordhoff, who defined as the bottom line the board's expectations that the superintendent of health should work productively with the city manager, observed that Newman has a different style from his predecessor's and tends to stay out of the day-to-day affairs of the department. I would therefore table the dismissal motion until I could talk with Newman and outside counsel.

"I believe counsel would agree that the board can't successfully fire Reese for no reason under the employment-at-will doctrine. I am as wary of the substance of Judge Belanger's remark as I am of his ethics in making it. It has been *adjudicated* that the proximate cause of Reese's firing was his exercise of constitutionally protected free speech. Firing him again, ostensibly for no reason, would seem a flimsy disguise. If Reese sued in a state where the courts do not always follow the at-will theory—especially where public policy issues are involved—the board could be assessed punitive damages for its continuing 'harassment' of him.

"The board must consider if it really wants to terminate Reese given

that the press is following the case and is sympathetic to Reese over the free speech issue. Board members are elected officials, after all, and the *Sentinel* does influence public opinion. Moreover, if we fire Reese arbitrarily, what message are we giving the city employees who *so far* have not seen a need to organize? And what message would we be giving potential candidates for Reese's position?

"These questions suggest that the board would be better served by bringing Reese quietly back on the team. Our failure to work productively with him stems partly from the lack of objective performance standards for his job. We have given him little help. When he sought guidance in handling Griffith's demeaning response to his proposal, we told him to work it out himself. Until Reese learns to work with our informal organization, someone must act as his mentor in dealing with the city manager and board members. Replacing Reese won't eliminate that need. Whenever professionals must work under administrators who are nonprofessionals, there is a natural friction; hospitals deal with this constantly.

"A frank discussion with Reese and Chuck Sands would be an important early step. We must assure Reese that we intend to develop more structure in his job and in our relationships. Design of performance standards for Reese's work will be a key part of this plan. I'd give Crawley and Hartle roles. Crawley is a personnel director by profession, and Hartle, a medical professional who needs both recognition and a better appreciation of the need for objectivity in assessing job performance. Definition of specific job objectives and periodic reports to the board would be essential. Someone should work with Reese as a coach on a continuing basis.

"Perhaps Adrian Reese holds values and feelings that are incompatible with a small-town political environment. If this is the case, Reese will ultimately leave on his own or will be properly terminated for cause."

Improving the chemistry

Among executives, one of the most bothersome questions about a situation like that of the Marshall City board of health is the problem of "chemistry." How can you hope to achieve a high standard of operating efficiency when you have personality conflicts between key people as, in this case, Hartle and Reese or Reese and Griffith? Doesn't an executive's right to manage imply freedom to hire and fire so that the best possible team can be put together?

Our commentators don't have clear answers to these questions. In different ways they indicate their beliefs that the board has an obligation to try harder to work things out with the present personnel. Down the road, yes, the board may indeed need to shake things up. But first it must make a serious effort to work with the current superintendent.

Renzel addresses this issue as follows:

"The board should not fire Reese at this time. Since Griffith is gone, one part of the conflict is absent. Reese evidently has some very positive attributes and the potential to do well. The board should sit down with Reese, go over its concern regarding past behavior, and establish authorities, specific expectations, and objectives for future performance. It should define when he needs concurrence and to whom he should turn for clarification. It should assure him that he is starting with a clean slate to demonstrate his capabilities, judgment, and interpersonal skills. To the extent that parameters and policies were not appropriately defined or delineated to Reese previously, conflicts and issues were failures of the board."

But what about the board members themselves? If difficult personalities like Hartle's are part of the problem, as some would perceive it, is the solution to remove *them*? An alternative to terminating Reese would be to force a change in Hartle's behavior or maneuver him off the board. Presumably Jarvis could accomplish this;

one commentator made the intriguing suggestion that Hartle be assigned to coach Reese. If the doctor could be sold on doing this, a giant step might be taken to improving the climate.

If Jarvis runs into a stone wall in his efforts to change Hartle, he might try to convince him to resign or at least not run for reelection. Admittedly, these would be difficult steps to take, but if Jarvis has the conviction and the leadership qualities, he might find this approach well worth taking.

PR & legal issues

For some executives the worst thing about an employee objector is the possibility of bad publicity. Significantly, our three commentators attach more importance to the management questions than to the prospect of a bad press.

To quote **Renzel** again:
"The public relations issues, though important, should be secondary to the question of what is the right action to take from a personnel and management perspective. Public bodies must be willing to live with their decisions despite negative press, but they should be convinced that their action is correct. In my opinion, by firing Reese and then losing the case, the board has already received its black eye. Firing him again for no reason would only indicate vacillation and retaliation in the eyes of the public. If Reese, given a fair chance, causes problems in the future by disregarding specified expectations and authorities, the board can then take disciplinary action based on sound grounds, thus minimizing the risk of another black eye."

All three commentators fault Nimmo and Judge Belanger for their apparent insensitivity to the question of Reese's rights as a public employee. Whether due process has been denied him and whether his constitutional right to free speech has been violated are issues that many judges and attorneys these days would look at carefully.

In addition, Reese could have a contractual right to be terminated only for just cause. Jarvis mentioned that "two years ago we [the board] appointed him permanent superintendent of health." If it can be verified that such a commitment was made, Reese may be out of the board's firing range, depending on the attitude of the state's courts. In New York, Michigan, California, and some other states, the courts would be expected to side with Reese.[1]

In sum, our commentators offer strong evidence that in the eyes of managers as well as of judges and industrial relations authorities, discharge is no longer a simple, personal, seat-of-the-pants decision. Though many managers view this trend uneasily, employees and the public generally seem to approve of it.

Especially when jobs are hard to come by, public opinion crystallizes in favor of due process for employees—not due process in the formal, legal sense that lawyers think of it, but in the sense of managerial guarantees that employees will be given a fair chance to keep their jobs.

This doesn't mean that anyone, subordinate or superior, "owns a job" but that an employer organization has an obligation to deal equitably with employees when conflicts arise between them and their superiors. Managers who violate this notion can get their organizations into trouble just as surely as can employees who work incompetently at their assigned tasks. ▽

Reprint 83504

---

1 See my article "Your Right to Fire," HBR March-April 1983, p. 38.

A long-buried report triggers a crisis of integrity, loyalty, and ethics.

The Case of the Willful Whistle-Blower

by SALLY SEYMOUR

When Ken Deaver, CEO of Fairway Electric, promoted me to vice president of the nuclear division, I was on top of the world. Now, just a month later, it feels like the world's on top of me. I'm used to having a team to share the problems, but now I'm on my own. At least Ken's door has always been open to me. He's been my mentor since I began at Fairway eight years ago, and he's really responsible for my success here. I owe him a lot. But when I think back over the last few weeks, I have to wonder whether I should have listened to him on this one.

It started the morning I walked into my office to find Jim Bower, one of my old teammates, waiting for me. He apologized for taking my time but said it was really important. I had worked with Jim for more than four years. If he says it's important, it's important.

"What's up?" I asked.

"Bob," he said, "I've run up against something I can't handle alone. I hate to dump this on you when you're just starting your new job, but it's the sort of thing I should take to my boss, and that's you now."

"Sure, Jim. Whatever it is, you've got my help."

He took a couple of deep breaths before he continued. "You know how we're cramped for space downstairs. Well, yesterday I asked my secretary to clear out any files over five years old. Before she left for the day, she stacked the old files on my desk so I could glance through them. And I couldn't believe what I found."

Jim pulled a red notebook from his briefcase.

"I found this report written 15 years ago by two engineers in the nuclear division. It's about a flaw in our design of the Radon II nuclear reactor. Apparently there was a structural problem in the containment unit that would show up as the power plant was being built. It wasn't a safety hazard, but it would hold up construction and cost a lot to fix. The report says that Fairway was going to rework the design. But listen to this memo from the head of the nuclear division." Jim opened the notebook and read from a sheet stapled to the inside cover.

"'The potential problems in the design of the Radon II are disturbing. They do not, however, present a safety hazard. It therefore would be counterproductive to discontinue sales of the design. If there are problems with fittings, they will show up as the plant is built, at which point the necessary corrections can be made. The need for retrofitting is not uncommon. Our experience has been that customers rarely complain about such extra costs.'"

Jim closed the notebook and looked up.

"This memo makes me sick, Bob. I can't believe Fairway would risk its reputation by selling plans they knew were flawed. Those customers bought the designs thinking they were the best on the market. But the Radon II took longer to build and cost a bunch more money than what Fairway told customers. That's misrepresentation. Maybe the reason the utilities never complained is because they could pass the cost on to the rate payers. But that's a real rip-off, and the top guys at Fairway knew about it."

Jim threw the notebook on my desk and looked at me, his face flushed.

"Don't you think engineering ought to know about this?" he said.

I'd never seen Jim so steamed up. Of course, I was pretty upset myself. That report was new to me too. But I had a lot of faith in Fairway, so I wasn't going to

Sally Seymour is on the faculty of the Harvard Business School, where she teaches management communication.

leap to conclusions. I told Jim I'd ask some questions and get back to him by the end of the day.

I headed straight for Ken's office, recalling along the way everything I could about the Radon II reactor. I knew that we'd had problems with it, but it never occurred to me that our original designs were flawed. Jim was right that no one ever complained about the delays and costs of refitting. But I remembered one instance where a utility converted a Radon II to a coal-fired plant because of the cost overruns. In that case, the utility paid for the conversion and it didn't go into the rate base.

When I showed the report to Ken, he recognized it right away.

"How did Jim get ahold of this?" he asked.

"He discovered it by accident—cleaning out old files," I said. "He's pretty disturbed about it, and I can't say I blame him." Ken's office was suddenly very still.

"I thought this report was dead and buried," he said. "Have you read it?"

"Enough to get the drift," I said. "Apparently we sold a power plant design when we knew there were flaws in it."

"Yes, but you've got to understand the context. Back then we were in the middle of an energy crisis. Everyone was rushing to build nuclear power plants. We were under tremendous pressure to come up with a winning design, and Radon II was what we decided on. After a few plants went under construction, some problems surfaced, so we put a couple of engineers on it. But by the time they wrote this report, it was too late for us to go back to the drawing board. We

---

> ## Jim: "I had a moral obligation to make the information public. Now you want to fire me?"

---

wouldn't have had any customers left. We figured we'd solve the problem as soon as we could, but we'd sell the original design in the meantime. It was basically a very good one. And it was safe."

"I can't believe we would risk our reputation like that."

"I know it's not the way we usually operate, but that shows you the pressure we were under," Ken said. "The whole division would have gone down. There was no other way."

I was uncomfortable putting Ken on the defensive. I'd always trusted his judgment. Who was I to grill him about something that happened 15 years ago when I wasn't even around? Still, I needed to press the point.

"So what do I tell Jim?" I asked.

"Nothing. It's ancient history. The engineers who wrote that report are long gone. Look at it this way, the fact that we ordered a study of the problem shows that we care about quality. We eventually got the bugs out. Besides, it was never a question of safety. It was merely a matter of some extra work during construction."

"But what about all the cost overruns? If Fairway didn't swallow them, someone else must have—like the utilities or their customers."

"Look, Bob, what's past is past. What would we gain by bringing this into the open today? But I guarantee we've got a hell of a lot to lose. The regulators and some shareholders would love to blame us for all the exorbitant cost overruns. And the antinuclear groups would have a field day. We've got enough problems getting licenses as it is.

"We'd lose a lot of business, you know. I'm talking about hundreds of jobs here, and the very survival of this company. Maybe we're not perfect, but we're the most conscientious, quality-conscious corporation I know of."

"And what do I do with this report?" I asked.

"Deep-six it. As we should have done long ago. Tell Jim Bower what I told you, and explain why there's no reason to make an issue of it at this late date."

I nodded in agreement and headed back to my office. I found Jim waiting.

He scowled when I reported Ken's reaction.

"So you're telling me to forget I ever saw the report? And I suppose that means you're going to forget I showed it to you."

"Look, Ken's got some good reasons for not wanting to make an issue of it. I may or may not agree with him, but he's running the show."

"Damn it, Bob!" Jim shouted. "If we go along with this, we're just as guilty as the people who sold those bad designs 15 years ago."

"Cool down, cool down. I know what you're saying, but Ken is just being realistic. After all, no one got hurt, the cost was spread over a lot of people, and the problem's been corrected. If this gets exposed, it could really hurt us."

"No, I won't cool down. Maybe it seems like ancient history to Ken, but unless we make a clean slate now, it could happen again. One of the reasons I took this job is because Fairway is a company I can respect. What am I supposed to think now?"

"I see your point," I replied, "but I also see Ken's. And he's the boss. Maybe you should talk to him."

"If I can't get through to you I don't see how I'll get through to him. So I guess that's it."

As it turned out, that wasn't it. When Jim left my office, he didn't go straight back to work. First he went to the newspaper, and the story appeared two days later.

FAIRWAY SOLD DEFECTIVE REACTORS – REPORT WARNED OF HAZARD

Naturally, the reporter got it all wrong and blew the problem out of proportion. He didn't even have a copy of the report. I suppose we hadn't helped matters though. When the reporter called for a comment, Ken asked him to call back in a couple of hours. Then Ken and I met with our public relations officer, Amy Thone, to discuss how to handle the situation. Amy thought we should come clean – admit we made a mistake and stress the fact that our record for the past five years had been excellent. But Ken felt that the less we said, the sooner it would blow over. I went along with him. When the reporter called back, Ken's response was "no comment."

The article did say that the anonymous source still thought Fairway was a reliable builder of nuclear plants and that it was a good company with many skilled and highly principled employees. The source had gone to the newspaper because he felt it was his ethical duty to the consumers who had been forced to pay for Fairway's mistakes. But that part of the story was buried in the next-to-last paragraph.

Needless to say, the public outcry was intense. Antinuke activists went berserk, and politicians made holier-than-thou speeches. After a couple of days hearing phones ring off the hook, we realized that stonewalling was compounding our problems. So we made a clean breast of it. We drafted a statement to the press saying that Fairway engineers had in fact discovered design flaws in 1973 but that the company had corrected the problem within 14 months. Ken made himself available to answer questions, and he and Amy arranged to meet with community leaders. They even invited experts from the university to answer the technical questions. The thrust of these efforts was to assure the public that no flaws had been discovered since 1973 and that all Fairway's designs were safe.

Thanks to Amy and Ken, the controversy finally died down. I was proud of the way they handled things. I was also glad that Ken didn't fire Jim. At the height of the crisis, someone at headquarters had suggested that he "get rid of the troublemaker," but Ken thought that would only make matters worse. I didn't want to fire Jim either. I felt he was still a valuable employee. I knew he was committed to Fairway, and we sure needed his skills.

We weathered those difficult weeks with only a few outstanding lawsuits, but an ugly incident like that never has a simple ending. It keeps unraveling. Now we have another problem. Word got out that Jim was the whistle-blower, and now his life here is miserable. The feeling is that Jim can't be trusted. Last week, Lorraine Wellman, another former teammate, came to talk to me about the problem.

"You know, it's not that anyone hates Jim for what he did," she said. "It's just that no one can understand why he did it. They could understand it if someone

> ## Bob: "This is bad for you, your family, and your team. Wouldn't you be happier in another division?"

had been hurt or killed because of a bad design, but that wasn't the case. In their minds, he risked their jobs for something that happened ages ago.

"Morale is pretty low in the trenches," she added. "One guy told me he used to be proud of where he worked. Now his neighbors razz him about 'Radon-gate' and 'Three-Mile Radon.' No one wants to work with Jim, and it's affecting our output."

I felt terrible for Jim. Unlike the others, I understood why he did what he did, and I respected his integrity. On the other hand, I wasn't surprised that his coworkers resented him. I just wished everyone would forget the whole thing and get on with their work. But the situation seemed to be getting worse instead of better.

Yesterday Ken came to see me about the mounting problems in Jim's department. He suggested that Jim might want to resign and that we could give him a very generous package if he did. I knew what Ken was driving at. He didn't want to stir up trouble by firing a whistle-blower, but he thought we could get around it by pressuring Jim to leave on his own. That would solve all our problems. Of course Ken just wanted what was best for Fairway, but I resisted the idea. I asserted that the problems were temporary, and threw in a few remarks about Jim's outstanding performance. I figured I should defend him. After all, Jim had done the noble thing, and it didn't seem right that he should get the shaft. But Ken persisted. He was worried about meeting targets and didn't think one person should be allowed to make everyone else look bad. He asked me to talk to Jim.

Jim had been avoiding me since he showed me the report, and maybe I was avoiding him too. The worst thing about this whole situation is that it ruined our friendship. Still, he agreed to see me in my office. I tried to break the ice by extending my hand and saying that I missed seeing him. But he ignored the gesture and mumbled something about being busy. So I decided to jump right in.

"I've heard about the problems you've been having with the team. This thing is taking its toll—on Fairway, your department, and you."

"I can handle it. Or maybe that's not your point. Are you saying that the company doesn't want me around anymore?"

"Look Jim," I said, "I'm real sorry this happened. I hate to see you and your family suffering like this. Maybe a transfer to another office would be the best thing. There are other divisions that could use your talents."

"You just don't get it, do you, Bob? I haven't done anything wrong, and I'm the one who's suffering. People are blaming me for a report I didn't write and bad designs I didn't push on customers. And now I'm the one you want out. I figured the idea of firing me might occur to someone, but I can't believe you agreed to it. That's one I hadn't expected."

"No one has mentioned firing," I said. "I'm talking about a transfer. I see why you're angry about your teammates giving you a hard time, but why come down on me? I'm one of the few who understand your position, and I've tried to support you."

"You've tried to *support* me? Give me a break! I didn't want to get into this, but now that you've brought it up, I'm going to spell it out for you.

"I didn't ask to see that report. It fell into my hands. But once it did, I couldn't just pretend it wasn't there. What the company did was wrong—you know that and I know that. If someone didn't say something, Fairway could get away with it again.

"But I surely didn't figure you'd make me go this alone. I didn't expect you to run to the newspapers, but I did expect you to make a strong case to Ken for the company coming clean on this. And failing that, I expected you—as my supervisor—to take this off my shoulders by assuming the responsibility yourself.

"You've got more power than I have, and you certainly have more influence with Ken. But you acted like this whole thing had nothing to do with you—like you were just a messenger. You dumped Ken's answer in my lap and washed your hands of the whole affair.

"I never thought I'd say this, but it's beginning to look like you care way too much for your fancy new title and your tight relationship with Ken. Well, I won't quit and I won't transfer!"

Before I could respond, Jim was out the door. I don't know how long I sat at my desk in a daze. After a while I tried to get back to work, but I couldn't concentrate. The whole morning I kept going over what Jim had said. How could I defend Jim and the company at the same time? Was Ken wrong? Had Jim really done the noble thing after all?

WHAT WOULD YOU HAVE DONE?

We asked experts from human resource management, public relations, and industry what they would have done in this situation. Here are their responses.

RICHARD B. PRIORY *is vice president, design engineering, for Duke Power Company. His responsibilities include the design and licensing of the company's generating facilities and the management of corporate research and development. He is also chairman of the Nuclear Plant Standardization Study Group of the Atomic Industrial Forum.*

Let Honesty Build Profits

The realization that management sets the tone for how business is conducted throughout the company came too late to Fairway. Knowing that corporate integrity is an immeasurable asset would have saved the company a nuclear-sized headache. Who can calculate how much business Ken's ethics cost his company over the years, as long-term integrity and success were jeopardized for short-term considerations?

One problem is how Fairway handled the discovery of the design flaw. A supplier wanting profitable, enduring business associations with customers would have explained the problem, the solution, and how the solution would be implemented. Ken should have contacted his utility clients, illustrated the problem and solution, and assured them that Fairway would cover the extra hardware and work.

If he had believed that quality products and straightforward dealings with customers result in greater long-term profits—profits that would outweigh the savings from having utilities and customers pay for rework—Ken would have commended the engineers who identified the problem and the solution.

Then there is the nuclear issue. Public trust in nuclear power is fragile, even on the best of days. And the industry, for the most part, is judged on perception, not reality. Explaining the design problem and solution directly to the utilities early on, particularly since there was no safety issue, may well have minimized the damage at Fairway. Once we get to the report's exhumation, the damage to the company's credibility is done. Sackcloth and ashes make up the dress of the day.

Finally, there is the people problem. When the report reappears, Fairway doesn't just miss the boat, it falls in the water. Management practically forces the report to be made public in the worst possible way, then lets personnel problems deteriorate to unmanageable levels. By treating Jim as it did, the company forfeited the chance to find an ethical solution. Ken seemed interested mainly in protecting himself. And Bob didn't know how to react to Jim, an employee to whom situations were either black or white.

Here's a better scenario: Jim brings the report to Bob, who goes to Ken for background but not for a solution. Ken proposes that the report be reinterred, but Bob prepares him for the possibility that Jim won't buy that solution. Bob returns to Jim with the whole story: who did what, when, and why. Together they go over possible solutions and the risks of each. Together they decide that the best long-term solution is to make restitution to the companies that spent money fixing the design flaw but to do it in a way that minimizes damage to existing employees.

Bob works hard to convince Ken that the report is going to be made public and the only question is who will do it and how best to manage the beating. Bob begins a communication effort with his department to explain how employee concerns about management decisions are addressed. Now even if Jim is targeted by other employees as the instigator, the impact is lessened.

BETH A. LEWIS *has been involved in whistle-blowing cases as manager of work-related problem counseling for Control Data Corporation's Employee Advisory Resources program. She is currently a student in the MIT Sloan Fellows Program.*

Support the Messenger

Two common reactions to whistle-blowers are to respond to the message and ignore the messenger, or to avoid the message and, instead, shoot the messenger. Either reaction can cause problems. In this case, both reactions take place.

At first, Ken and Bob reacted to the discovery of the engineering report with little consideration of Jim. They discuss the seriousness of the report but do not discuss the seriousness of Jim's concern. Although Jim had clearly told Bob that he thought the issue was very important and "something I can't handle alone," Bob underestimated Jim's motivation when he passed on Ken's directive to "forget it."

Regardless of the seriousness or even validity of a whistle-blower's report, managers must acknowledge the person's beliefs and motivation. The first objective should be to agree on a timely action plan without implying consensus on the outcome. Bob did this initially when he told Jim he would ask some questions and get back to him by the end of the day. Bob did not, however, follow up by asking Jim what he was willing to do or what he expected.

Alternative channels of communication are very important in whistle-blowing cases. Jim went to the newspaper because he didn't see another avenue in Fairway. In many such cases, an employee may be reluctant to even discuss the concern with his or her own manager. Sensing personal risk, a whistle-blower often wants to deal with someone who is removed from the immediate situation, is perceived as having authority, and can be contacted on an anonymous basis (at least until trust is established).

Telephone hot lines set up for employee assistance programs, for corporate security, or to handle ethical concerns are one effective channel. Once a whistle-blower has called a hot-line number, alternative courses of action must be available. Some employees may be willing to report openly; some may want anonymity. Some may be willing to go through the management chain; others may want to deal with the legal, security, or human resource department. Also, there must be an escalation plan—a further channel for voicing concerns – in case the person is not satisfied with the initial result.

After Jim went to the newspaper, Ken and Bob continued to respond to the message and ignore the messenger. They dealt with external problems and avoided the growing internal one. Whistle-blowers perceive themselves as going out on a limb. The worst thing to do is cut them off. Even if the whistle-blower is anonymous, it is important to have follow-up communications, to report on what action is being taken, and to get closure.

At the end of the case, the management and co-workers wanted to shoot the messenger. This resulted partly from Bob's failure to deal with the reactions in the workplace. More important, the entire situation reflected the lack of a corporate position on ethical issues and management's unwillingness to assume responsibility. When the CEO appears concerned only with short-term objectives and avoiding problems, it is not surprising that Bob is left asking who was wrong or right.

It is time for Bob to support the messenger.

MYRON PERETZ GLAZER *is professor of sociology and anthropology at Smith College.*
PENINA MIGDAL GLAZER *is professor of history and dean of faculty at Hampshire College. They are currently completing a study on whistle-blowing that will be published by Basic Books.*

Don't Give Your Detractors Ammunition

The case portrays an employee so blinded by anger that he stands ready to jeopardize both his own career and his company's reputation. He is more a caricature than a recognizable whistle-blower.

Jim's *initial* reaction to the discovery of the report, however, was typical of the 60 whistle-blowers or, as we prefer to call them, ethical resisters we have studied during the past five years. He felt that service to the customer was paramount. He worked for superiors whom he trusted and he believed in both their competence and their willingness to distinguish between appropriate and lawless behavior. Moreover, Jim was convinced that if he pointed out a significant problem, his superiors would correct it immediately. Like other ethical employees, he was deeply disturbed when responsible superiors, people of integrity, refused to act within what he believed were the organizational norms.

Rather than press his concerns within the company, Jim inexplicably broke off the attempt to negotiate a just resolution and contacted the press. He neglected to ensure the accuracy of his allegations by withholding the very report that had so enraged him, thereby further undermining his position. Of course,

given his vociferousness, attempts at anonymity were doomed.

Jim's route to public disclosure was highly unusual. More typically, ethical resisters pursue avenues within their organizations. They go up the chain of command and attempt to persuade management to correct unethical or illegal decisions. Resisters also turn to coworkers and appeal to others' sense of ethics and concern for the organization. When coworkers join the protest, they validate the whistle-blower's stance and provide much needed emotional support. While such an alliance cannot ensure success, it does help negate the charges of treason that inevitably arise when the resister goes outside the company.

Jim's reaction is atypical in yet another essential way. Not one of the ethical resisters we have studied spoke against a 15-year-old or 10-year-old or even 5-year-old decision. In virtually all cases, employees protested internally and made public disclosure only about matters that directly affected their work. They acted only when they believed that their silence would make them complicit in ongoing fraud and misrepresentation, and harm unwary customers or constituents. Ethical resisters were not looking for trouble. Nonetheless, they refused to turn away with the rationalization that it wasn't their affair or that nothing could be done anyway.

The retaliation against Jim was also unusual. While superiors want to avoid the public condemnation that may come from punishing an ethical employee, they are seldom so gentle as to coax one to resign when his loyalty and judgment have been condemned. More often, whistle-blowers in industry are summarily dismissed. If they work for the government, they are often isolated, transferred, and later fired. Such action is virtually guaranteed when employees have no support from peers and have not cultivated the consistent attention of the media or legislators.

Jim may have believed he was on the side of the angels, but he gave his detractors sufficient ammunition to destroy his credibility. He remained totally isolated. The odds against ethical resisters are so high that they should not give their opponents such an overwhelming advantage.

ROBERT L. DILENSCHNEIDER *is president and chief executive officer of the public relations firm of Hill and Knowlton, Inc. His experience includes work with major corporations, regulatory agencies, and consumer groups. He directed communications activities during the U.S. Steel/Marathon merger, the Kansas City Hyatt disaster, the Three-Mile Island accident, and the Bendix/Martin-Marietta takeover.*

Consider Only Ethical Alternatives

Public relations firms are to clients what priests are to confessors; therefore, when clients are weighing alternatives that are unethical or illegal, we urge them not to do it. We will not even discuss such a scenario. Our hope is that careful consideration and our advice will dissuade them from it. Judgment must prevail. If clients are weighing a course of inappropriate action but have made no decision, then we have to presume their innocence and keep their confidence.

While the case is an interesting exercise, I can count on one hand the number of times something like this has happened in the past 20 years. We have succeeded in talking many clients out of poorly conceived, unethical, and sometimes even illegal actions. Rarely will a client defiantly tell us that they are going to pursue an illegal course despite our counsel. If the matter seems significant, we simply tell the client we want no part of it. Obviously, that usually ends our relationship.

The conversations in the case would not have happened between seasoned business executives. And the employee's decision to go to the media strikes me as an unsophisticated, knee-jerk reaction. The problem should have been settled internally and with the proper state and federal regulatory authorities. At that point it would have become a matter of public record for the media and any other interested individual or organization. I would think that executives at the level described in the case would know that, especially given their work histories.

Reprint 88111

Sally Seymour

The case of the mismanaged Ms.

It started out as one of those rare quiet mornings when I could count on having the office to myself. The Mets had won the World Series the night before, and most of the people in the office had celebrated late into the night at a bar across the street. I'm a fan too, but they all like to go to one of those bars where the waitresses dress like slave girls and the few women customers have to run a mine field of leers when they go to a ladies' room labeled "Heifers." Instead, I watched the game at home with my husband and escaped a hangover.

**Before I could say good morning,
she demanded to know what
business it was of the company
who she slept with and why.**

So I was feeling pretty good, if a little smug, when Ruth Linsky, a sales manager here at Triton, stormed past my secretary and burst into my office. Before I could say good morning, she demanded to know what business it was of the company who she slept with and why. I didn't know what she was talking about, but I could tell it was serious. In fact, she was practically on the verge of tears, but I knew she wasn't the type to fly off the handle.

Ruth had been with the company for three years, and we all respected her as a sensible and intelligent woman. She had been top in her class at business school and we recruited her hard when she graduated, but she didn't join us for a couple of years. She's since proved to be one of our best people in sales, and I didn't want to lose her. She fumed around the

Sally Seymour is on the faculty of the Harvard Business School, where she teaches management communication.

room for a while, not making much sense, until I talked her into sitting down.

"I've had it with this place and the way it treats women!" she shouted.

I allowed her to let off some more steam for a minute or two, and then I tried to calm her down. "Look, Ruth," I said, "I can see you're upset, but I need to know exactly what's going on before I can help you."

"I'm not just upset, Barbara," she said, "I'm damned mad. I came over to Triton because I thought I'd get more chances to advance here, and I just found out that I was passed over for director of the marketing division and Dick Simon got it instead. You know that I've had three outstanding years at the company, and my performance reviews have been excellent. Besides, I was led to believe that I had a pretty good shot at the job."

"What do you mean, 'led to believe'?"

"Steve heard through the grapevine that they were looking for a new marketing director, and he suggested I put in my name," she said. "He knows my work from when we worked together over at Forge Techtronics, and he said he'd write a letter in support. I wouldn't have even known they were looking for someone if Steve hadn't tipped me off."

Steve Baines is vice president of manufacturing. He's certainly a respected senior person in the company and he pulls some weight, but he doesn't have sole control of the marketing position. The hierarchy doesn't work that way, and I tried to get Ruth to see that. "Okay, so Steve wrote a letter for you, but he's only one of five or six VPs who have input in executive hiring decisions. Of course it helps to have his support, but lots of other factors need to be considered as well."

"Come off it, Barbara," Ruth snapped. "You know as well as I do there's only one thing that really matters around here and that's whether you're one of the boys. I've got a meeting this afternoon with my lawyer, and I'm going to file a sexual discrimination suit, a sexual harassment suit, and whatever other kind of suit she can come up with. I've had it with this old-boy crap. The only reason I'm here is that, as human resources director, you should know what's going on around here."

So the stakes were even higher than I had thought; not only did it look like we might lose Ruth, but we also might have a lawsuit on our hands. And to top it off, with the discrimination issue Ruth might be trying to get back at us for promoting Dick. I felt strongly about the importance of this legal remedy, but I also knew that using it frivolously would only undermine women's credibility in legitimate cases.

"Ruth," I said, "I don't doubt your perceptions, but you're going to need some awfully strong evidence to back them up."

"You want evidence? Here's your evidence. Number one: 20% of the employees in this company are women. Not one is on the board of directors, and not one holds an executive-level position. You and I are the only two in mid-level positions. Number two: there's no way for women to move into the mid-level positions because they never know when they're

---

Every time I go to a sales meeting, I feel like I've walked into a locker room.

---

available. When a vacancy comes up, the VPs—all men, of course—decide among themselves who should fill it. And then, over and over again I hear that some guy who hasn't worked half as hard as most of the women at his level has been given the plum. Number three: there are plenty of subtle and sometimes not-so-subtle messages around here that women are less than equal."

"Ruth, those are still pretty vague accusations," I interrupted. "You're going to have to come up with something more specific than feelings and suppositions."

"Don't worry, Barbara. Just keep listening and maybe you'll learn something about how this company you think so highly of operates. From the day Ed Coulter took over as vice president of marketing and became my boss, he's treated me differently from the male sales managers. Instead of saying good morning, he always has some comment about my looks— my dress is nice, or my hair looks pretty, or the color of my blouse brings out my eyes. I don't want to hear that stuff. Besides, he never comments on a guy's eyes. And then there's that calendar the sales reps have in their back office. Every time I go in there for a sales meeting, I feel like I've walked into a locker room."

So far, this all seemed pretty harmless to me, but I didn't want Ruth to feel I wasn't sympathetic. "To tell you the truth, Ruth, I'm not so sure all women here find compliments like that insulting, but

maybe you can give me other examples of discriminatory treatment."

"You bet I can. It's not just in the office that these things happen. It's even worse in the field. Last month Ed and I and Bill, Tom, and Jack went out to Dryden Industries for a big project meeting. I'll admit I was a little nervous because there were some heavy hitters in the room, so I kept my mouth shut most of the morning. But I was a team member and I wanted to contribute.

"So when Ed stumbled at one point, I spoke up. Well, it was like I had committed a sacrilege in church. The Dryden guys just stared at me in surprise, and then they seemed actually angry. They ignored me completely. Later that afternoon, when I asked Ed why I had gotten that reaction, he chuckled a little and explained that since we hadn't been introduced by our specific titles, the Dryden guys had assumed I was a research assistant or a secretary. They thought I was being presumptuous. But when Ed explained who I was, they admitted that I had made an important point.

"But that wasn't all," she went on. "The next day, when we explained to them that I would be interviewing some of the factory foremen for a needs assessment, one of the executives requested that someone else do it because apparently there's a superstition about women on the factory floor bringing bad luck. Have you ever heard of anything so stupid? But that's not the worst of it. Ed actually went along with it. After I'd pulled his bacon out of the fire the day before. And when I nailed him for it, he had the gall to say 'Honey, whatever the client wants, the client gets.'

"Well, we got the contract, and that night we all went out to dinner and everything was hurray for our team. But then, when I figured we'd all go back to the hotel for a nightcap, Ed and the guys just kind of drifted off."

"Drifted off?" I asked.

"Yeah. To a bar. They wanted to watch some basketball game."

"And you weren't invited?"

"I wasn't invited and I wasn't disinvited," she said. "They acted like they didn't know what to say."

By this point Ruth had cooled down quite a bit, and although she still seemed angry, she was forthright in presenting her case. But now her manner changed. She became so agitated that she got up from her chair to stare out the window. After a few minutes, she sort of nodded her head, as if she had come to some private, difficult decision, and then crossed the room to sit down again. Looking at her lap and twisting a paper clip around in her hands, she spoke so softly that I had to lean forward to hear her.

"Barbara," she began, "what I'm going to tell you is, I hope, in confidence. It's not easy for me to talk about this because it's very personal and private,

"If I have any say about it, when the history of this company is written, it will be a pack of lies."

but I trust you and I want you to understand my position. So here goes. When Steve Baines and I were both at Forge, we had a brief affair. I was discreet about it; it never interfered with business, and we ended it shortly after we both came to work here. But we're still very close friends, and occasionally we have dinner or a drink together. But it's always as friends. I think Ed found out about it somehow. The day after I notified the head office that I wanted to be considered for the director position, Ed called me into his office and gave me a rambling lecture about how we have to behave like ladies and gentlemen these days because of lawsuits on sexual harassment.

"At the time, I assumed he was referring somehow to one of our junior sales reps who had gotten drunk at the Christmas party and made a fool of himself with a couple of secretaries; but later I began to think that the cryptic comment was meant for me. What's more, I think Ed used that rumor about my relationship with Steve to block my promotion. And that, Barbara, is pure, sexist, double-standard hypocrisy because I can name you at least five guys at various levels in this company who have had affairs with colleagues and clients, and Ed is at the top of the list."

I couldn't deny the truth of Ruth's last statement, but that wasn't the point, or not yet. First I had to find out which, if any, of her accusations were true. I told her I needed some time and asked if she could give me a week before calling in a lawyer. She said no way. Having taken the first step, she was anxious to take the next, especially since she didn't believe things would change at Triton anyway. We dickered back and forth, but all I could get from her was a promise to hold off for 24 hours. Not much of a concession, but it was better than nothing.

Needless to say, I had a lot to think about and not very much time to do it in. It was curious that this complaint should come shortly after our organization had taken steps to comply with affirmative action policies by issuing a companywide memo stating that we would continue to recruit, employ, train, and promote individuals without regard to race, color, religion, sex, age, national origin, physical or mental handicap, or status as a disabled veteran or veteran of the Vietnam era. And we did this to prevent any problems in the future, not because we'd had trouble in the past. In fact, in my five years as HRM director, I'd never had a sexual discrimination or harassment complaint.

But now I was beginning to wonder whether there had never been grounds for complaint or whether the women here felt it was useless or even dangerous to complain. If it was the latter, how had I contributed to allowing that feeling to exist? And this thought led me to an even more uncomfortable one: Had I been co-opted into ignoring injustices in a system that, after all, did pretty well by me? Was I afraid to slap the hand that buttered my bread?

Questioning one's own motives may be enlightening, but it's also time consuming, and I had more pressing matters to deal with before I could indulge in what would likely be a painful self-analysis. I asked my secretary to find George Drake, CEO of Triton, and get him on the phone. In the meantime, I wrote down as much as I could remember of what Ruth had just told me. When George finally called, I told him I knew his schedule was full but we had an emergency of sorts on our hands and I needed an hour of his time this morning. I also asked that Ed Coulter be called into the meeting. George told me I had the hour.

When I got to George's office, Ed and George were already waiting. They were undoubtedly curious about why I had called this meeting, but as I've seen people do in similar situations, they covered their anxiety with chitchat about ball games and hangovers. I was too impatient for these rituals, so I cut the conversation short and told them that we were going to have a serious lawsuit on our hands in a matter of days if we didn't act very quickly. That got their attention, so I proceeded to tell Ruth's story. When I began, George and Ed seemed more surprised than anything else, but as I built up Ruth's case their surprise turned to concern. When I finished, we all sat in silence for I don't know how long and then George asked Ed for comments.

"Well, George," Ed said, "I don't know what to say. Ruth certainly was a strong contender for the position, and her qualifications nearly equaled Dick's, but it finally came down to the fact that Dick had the seniority and a little more experience in the industrial sector. When you've got two almost equally qualified candidates, you've got to distinguish them somehow. The decision came down to the wire, which in this case was six months seniority and a few more visits to factory sites."

"Were those the only criteria that made a difference in the decision?" George wanted to know.

"Well, not exactly. You know as well as I do that we base hiring decisions on a lot of things. On one hand, we look at what's on paper: years at the company, education, experience, recommendations. But we also rely on intuition, our feel for the situation. Sometimes, you don't know exactly why, but you just feel better about some people than others, and I've learned that those gut reactions are pretty reliable. The other VPs and I all felt good about Dick. There's something about him—he's got the feel of a winner. You know? He's confident—not arrogant—but solid and really sharp. Bruce had him out to the club a couple of times, and I played squash with him all last winter. We got to know him and we liked what we saw; he's a family man, kids in school here, could use the extra money, and is looking to stick around for a while. None of these things mean a lot by themselves, of course, but together they add up.

We've got lawsuits if we don't advance Dick and lawsuits if we don't advance Ruth.

"Don't get me wrong. I like Ruth too. She's very ambitious and one of our best. On the other hand, I can't say that I or any of the VPs know her as well as we know Dick. Of course, that's not exactly Ruth's fault, but there it is."

I had to be careful with the question I wanted Ed to respond to next because Ruth had asked for my confidence about the affair. I worded it this way: "Ed, did any part of your decision take into account Ruth's relationship with anyone else at the company?"

The question visibly disturbed Ed. He walked across the room and bummed a cigarette from me—he had quit last week—before answering: "Okay, I didn't want to go into this, but since you brought it up .... There's a rumor—well it's stronger than a rumor— that Ruth is more than professionally involved with Steve Baines—I mean she's having an, ah, sexual affair

with him. Now before you tell me that's none of my business, let me tell you about some homework I did on this stuff. Of course it's real tricky. It turns out there are at least two court cases that found sexual discrimination where an employer involved in a sexual relationship with an employee promoted that person over more qualified candidates.

"So here's what that leaves us with: we've got Steve pushing his girlfriend for the job. You saw the letter he wrote. And we've got Dick with seniority. So if we go with Ruth, what's to keep Dick from charging Steve and the company on two counts of sexual discrimination: sexual favoritism because Ruth is Steve's honey and reverse discrimination because we pass over a better qualified man just to get a woman into an executive position. So we're damned if we do and damned if we don't. We've got lawsuits if we don't advance Dick, and, so you tell me, lawsuits if we don't advance Ruth!"

We let that sink in for a few seconds. Then George spoke up: "What evidence do you have, Ed, that Steve and Ruth are having an affair?" he asked.

"Look, I didn't hire some guy to follow them around with a camera, if that's what you mean," Ed said. "But come on, I wasn't born yesterday; you can't keep that kind of hanky-panky a secret forever. Look at the way she dresses; she obviously enjoys men looking at her, especially Steve. In fact, I saw them having drinks together at Dino's the other night and believe me, they didn't look like they were talking business. All that on top of the rumors, you put two and two together."

Well, that did it for me. I'd been trying to play the objective observer and let Ed and George do all the talking, but Ed's last comment, along with some budding guilt about my own blindness to certain things at Triton that Ruth had pointed out, drove me out in the open. "Come off it, Ed," I said. "That's not evidence, that's gossip."

Now Ed turned on me: "Look," he shouted, "I didn't want to talk about this, but now that you've brought it up, I'll tell you something else. Even if we didn't have to worry about this sexual discrimination business, I still wouldn't back Ruth for the director's job." He calmed down a bit. "No offense, Barbara, but I just don't think women work out as well as men in certain positions. Human resources is one thing. It's real soft, person-to-person stuff. But factories are still a man's world. And I'm not talking about what I want it to be like. I'm talking facts of life.

"You see what happens when we send a woman out on some jobs, especially in the factories. To be any good in marketing you have to know how to relate to your client; that means getting to know him, going out drinking with him, talking sports, hunting, whatever he's interested in. A lot of our clients feel uncomfortable around a woman in business. They know how to relate to their wives, mothers, and girlfriends, but when a woman comes to the office and wants to talk a deal on industrial drills—well, they don't know what to do.

"And then there's the plain fact that you can't depend on a woman the way you can on a guy. She'll get married and her husband will get transferred, or she'll have a baby and want time off and not be able to go on the road as much. I know, Barbara, you probably think I'm a pig, or whatever women's libbers call guys like me these days. But from where I'm sitting, it just made good business sense to choose Dick over Ruth."

I saw them having drinks together, and they didn't look like they were talking business.

"Ed, I don't believe it," I said. "The next thing you'll tell me is that women ought to stay at home, barefoot and pregnant." There was a long silence after that—my guess was that I had hit on exactly what Ed thought. At least he didn't deny it. Ed stared at the rug, and George frowned at his coffee cup. I tried to steer the conversation back to the subject at hand, but it dwindled into another silence. George took a few notes and then told Ed he could go back to work. I assumed I was excused too, but as I started to leave, George called me back.

"Barbara, I'm going to need your help thinking through this mess," he said. "Of course we've got to figure out how we can avoid a lawsuit before the day is out, but I also want to talk about what we can do to avoid more lawsuits in the future. While Ed was talking I took some notes, and I've got maybe four or five points I think we ought to hash out. I'm not saying we're going to come up with all the answers today, but it'll be a start. You ready?"

"Shoot."

"Okay, let's do the big one first," he began. "What should I have done or not done to avoid this situation? I mean, I was just patting myself on the back for being so proactive when I sent out that memo letting everyone know the company policy on discrimination. I wrote it not thinking we had any problem at Triton. But just in case we did, I figured that memo would take care of it."

"Well, it looks like it's not enough just to have a corporate policy if the people in the ranks aren't on board. Obviously it didn't have much of an effect on Ed."

"So what am I supposed to do? Fire Ed?"

Being asked for my honest opinion by my CEO was a new experience for me and I appreciated it, but I wasn't going to touch that last question with a ten-foot pole. Instead I went on to another aspect: "And even if you get your managers behind you, your policy won't work if the people it's supposed to help don't buy it. Ruth was the first woman to complain around here. Are the others afraid to speak up? Or do they feel like Ed about a woman's place, or have husbands who do? Maybe they lack confidence even to try for better jobs, that is, if they knew about them."

"Okay," he said, "I'll admit that our system of having the VPs make recommendations, our 'old-boy network,' as Ruth called it, does seem to end up excluding women, even though the exclusion isn't intentional. And it's not obvious discrimination, like Ed's claim that Ruth is unqualified for a position because she is a woman. But wouldn't open job posting take away our right to manage as we see fit? Maybe we should concentrate instead on getting more women into the social network, make it an old boys' and old girls' club?"

"To tell you the truth, George, I don't much want to play squash with you," I replied, "but maybe we're getting off the subject. The immediate question seems to be how we're going to get more women into executive positions here, or, more specifically, do we give Ruth the director of marketing position that we just gave Dick?"

"On that score, at least, it seems to me that Ed has a strong argument," George said. "Dick is more qualified. You can't get around that."

I had wanted to challenge Ed on this point when he brought it up earlier, but I wasn't quite sure of myself then. Now that George was asking me for advice and seemed to be taking what I had to say seriously, I began to think that I might have something valuable to offer. So I charged right in. "George, maybe we're cutting too fine a line with this qualifications business. I know a lot of people think affirmative action means promoting the unqualified over the qualified to achieve balance. I think that argument is hogwash at best and a wily diversion tactic at worst. To my mind, Ruth and Dick are equally qualified, or equal enough. And wouldn't it make good business sense to get a diverse set of perspectives—women's, men's, blacks', whites'—in our executive group?"

"But isn't that reverse discrimination—not promoting Dick because he's a man? How would a judge respond to that? That's a question for a lawyer."

George leaned forward. "Let's talk about my last point, the one I think we've both been avoiding. What about this affair between Ruth and Steve? Boy, this is one reason why women in the work force are such trouble—no, just joking, Barbara, sorry about that. Look, I don't like lawsuits any more than anyone else, but I'd do anything to avoid this one. We'd be a laughing stock if it got out that Triton promoted unqualified people because they slept with the boss. I don't know how I'd explain that one to my wife."

"Look, George," I said, "in the first place, Dick's superior qualifications are debatable; in the second place, we have no proof that Ruth and Steve are involved in that way; and in the third place, what if they were once involved but no longer are? Does a past relationship condemn them for life? Isn't there a statute of limitations on that kind of thing, or are we going to make her put a scarlet letter on her briefcase? I thought these discrimination laws were supposed to protect women, but now it looks like a woman can be denied a promotion because someone thinks she's a floozy."

"Wait a second, Barbara. Don't make me look like such a prig," George said. "I realize that when men and women work together sexual issues are bound to crop up. I just don't know what I'm supposed to do about it, if anything. In some cases a woman may welcome a guy coming on to her, but what if it's her boss? And then there's that subtle stuff Ruth brought up – the calendar, dirty jokes, the male employees excluding women by going to bars to watch TV – and other women. And Ruth's treatment at that factory – how can we control our clients? I'm not sure these are things you can set policy on, but I am sure that I can't ignore them any longer."

And there we were. All the issues were on the table, and we had about 21 hours to make our decisions and act on them.

What would you do?

We asked the following business leaders – people who actually have to deal with such problems – how they would solve this dilemma. Here are their responses.

Donald J. Comeau *is corporate senior vice president of the Stop & Shop Companies, Inc., where he has served in a variety of positions since 1960.*

The facts indicate clear discriminatory practices.

It is clear that Triton's historical methods of hiring, developing, and ultimately promoting its people systematically discriminate against women. The mere issuance of a "policy statement" from the CEO without the proper training and understanding of the people who must carry out the policy is ludicrous. Triton has obviously made an attempt to bring in qualified, high-potential women but has paid no attention to integrating them into the old-boy network, and even less attention to evaluating their qualifications on a nondiscriminatory basis.

It's not unusual that these issues came to light as a result of a specific situation. As Triton brings more highly educated and trained women into the company, management must change its policies on development and promotion.

The facts as presented indicate clear discriminatory practices. Since a possible lawsuit is a real threat, Barbara and George's time should be spent deciding: how they will handle the decision to promote Dick ahead of Ruth, what steps must be taken to correct the practices that put them into this situation, and how to handle Ruth.

The decision to promote Dick must stand. To do otherwise would put Triton at risk of losing two very good people – Dick and Ruth. Reversing the decision, while it would make Ruth director of the marketing division, would also position her for failure. The organization would perceive the reversal to have occurred simply because she was a woman, not because of her qualifications and ability to do the job. Dick, on the other hand, might resign and/or file his own lawsuit.

George as CEO must institute an affirmative action plan that his office controls and follows up. It must be understood and practiced at all levels of the organization and be recognized as part of the company's business plan, on which managers are evaluated. Important elements in the plan must include but not be limited to:

Elimination of the old-boy network.

A promotion policy based on qualifications – perhaps a bid system or other nondiscriminatory method of judging abilities.

A comprehensive development program for all managers to immediately begin educating them in Triton's affirmative action plan, with ongoing follow-up sessions.

Individual counseling that addresses women in management and how to deal with the issues, for example, for people like Ed. In this case, an affair should only be a consideration when job performance is affected, and that applies equally to men and women.

Communication of the plan to all employees and clients.

Once the outline of this plan is put on paper, George and Barbara should sit with Ruth and talk with her about the following:

The decision on Dick and the reasons for going ahead with him as the new director of the marketing division.

Plans for revitalizing an affirmative action strategy.

Since Ruth obviously has some strong and constructive feelings about integrating women into Triton, offer her the opportunity to work directly with Barbara and George to develop and implement the revitalized affirmative action plan.

If after this discussion Ruth decides to file a lawsuit, then she should do so; the affirmative action plan, however, must be carried out.

Zoe Coulson, *the first woman corporate officer of Campbell Soup Company, is vice president—consumer issues. Previously, she held positions at the Good Housekeeping Institute, J. Walter Thompson, and Leo Burnett Company in Chicago, and Donnelley/Dun & Bradstreet in New York.*

It takes more than a memo to promote qualified women.

Women—and men—climbing career ladders need to recognize that so-called old-fashioned values, ethics, and morals still have credence. Many men and women heading today's major American companies and participating on boards of directors have been molded by another era; it is not surprising that they use their own standards when evaluating the personal traits of someone being considered for advancement.

In this case, Ruth's corporate accomplishments are not reported as exceptional to the man's; in fact, Dick "had seniority and a little more experience in the industrial sector," according to Ed, a vice president. Ed's subjective evaluations, however, seemed to be influenced by traditional views some men have about women; a woman working in industry may be unsettling to a man raised in a background where women only worked at home.

Since men like Ed make management decisions, it is essential for women with high corporate goals to recognize the corporation's customs as well as management's standards on personal characteristics, and act accordingly. After the successful team project, Ruth did not mention if each male specifically was invited to celebrate afterwards; it sounds as if a spontaneous team event happened and Ruth didn't "read" it. While some men also don't correctly evaluate such customs, women, who may be new to these environments, need to be especially aware.

Different corporations have different customs, and if a company's atmosphere is tightly traditional, people of high ambition should respond accordingly. In this case, when Ruth was employed in another company, she did not consider the implications of her personal actions (her affair with Steve) if she changed companies. But the custom of informal meetings between candidates and other officers was one of Ed's methods of evaluating promotability, and Ruth's "reputation" didn't encourage the informal interview custom. In today's world of corporate mergers and executive job changing, managers overlap between companies and, indeed, areas of the country, so implications can be far-reaching.

While the people in this case are in middle management, they should be aware that traditional values and customs are important to upper management in many of today's big companies. And top executives send down signals; how they act is how they expect their peers to act. They may not promote someone with entirely different customs from theirs.

Ruth commented that at the previous company her brief affair with Steve "was discreet; it never interfered with business, and we ended it." Her previous personal behavior introduced an issue.

This case does not state the marital status of these employees. As the legal counsel of a big corporation commented recently, "When a senior manager 'bends the rules' on one corporate policy, he sends a message that his employees apply to lots of rules," which can lead to staff dishonesty. Marriage, of course, is a legal contract, as well as a personal commitment; therefore, some corporate managers use fidelity as one criteria when promoting someone.

In another corporation, the chief executive officer was removed by his board of directors a few years ago because of an extramarital affair. In another company, an officer was asked to resign because of his approach to a secretary. In yet another, the president suggested to a divorced senior executive that he marry the woman with whom he was living; the board chairman was a traditionalist. The man married the woman and probably removed a concern of the board.

Since these situations have affected men's careers, women need to be doubly cautious. Meeting with a male business friend occasionally for a drink or dinner should cause no stir in today's world if the ambiance of the place is pleasant and if the couple's demeanor portrays friendship, not sex; many corporate cultures accept this. In other environments, however, even a meeting with a nonemployee date that might reveal sexual overtones should take place in private, or at least not in a public place where a "message" might be extended.

Since Ruth seems to be one of few women in her company, she is more visible than a man, whether she likes it or not. She needs to recognize that she is being reviewed at all times.

All this is not to say there is no problem. Even though George sent a policy statement to staff on affirmative action, women in this corporation are still at risk. It takes more than a memo to promote qualified women! Senior management could consider these and perhaps other steps to send strong signals to employees:

Should men be trained in reviewing women's qualifications?

Should there be special programs for all minorities on "keys to success"?

Can top officers become informal mentors to potential executive women – and men – so that they better understand the company's customs?

Should male managers be evaluated on their progress in promoting women?

Since Ruth has stated her dissatisfaction, in my opinion she has two courses of action. She could continue to execute her job as well as possible and avoid situations that might be misinterpreted by associates. Or she could go work for another company and learn its pattern at the beginning.

With more dedicated, educated women in the work force, some discriminatory beliefs about women's roles indeed will erode in the future. Women like Ruth, however, should learn now how to put themselves in the man's chair, to better understand and respect male values. Also, women who are achievers are setting examples for women who follow them, so they have another responsibility.

Top executives can make efforts to discuss their values (and practice them), so aspiring men and women managers can learn their scoring system.

It is to be hoped that Ruth will now understand the scorecard at her company better so that next time an opening occurs she will be judged with higher points.

R. Marilyn Lee *is corporate director of human resources for The Times Mirror Company. Before joining Times Mirror, she was a deputy city attorney for the city of Los Angeles.*

All employees should feel comfortable and have an equal chance to advance.

Triton is about to have its first sex discrimination and sexual harassment complaint. This case has it all – a predominantly male work force with an old-boy environment, a secretive promotion sys-

tem, a qualified woman loses a job to a qualified man, rumors of a personal relationship, sexual stereotypes, and good old-fashioned bias.

How did a nice company like Triton with a concerned CEO like George end up in a mess like this? From the facts given, it appears that Triton hasn't done well in keeping pace with a changing workplace. Women generally make up more than 45% of the nation's employees, yet Triton has only 20%, low for even an industrial setting. There are no women in the executive group at Triton and only two in middle management. From Ruth's perspective, the women at Triton are made uncomfortable by the good-old-boy atmosphere of talking sports and going to bars. Management has an antidiscrimination policy but apparently has taken no steps to make the work environment hospitable for all employees.

The case does not look good for Triton. Ed found Dick's and Ruth's qualifications to be nearly identical. The additional criteria that Ed considered – intuition, socializing with Dick at club events, Dick's being a family man who needed the extra money – were subjective at best and irrelevant at worst. Add Ed's belief that women don't belong in certain work settings, his discriminatory treatment of Ruth, and his hasty assumptions about Ruth's relationship with Steve, and this case could be a plaintiff lawyer's dream come true.

Can the problem be resolved in the next 24 hours? Probably not, but there is time for Barbara to review the facts and discuss options with George and Ed. Triton's legal department or outside lawyers should be consulted as management proceeds.

Here is one approach the company might take. Barbara could meet with Ruth the next day and explain that the company takes seriously her claims of discrimination. Let Ruth know that George has been briefed and has asked Barbara to immediately proceed with an investigation that will include more detailed interviews with Ruth, Ed, and others.

It would also be a good idea to find out what Ruth wants at this point. When she first saw Barbara, she was very upset. Barbara needs to find out if Ruth really would like to continue working for Triton, or have recent events soured that possibility? If the situation is salvageable, Barbara should ask Ruth to give the company time to do the right thing. (That does not mean giving her the disputed promotion. Since it appears that the company's selection of Dick has been announced, it would be unwise to reverse the decision and thereby create a second personnel dispute.)

Either Ruth will agree to work with the human resources manager on the complaint, or she will tell her that it has gone too far and she would rather go to court. Perhaps the prospect of a future promotion for Ruth can be suggested and discussed with George. In either event, the company should investigate her claim, take appropriate corrective action, and move forward with new personnel programs.

The long-term goal for Triton's management should be to open up the atmosphere so that all employees are comfortable and have an equal chance to advance. Some steps are quite simple.

First, an internal job posting procedure should be established. Promotional openings should not be communicated only through the grapevine. Job posting increases accountability in hiring decisions and encourages women and minorities to apply.

Second, supervisory training on equal opportunity and a diversified work force is clearly needed. Managers and supervisors should understand that offensive language and insensitive actions can create a hostile, discriminatory environment. Ruth's case contains several examples: calling her "honey," not introducing her on sales calls, not including her in social activities on business trips, and allowing locker-room calendars to be posted on office walls. Many men are genuinely surprised that some of these actions are offensive. A discussion between male and female colleagues, including suggested ways to handle travel assignments and introduce new employees, would help.

In addition, training can address sexual stereotyping. For instance, Ed assumes that a saleswoman would not relate well to a client in a factory setting because she may not talk about hunting or sports. Ruth has already shown that notion to be false because she is one of Triton's best salespeople. Ed also wrongly assumes that women leave jobs at a greater rate than men. Men tend to leave jobs just as often—for promotional opportunities, career changes, and, yes, even because their wives have been transferred to new jobs.

A good training program will also develop ways to deal with customers who seem to prefer a male account executive. Here Ed might have suggested to Dryden Industries that Ruth was one of Triton's top people and capable of doing the needs assessment, or that Ruth work with a man to do the survey more quickly.

Training can instill a better understanding of affirmative action and employment law generally. Ed, playing armchair lawyer, is confused about reverse discrimination. Selecting a qualified woman candidate over a qualified man is lawful when women are underrepresented in that job category—certainly the case at Triton.

Training classes could review Triton's employment data and identify the problem areas. Affirmative action hires and special attention to the promotion of women and minorities may be needed until the work force is more balanced. Once employees understand that concept, some of the anxiety about affirmative action is eased.

Ed will need some individual coaching since he obviously has strong opinions on this subject and may adversely influence others he supervises.

Third, Triton's management must show that its affirmative action policies have a clear direction. Issuing an antidiscrimination policy is fine but is a small piece of a larger pie. The company needs to take firm steps to increase the number of women in the general work force and in management.

A directive from the top is always the best way to start. George should meet with his vice presidents and convey his expectations: that they will increase the number of women employees in each department where women are underrepresented and establish programs to assure career development for women. George could make affirmative action goals a part of each executive's annual bonus plan and withhold payment if goals are not met. It is not surprising to find that those people who are good at meeting sales and other business goals become equally good at meeting affirmative action goals, once the company's commitment is made clear.

Last, the human resources department should become more involved with the promotion process. If Triton had well-defined affirmative action goals, Barbara could have advised Ed that all things being equal, Ruth should have been selected over Dick in order to diversify the director group. Promotional selection by a committee of vice presidents appears to be a holdover from the old days and does cloud the issue of who is actually making the promotional decision. Hence, Ruth's past affair with Steve is brought up even though Ruth, in marketing, does not have a direct reporting relationship to Steve, in production.

As Triton implements some of these long-range solutions, there will be plenty of questions and issues to address along the way. Barbara is perceptive to acknowledge that other women may also have complaints but may have been afraid to come forward. The issues are clearly under the surface, and it would be far better to take remedial action now before another "case of the mismanaged Ms." appears.

Joseph Posner *is a trial and appellate lawyer in the Los Angeles area. His practice concentrates on representing plaintiffs in wrongful firing and employee harassment cases.*

Coulter has to go.

Ed Coulter is going to cost this company some real money. Any way you look at it, the company is going to have to pay some big bucks to get out of the mess in which it finds itself and, perhaps more important, to prevent the same thing from happening in the future.

Apparently, Triton already gave Dick Simon the promotion to director of the marketing division. Even without considering the issue of reverse discrimination, the company can't very well take the promotion away from him. If it tried to do this, Dick would probably have a good lawsuit against the company without regard to whether the action constituted reverse discrimination. At least under California law, I think that he could sue and win.

When Ruth came into Barbara's office, she had more suspicions than facts. But her suspicions proved to be far more true than even Ruth probably realized. It is apparent to me that this company, which seems to be a fairly good-sized operation, has engaged in a systematic pattern of making it virtually impossible for a woman to receive any significant promotion. On the one hand, you had Ruth with an outstanding record, a sensible, intelligent person, and quite stable; the fact that she was provoked by this incident is not only understandable because of its gravity but it also shows the extreme impact on her.

Taken by itself, deciding to promote Dick or to promote Ruth to the director's job could probably each be defended, as they appear evenly matched. But when I see: (1) all the top jobs controlled by a tight group in the old-boy network and the openings not made known to others; (2) the situation at the customer's factory where Ed refused to back up Ruth by telling the customer that Ruth was the person in charge and had to do the interviewing; (3) the use of a mere suspicion about a subject which is none of Ed's business in the first place, i.e., Ruth's friendship with Steve; (4) Ed's admission that a factor in promotions is off-hours socializing at the country club (leading to the conclusion that off-hours socializing at the local bar is a part of business activities); (5) Ed's candid statement that he doesn't think women are good for certain jobs because they should stick to things that are in his words "real soft, person to person"; (6) his statement that women aren't dependable because of marriage, dependence on a husband, pregnancy, or the like—these factors all add up to the reality that the company did exactly what Ruth suspected it of doing.

In that connection, the other points, such as the fact that there is a pinup calendar in the sales room, don't carry a lot of weight with me. In a trial, these, however, as well as the most important factors I already mentioned, would certainly be something for the jury to think about.

In my opinion, Ed Coulter has to go. The company simply cannot afford to keep a man in his position with his attitudes and demonstrated actions. Perhaps a transfer could be arranged for him and/or a job found for him at another company or related entity. But one thing is for sure—the longer he is there, the more he is going to cost the company, if not today, then later.

Next, even George, the president, needs to have his consciousness raised. He is not in the same league with Ed, by any means, but he needs to realize that he has a problem, and he needs to do something about it. That would include calling together the five or six remaining vice presidents and laying the law down in no uncertain terms that the way people are selected for the top jobs is going to change, and change now. And then George has to monitor the situation to see that his subordinates do what he tells them.

This leaves us with the big question, what to do about Ruth, and this is a real dilemma. If Ruth were to sue, and if she ever could get testimony about the conversation in George's office, she would win in a walk. And since the company appears to have been selecting people for the top jobs this way for some time, I am willing to bet that there are more "Ruths" out there.

The company should think about a substantial monetary settlement with Ruth *right now*, whether she stays with Triton or not. Certainly, nothing should be said to her about leaving, and she should be promised that she would be the preferred candidate for the next slot that opens up. Moreover, Triton should look around to see if there are any such positions to which she could be promoted now. In addition, the company should think about doing some reorganization, if that is possible and makes good business sense. The one thing that Ruth will have to accept is the fact that Triton can't very well take back its promotion of Dick Simon.

T. Gary Rogers *is chairman of the board and chief executive officer of Dreyer's Grand Ice Cream, Inc. and director of several other corporations and associations.*

Put the responsibility for human resources where it belongs.

If George Drake were to ask me for advice on dealing with the issues raised by the Ruth Linsky controversy at Triton, I would offer him the following five observations:

1   Triton's policy is equal opportunity, and Ruth hasn't had it yet. Affirmative action has to be more than a toothless memo. Equal opportunity in hiring means the person with the best *relevant* qualifications (more on that below) gets the job. Triton has an obligation to let its people know when an opening occurs and to interview any applicants from within the company who may be qualified. Because minorities and women *are* often discriminated against in hiring decisions, Triton must be especially careful to ensure such candidates for promotion a fair opportunity to present their credentials and make their case. Ruth clearly deserved an interview for this job, but

she did not really get one, and this must be remedied immediately.

2 The relevant qualifications are only those related to job effectiveness. Triton's first responsibility is to its shareholders. Its managers should be selected on the basis of their ability to further the company's goals and maximize its earnings. In choosing between Ruth Linsky and Dick Simon for director of the marketing division, only factors that affect job performance in that role should pertain. Ruth's relationship with Steve Baines is irrelevant unless it somehow affects her ability to perform the job. The assertion that she will get married and move or want time off to have a family is not germaine unless those really are her plans. Similarly, Dick's being a family man, or needing a raise, or playing squash obviously should not enter into the equation.

On the other hand, it *is* appropriate to consider that a director of marketing in the industrial drill business has to deal and be effective with many types of men, including some who have deep-seated (albeit unfair) prejudices toward women in business. Triton has no obligation to change the culture of its industry and has to be realistic about the skills and attitudes its managers require to cope effectively within that culture. Therefore, it *is* appropriate to compare Ruth and Dick in terms of their maturity, experience, and demonstrated ability to function in what is largely a "man's world," even though that requirement poses a much tougher challenge for Ruth than it does for Dick.

3 Let Ed Coulter make the decision, but require him to explain his thinking. Ed is charged with responsibility for marketing at Triton and has the right and duty to select the management team for his department. If Ed wants the advice of the other vice presidents, that's fine, but the final decision should be his responsibility alone—not that of a committee. In making his decision, however, Ed must comply with the company's affirmative action program and be able to satisfy his boss that he has done so.

Given the sensitivity of this matter and the questions about Ed's understanding of the issues, George should have a long talk with Ed about equal opportunity, relevant hiring criteria, and the law. At the end of this discussion, George should ask Ed to interview Ruth with an open mind, reconsider his decision, and then come back and share his thinking with George. In his conversation with Ed, George should be careful to have Ed understand that he is not campaigning for Ruth but only ensuring that she receive fair consideration as an applicant for the job.

4 Don't let potential lawsuits affect your business decisions. The real issue for George is whether Triton's policies and practices comply with his desires (and the law) on an ongoing basis. If they do, George should assume Triton will prevail, if sued. Unfortunately, defending lawsuits, particularly in the personnel arena, has become a cost of doing business, even for the best-managed companies. If George is satisfied that Triton is acting appropriately, then he should not let Ruth's threat of legal action affect his thinking—except, perhaps, as an indication of immaturity or poor judgment on her part.

5 Consider reassigning human resources responsibilities at Triton. The first and most important responsibility of any manager is for his (or her) human resources, and good managers will demand direct control over the hiring, training, motivating, and developing of their people. Triton appears to exhibit a problem common to many companies with a high-profile human resources department—management has abrogated much of its most important responsibility. Triton's managers should understand, be thinking about, and be experienced with the subtleties of equal opportunity and other people-related issues. At Triton, it appears the human resources department "takes care of that."

For example, it would have been much more appropriate and efficient for Ruth to take her complaint directly to Ed—or to George, if necessary—rather than to the human resources department. Choosing properly between Ruth Linsky and Dick Simon requires integrating judgments about job requirements, industry culture, and individual capabilities. If Ed Coulter is qualified for his job, he should be able to make these judgments appropriately without help from a staff department. If Ed cannot be trusted to do this, he should be replaced. George should reduce the role of his corporate staff in personnel matters to only technical support and record keeping and put the responsibility for human resources where it belongs—squarely in the hands of his managers. ▽

Reprint 87614

Dominion-Swann management acquires technology to support employees — or control them?

The Case of the Omniscient Organization

by Gary T. Marx

The following is an excerpt from Dominion-Swann Industries' 1995 Employee Handbook. DS is a $1 billion diversified company, primarily in the manufacture of electrical components for automobiles. This section of the handbook was prepared by the corporate director of personnel, in consultation with the human resource management firm Sciex-Plan Inc.

Dominion-Swann's new workplace: Hope for industry through technology

We are a technology-based company. We respect our employees, whose knowledge is the core of the technological enterprise. We care about the DS community. We value honesty, informed consent, and un-fettered scientific inquiry. Our employees understand company strategy. They are free to suggest ways to improve our performance. We offer handsome rewards for high productivity and vigorous participation in the life of our company. Committed to science, we believe in careful experimentation and in learning from experience.

Since 1990, we have instituted changes in our work environment. The reasons for change were clear enough from the start. In 1990, DS faced an uncertain future. Our productivity and quality were not keeping pace with overseas competition. Employee turnover was up, especially in the most critical part of our business—automotive chips, switches, and modules. Health costs and work accidents were on the rise. Our employees were demoralized. There were unprecedented numbers of thefts from plants and offices and leaks to competitors about current research. There was also a sharp rise in drug use. Security personnel reported unseemly behavior by company employees not only in our parking lots and athletic fields but also in restaurants and bars near our major plants.

In the fall of 1990, the company turned to SciexPlan Inc., a specialist in employee-relations management in worldwide companies, to help de-velop a program for the radical re-structuring of the work environment. We had much to learn from the corporate cultures of overseas competitors and were determined to benefit from the latest advances in work-support technology. The alternative was continued decline and, ultimately, the loss of jobs.

Frankly, there was instability while the program was being developed and implemented. Some valued employees quit and others took early retirement. But widespread publicity about our efforts drew to the program people who sincerely sought a well-ordered, positive environment. DS now boasts a clerical, professional, and factory staff which understands how the interests of a successful company correspond with the interests of individual employees. To paraphrase psychologist William James, "When the community dies, the individual withers." Such sentiments, we believe, are as embedded in Western traditions as in Eastern; they are the foundation of world community. They are also a fact of the new global marketplace.

The fundamentals

Since 1990, productivity per worker is up 14%. Sales are up 23%, and the work force is down 19%. Employees' real income is up 18%, due in large part to our bonus and profit-sharing plans. Many of these efficiencies can be attributed to reform of our factories' production technologies. But we can be proud to have been ahead of our time in the way we build our corporate spirit and use social technologies.

At DS four principles underlie work-support restructuring:

1. Make the company a home to employees. Break down artificial and alienating barriers between work and home. Dissolve, through company initiative, feelings of isolation. Great companies are made by great people; all employee behavior and self-development counts.

Gary T. Marx is professor of sociology at Massachusetts Institute of Technology. He is author of Undercover: Police Surveillance in America *(University of California Press, 1988).*

2. Hire people who will make a continuing contribution. Bring in people who are likely to stay healthy and successful, people who will be on the job without frequent absences. Candor about prospective employees' pasts may be the key to the company's future.

3. Technical, hardware-based solutions are preferable to supervision and persuasion. Machines are cheaper, more reliable, and fairer than managers. Employees want to do the right thing; the company wants nothing but this and will give employees all the needed technical assistance. Employees accept performance evaluation from an impartial system more readily than from a superior and appreciate technical solutions that channel behavior in a constructive direction.

4. Create accountability through visibility. Loyal employees enjoy the loyalty of others. They welcome audits, reasonable monitoring, and documentary proof of their activities, whether of location, business conversations, or weekly output. Once identified, good behavior can be rewarded, inappropriate behavior can be improved.

These principles have yielded an evolving program that continues to benefit from the participation and suggestions of our employees. The following summary is simply an introduction. The personnel office will be pleased to discuss any aspect of community performance or breaches of company policy in detail with employees. (You may call for an appointment during normal business hours at X-2089.)

Entry-level screening

As a matter of course and for mutual benefit, potential employees are screened and tested. We want to avoid hiring people whose predictive profile—medications, smoking, obesity, debt, high-risk sports, family crises—suggests that there will be serious losses to our community's productivity in the future.

Job applicants volunteer to undergo extensive medical and psychological examinations and to provide the company with detailed personal information and records, including background information about the health, lifestyle, and employment of parents, spouses, siblings, and close friends. Company associates seek permission to make discreet searches of various databases, including education, credit, bankruptcy and mortgage default, auto accident, driver's license suspension, insurance, health, worker's compensation, military, rental, arrest, and criminal activity.

The company opposes racial and sexual discrimination. DS will not check databases containing the names of union organizers or those active in controversial political causes (whether on the right or the left). Should the company's inquiry unwittingly turn up such information, it is ignored. We also use a résumé verification service.

Since our community is made up of people, not machines, we have found it useful to compare physiological, psychological, social, and demographic factors against the profiles of our best employees. Much of this analysis has been standardized. It is run by SciexPlan's expert system, INDUCT.

Community health

We want employees who are willing to spend their lives with the company, and we care about their long-term health. The company administers monthly pulmonary tests in behalf of the zero-tolerance smoking policy. Zero tolerance means lower health insurance premiums and improved quality of life for all employees.

In cooperation with Standar-Hardwick, one of the United States's most advanced makers of medical equipment and a valued customer, we've developed an automated health monitor. These new machines, used in a private stall and activated by employee thumbprint, permit biweekly urine analysis and a variety of other tests (blood pressure, pulse, temperature, weight) without the bother of having to go to a health facility. This program has received international attention: at times, it has been hailed; at times, severely criticized. People at DS often express surprise at the fuss. Regular monitoring of urine means early warning against diabetes and other potentially catastrophic diseases—and also reveals pregnancy. It also means that we can keep a drug-free, safe environment without subjecting people to the in-

DRAWINGS BY CHUCK MORRIS

dignities of random testing or the presence of an observer.

The quality environment

Drawing on SciexPlan's research, our company believes that the physical environment is also important to wellness and productivity. Fragrant aromas such as evergreen may reduce stress; the smell of lemon and jasmine can have a rejuvenating effect. These scents are introduced to all work spaces through the air-conditioning and heating systems. Scents are changed seasonally.

Music is not only enjoyable to listen to but can also affect productivity. We continually experiment with the impact of different styles of music on an office's or plant's aggregate output. Since psychologists have taught us that the most serious threat to safety and productivity is stress, we use subliminal messages in music such as "safety pays," "work rapidly but carefully," and "this company cares." Personal computers deliver visual subliminals such as "my world is calm" or "we're all on the same team."

At the start of each month, employees are advised of message content. Those who don't want a message on their computers may request that none be transmitted—no questions asked. On the whole, employees who participate in the program feel noticeably more positive about their work. Employees may borrow from our library any one of hundreds of subliminal tapes, including those that help the listener improve memory, reduce stress, relax, lose weight, be guilt-free, improve self-confidence, defeat discouragement, and sleep more soundly.

On the advice of SciexPlan's dieticians, the company cafeteria and dining room serve only fresh, wholesome food prepared without salt, sugar, or cholesterol-producing substances. Sugar- and caffeine-based, high-energy snacks and beverages are available during breaks, at no cost to employees.

Work monitoring

Monitoring system performance is our business. The same technologies that keep engines running at peak efficiency can keep the companies that make engine components running efficiently too. That is the double excitement of the information revolution.

At DS, we access more than 200 criteria to assess productivity of plant employees and data-entry personnel. These criteria include such things as the quantity of keystroke activity, the number of errors and corrections made, the pressure on the assembly tool, the speed of work, and time away from the job. Reasonable productivity standards have been established. We are proud to say that, with a younger work force, these standards keep going up, and the incentive pay of employees who exceed standards is rising proportionately.

Our work units are divided into teams. The best motivator to work hard is the high standards of one's peers. Teams, not individuals, earn prizes and bonuses. Winning teams have the satisfaction of knowing they are doing more than their share. Computer screens abound with productivity updates, encouraging employees to note where their teams stand and how productive individuals have been for the hour, week, and month. Computers send congratulatory messages such as "you are working 10% faster than the norm" or messages of concern such as "you are lowering the team average."

Community morale

There is no community without honesty. Any community must take reasonable precautions to protect itself from dishonesty. Just as we inspect the briefcases and purses of visitors exiting our R&D division, the company reserves the right to call up and inspect without notice all data files and observe work-in-progress currently displayed on employees' screens. One random search discovered an employee using the company computer to send out a curriculum vitae seeking employment elsewhere. In another, an employee was running a football pool.

Some companies try to prevent private phone calls on company time by invading their employees' privacy. At DS, encroachments on employees' privacy are obviated by telecommunications programs that block inappropriate numbers (dial-a-joke, dial-a-prayer) and unwanted incoming calls. In addition, an exact record of all dialing behavior is recorded, as is the number from which calls are received. We want our employees to feel protected against any invalid claims against them.

Video and audio surveillance too protects employees from intruders in hallways, parking lots, lounges, and work areas. Vigilance is invaluable in protecting our community from illegal behavior or actions that violate our safety and high commitment to excellence. All employees, including managers, check in and out of various workstations—including the parking lot, main entrance, elevator, floors, office, and even the bathroom—by means of an electronic entry card. In one case, this surveillance probably saved the life of an employee who had a heart attack in the parking lot: when he failed to check into the next workstation after five minutes, security personnel were sent to investigate.

Beyond isolation

Our program takes advantage of the most advanced telecommunications equipment to bind employees to one another and to the company. DS vehicles are equipped with on-board computers using satellite transponders. This offers a tracking service and additional two-way communication. It helps our customers keep inventories down and helps prevent hijacking, car theft, and improper use of the vehicles. Drivers save time since engines are checked electronically. They also drive more safely, and vehicles are better maintained since speed, gear shifts, and idling time are measured.

In addition to locator and paging devices, all managers are given fax machines and personal computers for their homes. These are connected at all times. Cellular telephones are provided to selected employees who commute for more than half an hour or for use while traveling.

Instant communication is vital in today's international economy. The global market does not function only from 9 to 5. Modern technology can greatly increase productivity by ensuring instant access and communication. Periodic disruptions to vacations or sleep are a small price to pay for the tremendous gains to be won in worldwide competition. DS employees share in these gains.

Great companies have always unleashed the power of new technology for the social welfare, even in the face of criticism. During the first industrial revolution, such beloved novelists as Charles Dickens sincerely opposed the strictures of mass production. In time, however, most of the employees who benefited from the wealth created by new factories and machines came to take progress for granted and preferred the modern factory to traditional craft methods. Today we are living through a Second Industrial Revolution, driven by the computer.

Advanced work-support technology is democratic, effective, and anti-hierarchical. DS's balance sheet and the long waiting list of prospective employees indicate how the new program has helped everybody win. To recall the phrase of journalist Lincoln Steffens, "We have been over into the future, and it works." We are a company of the twenty-first century.

HBR's cases are derived from the experiences of real companies and real people. As written, they are hypothetical, and the names used are fictitious.

Dominion-Swann Industries wants its employees to be productive, happy, and safe. Are they?

Four experts on technology and human resource management discuss Dominion-Swann's work-support technology.

Nothing is wrong with Dominion-Swann's admirable goals except their priority.

Like many companies, Dominion-Swann seeks to protect and maximize two vital resources critical to its ongoing success: the vast investment of the company in technology

JOSEPH MODEROW *is senior vice president and general counsel of United Parcel Service. He also serves on UPS's Technology Steering Committee.*

and its employees. Nothing is wrong with these admirable goals except their priority. People come second at DS, even in the handbook title which points to technology as the hope for industry and the centerpiece of Dominion-Swann's new workplace.

DS management informs employees that necessary changes in the work environment have been instituted and justifies these changes with a trail of failures rather than a vision of success. But it lacks the curiosity—not to mention wisdom—to explore the causes of its workers' demoralized state.

Despite DS's disturbing actions, competitive companies do have the right to determine, direct, and even measure how employees perform their responsibilities. Anyone who has seen recent UPS commercials will likely identify us with the phrase "We run the tightest ship in the shipping business." When you observe the urgency and determination of our delivery drivers, you may be led to believe that we achieved such efficiency through a corporate culture like that of DS. That is not the case. UPS succeeds because of its conviction that control and efficiency must not be achieved at the cost of employee commitment.

Much of UPS's success is attributable to continuous effort to optimize the efficient use and allocation of people, facilities, equipment, and technology. We do utilize work measurement programs in which drivers are given specific quantitative goals to achieve. This is a valuable tool in properly allocating resources and reflects the fundamental philosophy of "A fair day's wage for a fair day's work." This scientific management is, however, balanced by our commitment to communications programs that allow for an open exchange with employees on matters affecting the work environment, including direct participation in forming and applying company policies.

The DS handbook is not the basic product of managers addressing the needs of the employees they work with; it is primarily the product of a consulting firm charged with developing a "radical restructuring of the work environment." This clinical work follows a well-organized but unjustified pattern. Each instituted change is preceded by an explanation intended to gain employees' understanding and consensus on the action taken. Theft is a problem; therefore the solution is employee monitoring. Poor attitudes have adversely affected production; therefore scents, music, and subliminal messages will alter the workers' perspective of the work environment. Closer scrutiny of any of the justifications reveals obvious self-serving motives for the imposed practices that undermine Dominion-Swann's credibility.

There are three underlying themes in the handbook that undermine its long-term viability as a workable tool to affect employee attitudes and conduct positively.

1. The handbook attempts to establish a model whereby existing and future employees will fit neatly into a "scientifically" developed mold. The baseline of this mold is the "physiological, psychological, social, and demographic factors" of DS's *best* employees, as determined by Sciex-Plan's expert INDUCT system. Such standardization does not allow sufficient latitude for a diverse work force where creativity can flourish. Corporate mavericks – not corporate clones – bring vitality and diversity to managerial work.

2. The scope of the handbook is particularly disturbing. There seems to be no limit to the areas of an employee's life that are not invaded by personnel practices. On the job, there is continuous monitoring and surveillance of virtually every movement. The camera watches even in the lounge. Leaving work does not provide the refuge of privacy either. Employees are required to be "connected at all times" to the company through the umbilical cord of paging devices, fax machines, and personal computer modems. Disruptions of vacations and sleep become part of the norm in the company's quest for competitive gain. With ever-tightening standards of performance and personal conduct, both on and off the job, a diminishing portion of employees will be able to "measure up," resulting in eroding morale and, probably, open challenges to the strict employment practices and rules.

3. Finally, and most troubling, is the removal of the human element of management and evaluation. This principle is clearly enunciated in the handbook, which establishes that "technical, hardware-based solutions are preferable to supervision and persuasion." It goes on to conclude that "machines are fairer than managers." While we must admit to a computer's edge in accuracy, can we accept that machines make fairer evaluations of people than people do? I think not.

In the final analysis, we are all human and make mistakes, especially when measured with unrelenting scrutiny against the strictest of standards. Under such conditions, I want someone managing me who shares some of my own human frailties and imperfections. A machine suffers only mechanical failures but lacks the spark of human imagination.

Dominion-Swann already exists. Some elements of its organizational strategy have been practiced for over 100 years.

SHOSHANA ZUBOFF *is associate professor at the Harvard Business School and author of* In the Age of the Smart Machine: The Future of Work and Power *(Basic Books, 1988).*

The future creeps in on small feet. Change in the contours of lives and things is incremental and fragmented. We do not awaken suddenly to a brave new world. Ten years ago, our lives *were* different – no PCs, no fax machines. But even as these inventions and the uses we put them to renovate our world, we continue to wake up in the same beds, drive the same routes to work, and look forward to turkey on Thanksgiving. In consequence, the future gets away with a lot, making itself at home in our lives before we've had a chance to say no thank you.

Dominion-Swann Industries sounds like a futuristic workplace, where life is saturated with comput-ers that measure everything from your productivity to your heartbeat, where dreams of a perfectly ordered, clockwork world, shorn of human conflict, can come true. But DS already exists. Its technology strategy is widely adhered to. Some elements of its organizational strategy have been practiced for over 100 years. Others have been implemented and perfected throughout the 1980s.

Dominion-Swann of 1995 rose from the ashes of its managers. Somehow, its managers had lost their authority. There appears to have been, in the late 1980s, a rupture in their relationship with the work force. This was probably because maintaining constructive relationships with workers is demanding. It requires the kind of face-to-face interaction that builds trust, shared values, and reciprocity.

The failure of authority at DS is clear from the symptoms that have made it into the official history – and note that it is the symptoms that were reported, not their causes. Thus we are told about falling levels of productivity, quality, and morale. Employee turnover was on the rise, as were accidents, theft, drug use, and "unseemly behavior."

What to do when authority fails? How do those in power ensure that their commands will be obeyed if they detect that others may doubt their right to leadership? What good is a command if no one takes it seriously? Let's look at the options DS management faced back in 1990. It could have thrown in the towel, liquidated its assets, been taken over. Or it could have chosen to renew and reinvigorate management's authority by creating a workplace based on a new sharing of knowledge and power, where people are entrusted to do the work they know best, and managers are educators, guiding the development of value creation. It could have shown some faith in human beings, could have striven for growth and learning in every employee. It could have demonstrated its belief in the enterprise of management and in the skills and untapped wisdom of the managerial group.

In 1990, there was a growing number of corporate models for such an approach, as many businesses throughout the United States, Europe, and Japan achieved unprecedented economic success pioneering new, more progressive and humane forms of organization – setting new standards for quality, service, and the development of human potential. We will never know why DS leaders chose not to take this approach, but we can guess. Such an approach takes leaders who confront problems when they see them, who believe that human ingenuity and integrity, combined with technical prowess, are our last, best hope for sustained competitiveness.

Instead, DS managers decided that the key to renewal lay in information technology and in so doing tapped into an ancient response to the age-old problem of failed leadership. DS's managers, like other rulers before them, established techniques of control as a fail-safe system to guard against the frailties of their uncertain authority. Feudal kings used to take hostages from a noble's family, just in case he might want to raise a fuss over paying taxes. States employ radar traps, in case someone doesn't obey a speed limit. It was for just such a purpose that DS turned to information technology. As their handbook puts it: "Technical hardware-based solutions are preferable to supervision and persuasion." The means are at hand to shape behavior through monitoring, surveillance, and detection without even the slightest managerial effort.

Technology itself is not to blame for this state of affairs. In fact, information technologies, which represent a radical discontinuity in industrial history, could well lead to more reciprocity in the workplace, not less. Earlier generations of machines were designed to do essentially what human bodies could, only faster, more reliably, and at less cost. With machines, work required less human intervention and, overall, fewer human skills. This process has come to be known as automation. The ideal of automation is the self-diagnosing, self-correcting machine system that runs perfectly without human assistance.

Information technology can be used to automate all sorts of work in factories and offices. But unlike other tools of automation, information technology simultaneously registers data about the conversion processes it governs. Take the example of an industrial robot. It looks like a classic piece of automation, but the same microprocessors embedded in the robot that tell it what to do are also registering data about its activities. That slice of the production process is logged in a very precise way, as the robot supplies data on dozens of variables that could never have been defined or measured without it.

Multiply this effect across a highly automated manufacturing process and what you get is not only a complex machine system doing its job *but also an enormous, dynamic, fluid electronic text*, displayed on video screens and in computer printouts, full of numbers, charts, words, and symbols that portray total plant functioning in a way that never existed – indeed, never could have been imagined – before. The same effect is present in the office environment where we see connections being made between transaction systems, communication systems, management information systems, financial systems, customer and supplier systems, EPOS systems, scanner systems, and imaging systems.

As the time frames in which data are collected and presented become more accelerated, as more sectors of data are integrated, and as access to the systems becomes more widely distributed, the business is rendered transparent, as never before, through a dynamic electronic text. Moreover, anybody with the wit to access the data can discern patterns and dynamics, anticipate problems and opportunities, and make connections.

When information technology works to create this new kind of transparency, it is doing far more than automating – it is performing a second function that I call *informating*. The informated business invites the whole work force to think strategically.

All of which brings us back to Dominion-Swann. For the potential of the informated workplace to be fulfilled, two conditions are critical: an organizational strategy that emphasizes learning and a leadership vision that understands how technology and the organization are integrated to generate more participatory approaches to value creation. The informated business redistributes authority, turns managers into educators, and devolves responsibility on those at the front line of the organization to use information quickly and creatively, where and when it counts.

Has DS created transparency? You bet. But transparency of what? For what? The short answer is transparency of human behavior for the purposes of total control. DS has tapped into the technology's informating power: almost every aspect of employee performance and behavior has been translated into and is displayed in the form of electronic data. But it is a transparency that allows unseen senior managers (the few who survived the demise of management) to monitor and control people and processes down to the tiniest detail, to shape behavior by recording everything and detecting all variances.

Does DS represent a brave new world of organizational trends? Ask Jeremy Bentham, who founded the utilitarian movement at the turn of nineteenth century, and also worried about the unproductive and "unseemly" behavior of workers, paupers, and convicts. Bentham conceived the "Panopticon," a polygonal structured prison-factory, consisting of a central tower from which rows of glass-walled cells emanated. With the use of mirrors fixed around the center tower, it was possible for an observer to see into each cell while remaining invisible to the cells' inhabitants. ("Universal transparency" was the term he liked.)

The assurance of permanent visibility, Bentham thought, would elicit "good behavior" from the inmates. The architecture itself was the guarantee of conformity. It promised observation but eliminated any way for workers or convicts to know for sure if they were being watched. In much the same way, DS relies on the certainty of panoptic power. Transparency is achieved, not through the architecture of a building but rather through the architecture of information systems. In DS language, this is "accountability through visibility." All optimum solutions are decided a priori by the few remaining managers. The only real challenges, they think, are to find a docile work force and design systems that will monitor everything.

In the end, the British government refused to build the Panopticon, and paid Bentham off—some £23,000. Dominion-Swann might have done better to pay off SciexPlan, for as history shows, most people will not remain docile for long. In subtle ways, they begin to develop techniques of defense as countermeasures to the techniques of control with which they must contend. For example, those knowledgeable about software will attempt to confound the systems operations in several ways. They may try to block the system's ability to monitor their behavior or attempt to "snow the computer" by finding ways to alter data traveling upward in the organization. Those with fewer computer skills are more likely to practice passive resistance. They will simply ignore what the computer tells them or blame it when their performance is not up to standard.

For others, the pressure of visibility is enough to reorganize behavior at its roots. Their coping strategy is what I call "anticipatory conformity." These employees so want to avoid the embarrassment of being singled out as a source of variance that they will go out of their way to conform to standards rather than risk detection. Don't count on these employees to figure out how to solve a customer's problem or initiate an improvement in the production process. They are simply too fearful to take any risks.

Finally, there is the intimidating rush of "objective" data about their work with which employees cannot argue and which, at times, they do not even understand. An individual's views count for less than the force of truth that shines through all these real-time facts.

Some humility is, of course, necessary for learning. But humiliation will cause people to give up. Don't count on these employees to detect errors or anticipate problems. It's not that they have stopped thinking but rather that they have ceased to value what they think.

Are things at Dominion-Swann as rosy as they seem? We have only the word of DS managers. And, for all we know, the handbook was itself written by consultants.

DS has failed to capitalize on the full potential offered by its investment in automation.

BILL HOWARD *is vice president of information technology at Bechtel Corporation.*

The date on Dominion-Swann's handbook should read 1895, not 1995. Rather than a company of the twenty-first century, DS brings to mind an organization firmly rooted in the first industrial revolution, one that has applied twenty-first century technology to nineteenth century management practice. Computers are used in much the same way as the tools of the late nineteenth and twentieth centuries: to monitor, audit, replace, deskill, and dehumanize staff and supervision, rather than to empower workers and management to realize a quantum leap in productivity.

In its effort to make the company a home to employees, DS has used computers and telecommunications to produce the modern-day equivalent of the company town or the company store. Every move is logged, monitored, and evaluated—even the bathroom at work and the bedroom at home. Privacy and individualism are severely impaired. The company uses technology to tie the employee to the company but fails to use technology to stimulate individuals to greater creativity and productivity.

The entry-level screening and community health programs capitalize on the vast amounts of information in databases around the country and the capabilities of medical monitoring equipment. DS is pushing the limits of society's tolerance for this type of inquiry and information gathering. It appears to be effective for DS, but management should not be surprised when market opportunities are missed and increasing legislative restrictions in this area of inquiry and discrimination start to appear. And, by its careful selection techniques, DS creates a mediocre and homogeneous group of followers. It also misses the opportunity to include the ideas and values of those creative contributors who fall outside the norm.

Teamwork and suggestions by employees for improved performance are encouraged by DS. But my perception of the DS team is more like a swim team made up of individual performers trying for "personal bests" to aggregate the maximum team score rather than the highly successful work team of the 1990s, which operates more like a basketball team made up of skilled performers who improvise together to capitalize on opportunities as they arise. Interaction is more important than the sum of the individual player's actions. A supervisor serves as the coach rather than as the commander.

For Dominion-Swann to fully exploit the potential of the latest advances in work-support technology, I would suggest.

1. Establish a dialogue among the human resource department, the information technology organization,

and representatives of all parts of the company affected by the use of information technology to sort out which systems enhance productivity and which systems or practices should be modified or abandoned because they induce fear or privacy concerns. All new systems should be planned and implemented with employees' involvement.

2. Use information technology to enhance the power of the individual to participate and to contribute his or her ideas to work rather than simply as monitoring tools. Promote interactive discussions and analysis in a team environment with participation of multiple disciplines at various levels of the organization. Develop systems that allow management to serve as coach or mentor rather than critic or enforcer.

3. Use information technology to establish closer links with business partners outside the company. Extend the reach of DS to a broader team concept that includes suppliers and the all-important customer.

4. Design systems to span across functional boundaries so that teams can be organized electronically to solve problems and contribute to productivity.

5. Train, train, train employees in the use of information systems, and use technology to enhance training so that workers and supervisors can fully understand and buy into delivering the full potential offered by the technology.

6. Encourage a new leadership model that is attuned to technology and that recognizes the need to change the organization and processes to match the tools of the twenty-first century. Identify managers who recognize the interdependence of the various business units and operating functions and who can bridge those boundaries to deliver crossfunctional solutions. Automating old processes and functions without taking into account the powerful capability of the new tools assures that the anticipated payback will not be realized.

7. Continue to reward performance of teams rather than individuals, provide technology to key players to eliminate the barriers of time and distance, encourage healthful lifestyles, reduce middle management layers that merely serve as switches and filters, assure that the company strategy continues to be understood at all levels.

8. Fire SciexPlan, Inc.

Some may be impressed with the five-year gains in worker productivity, employee income, and sales. However, in my view, sales, productivity, and performance in all areas must be measured against the best performers in industry to ensure maintaining a competitive position. I believe Dominion-Swann has failed to capitalize on the full potential offered by its investment in automation and will fall behind more enlightened competition in the last half of the 1990s. But it has no way of knowing that. Dominion-Swann is an underachieving organization because it has failed to see the true potential in information technology: to empower workers to deliver competitive solutions that were not possible without the information tools of the Second Industrial Revolution.

Not only are employees rejecting surveillance techniques, but the courts are too.

KAREN NUSSBAUM *is the executive director of 9 to 5, National Association of Working Women, and president of District 925, Service Employees International Union.*

What's wrong with this picture? Dominion-Swann Industries cares about its employees. DS is committed to its employees. Here's how managers show it:

☐ They weed out the old and infirm and those with family problems.

☐ They use highly personal information on employees and their families and friends to keep out those who don't fit the "norm."

☐ They test urine, check fingerprints, run data checks, inspect files, conduct video surveillance, track movements, monitor.

☐ They control minds, control movement, control substances, control association.

Does that sound like love? DS's policies are discriminatory, invasive, and counterproductive. And though few companies implement such an impressive package of organizational and technological measures, all of these policies exist in one form or another in American businesses – with poor results. I will reflect on a few of them.

Weeding the work force. Dominion-Swann's method for upgrading the work force is to screen for imperfections. Justifiable caution becomes an ugly effort to create an Aryan nation of employees when you start to ask questions about parents' health and lifestyle. In any case, advanced-selection processes are a shortsighted way to respond to a diverse work force in a tight labor market. We are entering an era marked by a shortage of skilled workers. Employers need to adapt to the needs of a variety of new workers – workers who are old, handicapped, foreign, female – instead of just culling the "best." Successful employers will learn how to be strengthened by diversity, instead of hiring only in their own image. Besides, it is still *illegal* to discriminate in hiring on the basis of age and handicap, as well as race, sex, and national origin.

Is there a boss under my bed? DS's surveillance, testing, control, and data-check methods keep tabs on employees round-the-clock, cradle-to-grave, and home-to-office. But what's the point? Most of the information is not very useful to the employers, and I've yet to find the worker who *likes* surveillance. Let's take monitoring, for example. A study by the Office of Technology Assessment (aptly titled *Electronic Supervisor*) said this about monitoring: "The knowledge that one's every move is being watched, without an ability to watch the watcher, can create feelings that one's privacy is being invaded and that one is an object under close scrutiny. Being subject to close scrutiny without an ability to confront the observer may mean the

loss of a feeling of autonomy....The employee may feel powerless and exposed under the gaze of electronic monitoring." In a word, fear.

Take the case of the United Airlines reservation clerk who was disciplined for comments she made to a coworker. She was courteous to an obnoxious customer and handled him well—management had no quarrel with her there. But after this three-minute call, which was monitored, she complained to a coworker. Management, listening in, put her on probation for her remark, then sent her to the company psychiatrist when she complained, and ultimately fired her.

An ad for networking software in the March 13, 1989 issue of *PC Week* makes the following claim: "Close-Up LAN brings you a level of control never before possible. It connects PCs on your network giving you the versatility to instantly share screens and keyboards....You decide to look in on Sue's computer screen....Sue won't even know you are there!...All from the comfort of your chair." Another airline employee got into trou-

ble because her monitoring system strictly enforced a 12-minute limit on bathroom breaks. When she went over by 2 minutes, she was disciplined, and ultimately quit in emotional crisis. A data processor in New York told me that her screen periodically flashed "You're not working as fast as the person next to you." A secretary from Florida told me that the thing she found most offensive about her (generally abusive) boss was that he calls up on *his* VDT the work she's doing, while she's doing it. This is "work support"?

Not just workers. The "higher professions" are being hit too. One reporter told me that as she was typing in her story, her computer flashed "I don't like that lead." A surreptitious editor was butting in on a first draft. This kind of thing makes one feel humiliated, harassed, and under the gun. A leading maker of monitoring software programs says, "Monitoring helps employees. It's the only way we can get everything on the permanent record." But I've never met even one highly poised professional who appreciates this kind of "feedback."

Not only are employees rejecting surveillance techniques, but the courts are too. Legal challenges to employer access to databases of personal information are expected to grow. And workers are filing privacy suits against their employers in unprecedented numbers. Between 1984 and 1987, *20 times* as many workplace privacy suits were decided by U.S. courts than in the three years before. Jury verdicts in favor of workers averaged $316,000—compared with 1979 and 1980 when no workers won compensation.

Why were they doing this anyway? If for no other reason, I'd advise managers not to follow Dominion-Swann's example because their policies are counterproductive. Studies repeatedly show that monitoring and surveillance of employees lead to high levels of stress, and stress-related diseases are now the most common occupational illness for workers under 40, costing U.S. business hundreds of millions of dollars each year. Even if you start with the Wheaties class

of employees, as DS has tried to do, after a period of increased productivity, workers will simply burn out.

Monitoring expert Alan Westin of Columbia University describes Federal Express's "people first" approach to office automation, which was supposed to downplay quantitative measures (recorded through monitoring) and elevate nine "quality" elements. However, the manager of customer service in one regional office, in contradiction to the organizational policy, enforced a campaign designed to "get the handle time down!" Before corrective actions raised quality back to where it had been, the staff experienced high rates of physical and psychological ill-health. Incidentally, once these corrective changes were in place, average handle time dropped below its level under the coercive regime.

And DS will be disappointed if its goal is to bring employees closer to management and create a "homey" team. A survey by the Massachusetts Coalition on New Office Technology shows deep alienation among monitored workers.

Corporate culture does need retooling. There are real problems facing employers, but substituting control and fear for supervision and training is not the answer. Dominion-Swann's new policies are the marks of the *failure* of management, not its crowning achievement. I endorse the call for commitment and professionalization of the workplace. To get there, we need education, training, and respect.

Reprint 90209